Museums After Modernism

New Interventions in Art History

Series editor: Dana Arnold, *University of Southampton*

New Interventions in Art History is a series of textbook mini-companions – published in connection with the Association of Art Historians – that aims to provide innovative approaches to, and new perspectives on, the study of art history. Each volume focuses on a specific area of the discipline of art history – here used in the broadest sense to include painting, sculpture, architecture, graphic arts, and film – and aims to identify the key factors that have shaped the artistic phenomenon under scrutiny. Particular attention is paid to the social and political context and the historiography of the artistic cultures or movements under review. In this way, the essays that comprise each volume cohere around the central theme while providing insights into the broader problematics of a given historical moment.

Museums After Modernism

Strategies of Engagement

Edited by

Griselda Pollock and Joyce Zemans

Blackwell
Publishing

BLACKWELL PUBLISHING
350 Main Street, Malden, MA 02148-5020, USA
9600 Garsington Road, Oxford OX4 2DQ, UK
550 Swanston Street, Carlton, Victoria 3053, Australia

The right of Griselda Pollock and Joyce Zemans to be identified as the Authors of the Editorial Material in this Work has been asserted in accordance with the UK Copyright, Designs, and Patents Act 1988.

First published 2007 by Blackwell Publishing Ltd

2   2007

Library of Congress Cataloging-in-Publication Data

Museums after modernism : strategies of engagement / edited by Griselda Pollock and Joyce Zemans.
   p.cm. – (New interventions in art history)
  Includes bibliographical references and index.
  ISBN: 978-1-4051-3627-3 (hardcover : alk. paper)
  ISBN: 978-1-4051-3628-0 (pbk. : alk. paper)   1. Art museums—Philosophy. I. Pollock, Griselda. II. Zemans, Joyce, 1940– III. Series.

N430.M795 2006
708.001—dc22

                      2006016597

A catalogue record for this title is available from the British Library.

Set in 10.5/13pt Minion
by SPi Publisher Services, Pondicherry, India
Printed and bound in Singapore
by COS Printers Pte Ltd

The publisher's policy is to use permanent paper from mills that operate a sustainable forestry policy, and which has been manufactured from pulp processed using acid-free and elementary chlorine-free practices. Furthermore, the publisher ensures that the text paper and cover board used have met acceptable environmental accreditation standards.

For further information on
Blackwell Publishing, visit our website:
www.blackwellpublishing.com

For Moshe, Elan, Galit, and Talia

Dedicated to the memory of Judith Mastai,
July 10, 1945 – February 17, 2001

Contents

List of Figures

Notes on Contributors

Ulla Arnell is Curator and Project Manager at Riksutställningar (Swedish Traveling Exhibitions), with a focus on contemporary art and art education. She has a BA from Uppsala University in sociology, art history, art theory, Nordic, and comparative ethnology. She contributes to Swedish art education journals and is a member of InSEA (International Society for Education Through Art) and organizer of international art education congresses.

Mieke Bal is Dutch Royal Academy of Sciences Research Professor, and Professor of Theory of Literature and founding director of the Amsterdam School for Cultural Analysis, Theory, and Interpretation (ASCA) at the University of Amsterdam. Her most recent publications include *Travelling Concepts in the Humanities* (2002) and *Quoting Caravaggio: Contemporary Art, Preposterous History* (1999). Among her many other books are *Narratology: An Introduction to the Theory of Narrative* (2nd rev. edn., 1997), *The Mottled Screen: Reading Proust Visually* (1997), *Double Exposures: The Subject of Cultural Analysis* (1996), and *Reading "Rembrandt": Beyond the Word–Image Opposition* (1991). She also edited a programmatic volume, *The Practice of Cultural Analysis: Exposing Interdisciplinary Interpretation* (1999), which gives a good idea of the nature and practice of cultural analysis. The breadth of Bal's research contributions can be seen in *Looking In: The Art of Viewing*, essay and afterword by Mieke Bal, with a commentary by Norman Bryson (2000). Her areas of interest include literary theory, semiotics, visual art, cultural studies, postcolonial theory, feminist theory, French, the Hebrew Bible, the seventeenth century, and contemporary culture.

Juli Carson is Assistant Professor of Art History and Curatorial Studies in the Department of Studio Art at the University of California, Irvine, and director of UCI's University Art Gallery. Her numerous publications include contributions to edited volumes and exhibition catalogues, and she is completing a book manuscript on recent neo-conceptual art practice titled *The Moebius Effect: The Conceptual Unconscious in Contemporary Art*. Carson is also the founding editor of Vel Press, which publishes books on theory, art, and culture.

The work of multidisciplinary artist **Vera Frenkel** addresses the forces at work in human migration, the learning and unlearning of cultural memory, the messianic fantasies of commodity cultures, and the increasing bureaucratization of experience. Her installations and new media projects have been shown at the Biennale di Venezia, *documenta* IX, MoMA, the National Gallery of Canada, the OK Centrum für Gegenwartskunst, Linz, the Georg Kargl Gallery, Vienna, the Setagaya Museum, Tokyo and the Freud Museum, London, and her writings have appeared in publications such as *Art Monthly, Canadian Art, FUSE Magazine, Intermédialités, Public*, and *n.paradoxa*. Frenkel's current project on the inner life of a dysfunctional cultural organization, *The Institute?: Or What We Do for Love* (<www.the-national-institute.org/tour>), received the 2004 Centre for Contemporary Canadian Art "Untitled" Art Award. A four-disc DVD/CD-ROM collection of the artist's videotapes, media works, and writings, *Of Memory and Displacement*, was released by Vtape Distribution in 2005. Frenkel is recipient of a number of the most significant prizes awarded to a living artist in Canada, most recently the 2006 Governor General's Award in Visual and Media Arts.

Janna Graham has developed collaborative and participatory programming with artists, activists, and community organizers at the Art Gallery of Ontario in Toronto since 1999. She has a BA in Geography and an MA in Cultural Studies from Leeds University. She has contributed to the *Journal of Visual Culture, FUSE Magazine*, and *The Journal of Cultural Studies*, and has worked on independent artistic, curatorial, and education projects with Artcirq (Igloolik), 16 Beaver (New York), Mercer Union, Art Metropole, and Alphabet City (Toronto), Walter Phillips Gallery (Banff), Theory in Practice II (Croatia), Project Art Centre (Dublin), Whitechapel Art Gallery (London), Vanabbe Museum (Eindhoven), and Centre CATH (Leeds). She is currently a PhD candidate in the Department of Visual Cultures at the University of London.

Reesa Greenberg (<www.reesagreenberg.net>) is an independent scholar and museum consultant whose research focuses on contemporary exhibition practices and display, in situ and online. Her publications include *The Exhibition as Discursive Event* (1995), *The Rhetoric of Arrangement: Seeing is Believing* (1996), *Thinking About Exhibitions* (co-edited with Bruce Ferguson and Sandy Nairne, 1996), and *Redressing Exhibitions: Partners and the Friedrich Christian Flick Collection* (2005). She is currently preparing two book manuscripts, *Blind Spots: Museums, Collectors, Display and the Holocaust* and *National Narratives and a New Canadian War Museum*.

Mary Kelly is Professor of Art and Critical Theory at the University of California, Los Angeles. Recent exhibitions include those at the Museo Universitario de Ciencias y Arte, Mexico City, Generali Foundation, Vienna, and the *2004 Biennial*, Whitney Museum of American Art, New York. She is the author of *Post-Partum Document* (1983, reprinted in English and German, 1998) and *Imaging Desire* (1996). *Mary Kelly*, a monograph on her work, was published in 1997.

Judith Mastai began her career as an actor, before moving into research into public education. Her doctoral research on adult education focused on community development. For many years she worked with government agencies in developing programs for public education around issues of alcohol, sexual abuse, and racism. From 1987 to 1994, she served as Head of Public Programs at the Vancouver Art Gallery, where she initiated a range of new initiatives to make "education" integral to programming and planning. Working with a range of conceptual artists, she became a critic and independent curator, organizing exhibitions and conferences, including the third Feminist Arts and Histories Network conference at the University of Reading, before becoming Director of Education at the Art Gallery of Ontario (1997–2000). She was co-founder and editor of the critical art magazine *Collapse: The View From Here*, published by the Vancouver Art Forum Society. At her untimely death, she was the Executive Director of the Canadian Craft Museum in Vancouver and was preparing her major study on the theme which gives this book its title. She had lectured extensively on her range of interests in contemporary artists and the challenge of rethinking the museum.

Gerald McMaster is Curator of Canadian Art at the Art Gallery of Ontario. He holds a PhD from the University of Amsterdam School for Cultural Analysis. From 1977 to 1981, he was both instructor and Head of the Indian Art Program at the Saskatchewan Indian Federated College

(SIFC). Since 1981 he has been Curator of Contemporary Indian Art for the Canadian Museum of Civilization, and until 2000 he was Curator-in-Charge of the Canadian Museum of Civilization's First Peoples Hall, where he produced many leading-edge exhibitions such as *In the Shadow of the Sun* (1989), *Indigena: Indigenous Perspectives on 500 Years* (1992), *Edward Poitras: The Venice Biennale Project* (1996), and, *Reservation X* (1998). He was Deputy Assistant Director for Cultural Resources for the Smithsonian Institution's National Museum of the American Indian (NMAI), where he oversaw the curatorial, repatriation, and archival departments. For NMAI he curated *First American Art* (2004) and *New Tribe New York* (2005–6). His awards and recognitions include the 2001 ICOM Canada Prize for contributions to national and international museology and he was selected to be Canadian Commissioner to the XLVI 1995 Biennale di Venezia.

Ruth B. Phillips is Canada Research Chair in Modern Culture and Professor of Art History at Carleton University. Her doctoral research in African art was published in her 1995 book *Representing Woman: Sande Masquerades of the Mende of Sierra Leone* (1995). Her current research interests in Native North American art and cultural exchange have led to several other books, including *Trading Identities: The Souvenir in Native North American Art from the Northeast, 1700–1900* (1998), *Native North American Art* for the *Oxford History of Art* (1998, with Janet Catherine Berlo), and *Unpacking Culture: Arts and Goods in Colonial and Postcolonial Worlds* (co-edited with Christopher B. Steiner). From 1997 to 2003 she served as director of the Museum of Anthropology at the University of British Columbia. Her curatorial projects include *The Spirit Sings: Artistic Traditions of Canada's First Peoples* (1988), *Across Borders: Beadwork in Iroquois Art* (1999), and, most recently, the indigenous component of the Portrait Gallery of Canada.

Griselda Pollock is Professor of Social and Critical Histories of Art and Director of the Centre for Cultural Analysis, Theory, and History at the University of Leeds. She works in/on social history of art, cultural studies, feminist studies in the visual arts, and modern Jewish studies. A series of strategic interventions into art history and cultural theory, starting from *Old Mistresses: Women, Art and Ideology* (with Roszika Parker, 1981), through *Vision and Difference* (1988, reissued 2004), to *Generations and Geographies in the Visual Arts: Feminist Perspectives* (1996) and *Differencing the Canon: Feminist Desire and the Writing of Art's Histories* (1999) have systematically challenged dominant phallocentric and Eurocentric models of art and cultural history while actively providing new methods for international and postcolonial feminist studies in the theory, practice, and analysis of the visual arts that breach the divisions between theory, practice, and history. She is currently working on trauma and cultural memory in a trilogy of books including a study of Charlotte Salomon, *Theatre of Memory* (Yale, 2007), and postmodern engagements with psychoanalysis and aesthetics in a book titled *Towards the Virtual Feminist Museum* (Routledge, 2007). Further information is on the website <www.leeds.ac.uk/cath/pollock>.

Shadya Yasin was one of the first members of the Art Gallery of Ontario's (Toronto) *Teens Behind the Scenes Program* in 1999. Since then, she has been involved as a youth mentor and a facilitator of partnerships between the AGO and a variety of community programs in Toronto. She coordinates youth and Somali culture programming in Toronto public housing facilities and libraries, is a spoken word artist and a student of African studies, international development, and community arts at York University in Toronto.

Joyce Zemans, CM, art historian, curator, and arts administrator, is Director of the MBA Program in Arts and Media Administration in York University's Schulich School of Business (Toronto). She holds the position of University Professor, and served as Director of the Canada Council for the Arts (1988–92). She was Dean of York's Faculty of Fine Arts (1985–8) and Chair of the Department of Visual Arts (1975–81). From 1966 to 1975, she taught at the Ontario College of Art, where she directed the Liberal Art Studies Program. Her research and teaching focus on both art history and cultural policy, with specific reference to the Canadian experience. She has curated exhibitions of and written about twentieth-century Canadian art. Her research has also focused on the work of Canadian women artists. She is the editor of the third volume of the *Ontario Association of Art Galleries Handbook* (2001). In cultural policy, her publications include *Where is Here? Canadian Cultural Policy in a Globalized Environment* (1996) and *Comparing Cultural Policy: A Study of Japan and the United States* (1999). Zemans has received honorary degrees from the University of Waterloo and the Nova Scotia College of Art. She is an Honorary Fellow of the Ontario College of Art and Design and a member of the Order of Canada.

Series Editor's Preface

New Interventions in Art History was established to provide a forum for innovative approaches to, and perspectives on, the study of art history in all its complexities. *Museums After Modernism* brings together essays from some of the most renowned commentators in the field to offer a unique mix of academic, practitioner, and curators' statements that expands the field of critical museum studies.

This volume brings fresh insight to the social and cultural contexts of the museum and offers an in-depth analysis of the new possibilities offered by the interaction of museological theory and practice. Indeed, it advances our understanding of the relationship between critical museological methods and processes, theories of public engagement, and contemporary artistic practice. But *Museums After Modernism* does so in a provocative and illuminating way, grounding itself in the influential work of Judith Mastai, and exploring the fate of art and art institutions after modernism.

The book is not, however, a Festschrift, nor is it a homage. Instead, it comprises discussions ranging from art-making to curation, exhibition and display to access, to histories, public reception, and pedagogy. Together, these issues combine to produce a radically new and productive rethinking of the museum and its function.

Museums After Modernism is, then, a lively collection that responds to an increasing interest in critical museum studies by offering new possibilities for the historical, conceptual, and analytical frameworks for study. This book is a welcome addition to the titles in *New Interventions* through its innovative and inventive analysis of a familiar topic. At the same time, it complements the volumes in the series that address the museum and notions of display, modernity, and criticism, and makes an essential contribution to the understanding of the museum as site of critical potentiality for new ways of seeing, thinking, and doing.

Dana Arnold
London, 2006

Preface

While I once described my working environment at the Vancouver Art Gallery as a laboratory, I now describe it as a performance in the sense that, every day, in many ways, my colleagues and I are engaged in performing a continually emerging institutional subjectivity. Change is not an interlude, but a condition of our work.

Judith Mastai, "Performing the Museum: Education, Negotiation, Art Galleries and their Publics" (unfinished manuscript)

This book came out of a collaboration between York University in Toronto, the Ontario Association of Art Galleries, and the AHRC Centre for Cultural Analysis, Theory and History at the University of Leeds. A small advisory group of Vera Frenkel, Johanne Lamoureux, Griselda Pollock, John O'Brien, and Joyce Zemans created the first stage: an international symposium in Toronto in 2002. This research laboratory brought together artists, curators, art historians, and cultural analysts to consider a theoretical and practical agenda that had been posed by the work and thought of Judith Mastai, whose untimely death in 2001 many of us not only personally mourned but intellectually and culturally lamented. A major book upon which she had been working through her complex practice of "performing a new institutional subjectivity" and reflecting upon the strategies for engagement remained drafted but incomplete. It was she who, borrowing the phrase "Museums After Modernism" from Eileen Hooper-Greenhill, insistently took up the challenge of questioning the complex and expanded forms of museum practices and museum encounters, while also forging in concrete programs new methodologies at both organizational and performative levels that worked in the firm belief that art is a deeply important form of thought and provocation to thought.[1]

The symposium had its own extended cast and still has a virtual existence with a full audio record that is available on the website: <www.yorku.ca/mam/>.[2] An audio webcast enables scholars and artists to access the full record of lectures, discussions, and panels whose significance lay specifically in the concept of transdisciplinary encounters between members of the complex art world who are often professionally divided from each other by role, function, and position. The program for the symposium reflected a series of points of intervention and strategies of engagement with the museum in its challenged and expanded present.

The second stage of the collaboration was to commission and collect a series of essays whose range of voices, interests, and practices would similarly perform an intervention in that space between art history and cultural studies now called Museum Studies, without conforming to the new genre. In this book, there are discussions about art-making, curation, exhibition, display, special projects, access, publics, communities, histories, controversies, public reception, and pedagogy. There are readings of exhibitions and explorations of exhibitions as readings of contemporary culture. What marks the core project for the book is our growing appreciation of the radical, productive, and challenging "teaching" of someone deeply involved in thinking about the museum, its time, its place, and its function now.

While much of Museum Studies in recent years has been propelled by Foucauldian analyses of the institution as discursive formation, of the museum as site of narratives and ideologies, and of debates about museums and their publics, few collections address the core idea of the museum as a place for discursive thinking. It is not a question of "the museum and its public," but in what sense the museum can be(come) a public place, publicly responsible for stimulating and housing critical thinking in and through art. In the age of increasing privatization, what is the scope for a public or civic institution to provoke and host public debate about issues of major relevance that are being attended to through the prism of art-thought, and art-practice, of cultural intervention? Does the museum that in the modernist era became either repository, educator, or entertainment venue have a future as a unique relic of the public sphere in which the showing, experiencing, and reading of art – meaning the full range of world aesthetico-symbolic practices – plays a role beyond tourism, the blockbuster, and nationalist pedagogy?

Can we recast the museum as critical site of public debate distinct from the museum as privileged manager or professionalized administrator of cultural heritage, authorizing selective stories and formalized pasts?

Drawing on her profound engagement with conceptual art and artists such as Terry Atkinson in and beyond Art & Language, and Mary Kelly, Judith Mastai's questions about the museum went to the heart of contemporary debates about the production, consumption, and distribution of art: how can we prevent art from being lost in the system of curation, as inert matter, the material support of museal discourses and institutional practices? As a serious reader of Arendt and Adorno, Judith Mastai also realized that we cannot operate outside these highly administered institutions and practices; thus any new museology must be considered as a working through of institutions that already exercise their hegemony within the modern system.

This is neither a Festschrift nor a homage. It is the creative extension/realization of a concept of intellectual performance, performing an intervention – as is the spirit of the series in which it appears – in art history (a discipline with many sub-divisions working across university and museum, studio and book, museology and curatorial studies, art practice and art theory), in art's histories (plural, diverse, contested, and dispersed), and in the present history of the modern museum/the museum in modernity as the privileged locus of their intersection. It registers and extends the influential legacy of an important but little known thinker about the art museum, about art, the museum, and the world. The structure of the book reflects a series of aspects of the legacy we wish to document in engaging with the racism of art and anthropology, the museum and traumatic histories, the diversity, inclusiveness, or exclusion of publics, archive, and amnesia.

It also demonstrates specific connections within the larger community of practices and theories that intersected with and informed the practices and theories of one particular catalyst to whose singular intervention we lend our many minds. Gender, difference, otherness, trauma, history, delivery, learning, exile, encounter, transformation, and archive shape the book, whose threads are provisionally woven together in the opening chapter, which argues, above all, for the necessity of a transdisciplinary "other" space beyond the idealizing art history paradigm or the museological critique, or popular images of the museum's class and cultural identity. Disembarrassed of vested interests, the space of transdisciplinary encounter enables each participant to work through their disciplinary specificity as historian, anthropologist, artist, or programmer, to think with the trained rigor of an experienced practice, and yet to recognize that if the borders between such necessary disciplines are too rigidly policed, we will not be able to meet the challenge of our own unstable, transformed, traumatized present: what Zygmunt Bauman diagnoses not as postmodernity but as "liquid modernity."[3]

Following Pollock's opening stage-setting, a chapter by Mieke Bal, a leading cultural analyst of the museum, offers a feminist reading of the exhibition *Rembrandt's Women* (2001, National Gallery of Scotland and Royal Academy of Arts, London). She inverts the terms of its title to ask how we might produce, in a different viewing, a "Women's Rembrandt" in contradistinction to the persistent creation of the Old Master-Genius defended by the current Rembrandt project. In the next chapter, First Nation artist and curator Gerald McMaster engages with a similar question of who reads whom in relation to the subject-viewing as well as subject-making position of the First Nations and the representation of their national histories and living cultures in contemporary art and anthropological museum displays into which First Nation artists intervene in their own varied strategic practices. Trained as an art historian and anthropologist, Ruth B. Phillips then examines displays of African art at major museums such as the British Museum and the Metropolitan Museum of Art, New York, analyzing the political effects of each positioning of the viewer's encounter with various African cultures.

Reesa Greenberg, a historian and theorist of the art exhibition and of installations in Jewish Historical Museums, next reflects on the creation and controversies associated with a challenging exhibition at the Jewish Museum in New York entitled *Mirroring Evil* (2002) in order to examine the ethics as well as the politics of the museum's responsibilities toward art, on the one hand, and to deeply invested constituencies of its public on the other. Vera Frenkel, storyteller, art-ethnographer, and video artist, whose works ... *from the transit bar* (1992) and *Body Missing* (1994) have dealt in multi-media and web-form with the cultural legacies of fascist criminality and the traumatic mark of the Holocaust, reflects on the impossibility of representation and trauma and the models developed in art and education for engaging with both traumatic legacies and traumatized times. Also exploring trauma and representability, as well as witnessing, Mary Kelly writes about her installation using both intaglio-printed lint and a commissioned musical score, *The Ballad of Kastriot Rexhepi* (2001), which explores the intersections of subjectivity and history inspired by a news report about a traumatic incident in the Balkan wars.

Swedish curator Ulla Arnell analyses the history of an innovative project in Sweden created to take art out from the metropolis and beyond the museum. This included producing "the exhibition train," which took a range of specially curated exhibitions around the country making the museum mobile. Janna Graham and Shadya Yasin create a dialogical history of a project to engage younger people from the diverse communities of Toronto with the Art Gallery of Ontario – a program created by Judith Mastai, still operative, and theoretically as well as practically influential. Judith Mastai is represented in this book by two short chapters, one on her negation of the concept of the visitor, and a second that documents her work as a research curator recovering a forgotten archive to recirculate a critical history of feminism and conceptual art from the early 1970s – a project that marks her understanding of both collaboration as a practice and its politics. Juli Carson provides an in-depth theoretically informed analysis of the New Museum of Contemporary Art, New York, established within the feminist problematic by Marcia Tucker as an intervention whose exhibition histories embodied some of the contradictions of feminist cultural politics in the 1980s that are also recovered and restaged by Carson's work as an art historian.

Griselda Pollock's opening chapter "frames" these case studies and reflections by analyzing Suzanne Oberhardt's notion of "framing" and the museum, and by exploring the many levels of meaning in the phrase museums after modernism: from the debates in revolutionary France about the very foundations of museums and their effects on art to Merleau-Ponty's critique of Malraux's "museum without walls" in the 1950s; from the foundation of the Museum of Modern Art in New York in 1929 to the emergence of a Marxist-feminist critique of that museum as discourse and ideological text offered by Duncan and Wallach in 1979; from Adorno's definition of our horizon as now "after Auschwitz" to Zygmunt Bauman's theses on liquid modernity.

"Museums after modernism?" was put on the table by Eileen Hooper-Greenhill as a question in 1992. Thinking about the impact of conceptual art on culture and intensely engaged with the debates about the trauma of the Holocaust, as well as being alert to issues of feminism and postcolonial theory, Judith Mastai took up the challenge in her practice in the art museum which she researched by relentless travel, creating dialogues with other innovators in museum education and programming, interviewing artists, convening transdisciplinary seminars,[4] teaching students, organizing international conferences, curating exhibitions, and directing the public programming of two very large international museums/art galleries. Intensely aware of the continuing relevance and necessity of the question, we now take up her reframing of the question to pass it through a range of artistic and intellectual visions. The premise is that we are situated in both history – modernity in its ever-changing and self-transforming modes – and in the histories of art which act within and upon history. The museum is paradoxically the product of modernity: of democracy, the creation of the public sphere, universal education, historical consciousness, nostalgia, mourning, imperialism, cultural looting, amnesia, and pedagogy. It is, therefore, a powerful feature of the way we experience art, culture, and ourselves. What has the museum become? What can the museum be now? What forces are directing its ever-increasing symbolic capital at the same time as it becomes less and less a public forum? What are artists telling us about its possibilities? How should those us of involved in the education of artists, art historians, curators, and publics be thinking about our work?

We are indebted to all who worked with us to make the book a reality, including the sterling editorial support of Joanne Heath. It is but a snapshot of larger projects, continuing art practices, and, above all, commitments to strategies of engagement.

Griselda Pollock and Joyce Zemans

Notes

1 Eileen Hooper-Greenhill, *Museums and the Shaping of Knowledge* (The Heritage: Care-Preservation-Management Programme; London: Routledge, 1992).
2 The conference was co-sponsored by York University, the Centre for Cultural Analysis, Theory and History at Leeds University, and the Ontario Association of Art Galleries. Its principal sponsors were the Canada Council for the Arts, the Social Science and Humanities Research Council of Canada, the Museums Assistance Program in the Department of Canadian Heritage, the Laidlaw Foundation, the Walter and Duncan Gordon Foundation, the Samuel and Saidye Bronfman Family Foundation, and the UK Arts and Humanities Research Council.
3 Zygmunt Bauman, *Liquid Modernity* (Cambridge: Polity Press, 2000).
4 Judith Mastai organized a seminar on "Museums after Modernism" at the University of Leeds on December 16–17, 2003, with Terry Atkinson, Sandy Nairne, Sunil Gupta, Jon Bird, Adrian Rifkin, Rita Keegan, Richard Gagola, and Griselda Pollock. A typescript was prepared and may soon be available as an occasional paper. In Mastai's files is also a very long interview with Toby Jackson, the innovative public programmer at the Tate Liverpool.

1

Un-Framing the Modern: Critical Space/Public Possibility

Griselda Pollock

Framing the Frames

In *Frames within Frames: The Art Museum as Cultural Artifact,* Suzanne Oberhardt argues that, from the inside, the museum effaces itself to become an invisible frame for the art or artifacts it appears merely to house, conserve, and exhibit.[1] To recognize that the institution itself produces meaning, we need to widen our focus to see its active framing of its contents and our experience. Pulling back even further, we can identify larger cultural frames within which the museum itself figures in popular discourses and representations about culture and society. Beyond even these supplementary cultural frames, Oberhardt proposes an open, other, critical space through which we can critically engage with the histories and possibilities of that distinctive product of modernity: the museum.

Creating a four-framed model on an axis running diagonally from profane to sacred, Oberhardt identifies the first, close-in Frame 1 as the adoring art-historical model, in which the museum positions art both on the side of the sacred, set apart from ordinary life, and as a source of moral authority. Its direct counter-frame is New Museology, a political critique of the museum as institution and ideology, situated in the colonial and imperial histories of modernity's constructions of nations, races, and genders.[2] Emerging in the early 1980s, this new discipline (often called Museum Studies) shifted the focus from the canonizing model of art-historical adoration of *the painting* (Oberhardt's term for all valued objects of the art-historical paradigm) to a postmodernist critique of institutions and representations in which the programming of display and the disciplining of the spectator create a pedagogic text: what Tony Bennett calls "the exhibitionary complex."[3] The third frame "scrutinizes the discourses of the art museum not through texts displayed *by* the art museum but rather through how the museum itself is represented and talked *about* in contemporary society."[4] Here the academic voice and its self- or counter-representations fade into a larger picture in which neither is central. Beyond lies yet another space in which no frame has dominance. Oberhardt concludes:

> What we can strive for, though, is the continued deconstruction of prevailing frames for the purpose of creating new ones: each attempt resisting odious and dominant world views and creating fresh meanings, identities, and fairer ways of life. In a shift from a relatively static culture to a global, corporate and electronic culture that constantly invents and reinvents itself, we can come to know the art museum differently.[5]

It is this knowing the art museum differently that goes beyond the opposing forces of Frames 1 (adoring art-historical) and 2 (new museological). Deconstruction accepts that there is neither an outside, utopic other place, nor a simple resolution of Manichean good and bad.[6] But our work on all frames alerts us to our capture by existing modes of knowledge and practice from which dystopia we cannot step outside into a utopian space. We inherit histories which position us; but we can think about them, deconstruct their terms, and displace the boundaries in a constant work that neither idolizes nor decries but reworks the inherent possibilities of the museum as public space.

In this book, some authors are artists, others are curators. Yet others are art historians or cultural analysts. All are committed to the significance of art-making as more than the production of luxury goods, entertainment, moral education, or ideological heritage. Art and our engagements with it are engagements with thought, with challenging questions posed ever more starkly in what Oberhardt calls the shift from static culture to the more fluid, rapidly changing, and electronically, digitally virtualized worlds that increasingly set the terms for global modes of living, dying, thinking, and making.

In his analysis of our contemporary condition not as postmodernity but as "Liquid Modernity," sociologist Zygmunt Bauman argues that the conjunction of globalizing international capital, untrammeled by former national political institutions that functioned as local constraints, unchecked by the balanced contest of world powers typical of the Cold War era, with the exponentially expanding cultures of the electronic and cyber-informational age, has produced a situation in which modernity is now in a relentless cycle of directionless self-modernization. There is no ultimate goal, no long-term narrative which leads to a revolutionary sweeping away of one order to be replaced by a new one, stable or as the consolidated modernity of the first age of industrial capitalism. Now the forces of economic and cultural modernization drive *themselves*, generating continual internal modernization for its own sake, transforming all aspects of our lives, loves, subjectivities, movement or lack of it, location and dislocations, sense of past, present, and future, work, leisure, humanity, and culture, infusing us with the feeling that life as well as things are transient, rapidly past their sell-by dates, throw-away and inherently unpredictable.

Thus the museum "after" what we might call the moments of solid modernism is a museum in the world of liquid modernity.[7] Oberhardt's notion of a constant deconstruction and reinvention, however, retains an ethical dimension, an aspiration drawn from both the adorational and the demonizing modes of museum discourse. Both, variously and divergently, invest in some aspiration to improvement; both adhere to a notion of a public purpose based on critical engagement. Something matters and art is part of what matters. Can there, however, be an ethical politics of the museum as a public forum in the endlessly shifting conditions of liquid modernity?

Frame 3 of Oberhardt's model is that of popular culture in which the world of knowledge and high culture may appear as an ideologically loaded sign. Focusing on the way in which the museum figures outside its own discourses in public life and imagination, she argues that "the art museum has a life in popular culture that has previously been ignored and/or misconstrued."[8] Cinema uses the museum as a signifier for several widely dispersed ideas and ideals that reflect a different place for the museum beyond its own art-world self-perception. Recall the central role of the San Francisco Legion of Honor in Alfred Hitchcock's *Vertigo* (1957). In the film, a conspiracy to commit and obscure a murder involves the fake Madeleine (Kim Novak) luring the psychologically invalided policeman Scottie (James Stewart) to the empty, still quietness of an art gallery, where, watched by Scottie, she is sitting in rapt attention before a painted portrait of her supposed ancestress. Identifying with the melancholy of the beautiful portrait of Carlotta Valdez, Madeleine will repeatedly attempt suicide. But it is Scottie's later recollection of the necklace in the portrait that will break the spell and lead to his discovery of the conspiracy to murder the real Madeleine in which his new lover Judy (Kim Novak) has played her part. The museum and a painting become central to the thematics of delusion, paranoia, obsession, death, and desire.

Alan Rudolph's *The Moderns* (1981) shares the theme of deception but thematizes the museum *of* modernism, converging at least three of the key frames in its final *mise en scène*.

Nick Hart (Keith Carradine) is an American artist living in Paris in the 1920s. The son of a famous forger, he has inherited the father's artistic gift but only scrapes a living together by drawing cartoons of expatriate characters for his friend L'Oiseau's (Wallace Shawn) weekly column in the *New York Herald Tribune*. Hart has a faithful gallery dealer, an ex-nun (Genevieve Bujold) who struggles to get his paintings noticed and finally manages to sell one to a newly rich industrialist. Surrounded by a glamorous Josephine Baker and a morose, drunken, and prosy Ernest Hemingway, hanging out at the Rue Fleurus salon of Gertrude Stein and Alice B. Toklas, Hart is finally persuaded by an divorcée of great wealth, Nathalie de Ville (Geraldine Chaplin), to "copy" her ex-husband's prized modernist collection of paintings by Matisse, Modigliani, and Cézanne so that she can sneak off to America with the originals. To Paris comes a self-made man, Bertram Stone (John Lone). He is "in rubber" and he wants to buy himself a large collection of art as a calculated form of economic investment and cultural legitimation. At the same time, he pours scorn on the value system that disdains his money-making and idolizes art. Stone is now married to Rachel (Linda Fiorentino), who, it transpires, is already married to Hart whom she suddenly and inexplicably left some years before he came to Paris after a torrid romance that has left him obsessed and embittered. Hart copies Nathalie de Ville's paintings, (un)consciously altering the faces of the women in the paintings by Matisse, Cézanne, and Modigliani to register his still deep attachment to Rachel. Deceived by Hart, and unsuspecting of the switch, Nathalie de Ville secretly breaks into his studio to take back her originals; in error, she steals Hart's copies. Hart's dealer sells the originals to Bertram Stone along with one of Hart's own paintings – which pictures Rachel lounging in her bath surrounded by adult male heads resting on wings in the manner of Raphael's most kitschy putti at the margins of the Sistine Madonna (Dresden, Gemälde-galerie). Stone has a party. Nathalie sees "her" paintings on the walls, and publicly declares them forgeries. Stone, wishing to show how little he cares for art itself, slashes and burns the now apparently worthless, yet what the viewer knows to be genuine, canvases. With the denouement of the sexual rivalry between Stone and Hart over Rachel, who promptly disappears, the columnist L'Oiseau fakes his own death, dresses as a woman and escapes with Hart from Paris to go to Hollywood, "where the pictures move." The already old and seedy world of Parisian modernism is to yield to the dynamically new of Hollywood movies – the industrial dream factory. As the train pulls out of the Paris station, Hart notices that his painting that was sold to Stone has been used for its overt eroticism as an advertisement for Stone's prime commodity: condoms. En route to Holly-wood, the two men stop off in New York. It is October 1929. They pause to visit the newly opened Museum of Modern Art (MoMA) at 53rd Street, New York.[9] There, beside a beautiful nude "by Modigliani," they see a label identifying this display of modernist paintings as *The Nathalie de Ville Collection.*

Hart wanders amongst his paintings, eavesdropping on a group of young college men being instructed in the mysteries of modern art by what we can only call "an art historian connoisseur." Speaking in rever-ential tones and calling on the young men to stand in silent awe before the mystery that is Cézanne, "a work of rare emotional delicacy, a revelation that cannot be taught or replicated," the connoisseur exposes the faith placed in the museum's authenticating frame, that has been undone by Hart's switch on Nathalie. When called to leave by L'Oiseau, Hart replies that listening to the connoisseur's talk "might help [him] to appreciate [his own] work." Blurred by camera angle and movement, Rachel then appears, standing before Hart's recasting of a Matisse odalisque who bears her features. All three then leave to make their way to Hollywood and the future, passing Hemingway, on his way into the "cathedral of art," ram-bling about his memories of Paris in the 1920s that will appear later in his *A Moveable Feast* (1964).

The Moderns dramatizes the paradox at the heart of the modern museum from the place that must be called "after modernism," a phrase that critically distinguishes itself from the delusional aspects of postmod-ernism. For what would come to be known as "modernism" was the product of its demise, in part as a result of its musealization in a particular and contestable narrative of modern art created by MoMA. Modernism was always trapped in the contradiction that, at the moment of its recognition as the modern, it had ceased, by definition, to be anything of the sort. For, as a product of that paradoxically historicist consciousness we call modernity, the museum produces an image of history as the other of the modern it thereby creates and annuls in the same moment. In historicizing the present, the museum creates both retrospect and teleology. For its contemporary mourners, modernism can only now be the object of an archaeological impulse in which the critical rereading of what at any point was institutionalized as modernism becomes the site of a critical release from some of the aporias and amnesias of the postmodern present.

The Moderns frames the museum's institutionalization of early twentieth-century European modernism as a closure, rightly suggesting that by 1929–32, the modern was "over" and ready to be consumed in terms no longer avant-garde. It also reflexively plays on the competition between high art and its popular other, the movies, not art but entertainment. Cinema is, however, being used to reflect back upon that constitutive moment that Alfred H. Barr, first director of MoMA, would himself attempt to grasp when he proposed to the founding Trustees in 1929 a new kind of museum as multi-departmental collector and historian of *everything* that was modern.[10] It would take most of the next decade to persuade the conservative Trustees to realize his total vision, including departments of architecture, film, photography, and design. Most radically, there was to be a very active division of what we would now call public programming, an educational wing that would circulate exhibitions, foster understanding, and reach out to share with an as yet unconvinced public the vitality and significance of the culture of their own moment: the modern. The catalogue and the traveling exhibition as forged by Barr were to be the tools of this outreach.

Although as late as 1953, cultural critic Dwight Macdonald would write admiringly of Barr's MoMA as "a nine-ringed circus," in January 1943 Barr had been sacked as Director by his Trustees for daring to exhibit a Sicilian New Yorker's shoeshine stand as part of his own commitment, not shared by the elite Trustees, to record and celebrate modern design.[11] Barr's demotic radicalism has perhaps been under-appreciated. Instead, the displaced sacralization of the modern as art by elite collector and art historian connoisseur has been institutionalized in the face of the very force of modernity to confuse, undo, and reconfigure the relations between industrial and aesthetic, art and design, high and popular.

In their founding study of the choreography of the space and iconographic layout of the modern art museum, Carol Duncan and Alan Wallach used anthropological studies of ritual and ritual space to explain how modern art museums use architectural framing to promote specific belief systems – ideologies.

> Museums, as modern ceremonial monuments, belong to the same architectural class as temples, churches, shrines and certain kinds of palaces. Although all architecture has an ideological perspective, only ceremonial monuments are dedicated exclusively to ideology. Their social importance is underscored by the enormous resources lavished upon their construction and decoration. Absorbing more manual and imaginative labour than any other type of architecture, these buildings affirm the power and social authority of the patron class. But ceremonial monuments convey more than class domination. They impress upon those who see or use them a society's most revered values and beliefs.[12]

This was written before the massive "boom" in museum building since the 1990s, when the world's leading architects were commissioned to create a radically new genre. Whereas the museum of solid modernity from the Louvre to the National Galleries of many Western nations called on the examples of the Classical Temple or Renaissance Palace to create the semantics of unbroken cultural authority, the museums built in postmodern (Charles Jencks's term) mode are generating their own rhetoric of otherness.[13] Frank Gehry's Guggenheim Museum at Bilbao is perhaps the most vivid example, itself a development from his first art museum, the Frederick R. Weisman Art Museum at Minneapolis (Figure 1.1).[14]

Duncan and Wallach analyzed the ideological effects of the layout of MoMA, which was rebuilt in the internationalist style in 1939 and expanded again in 1964. In "MoMA: Ordeal and Triumph on 53rd Street," the authors call the museum the "Chartres of mid-twentieth century art museums." They identified its "iconographic program," in which the normal relations are reversed. We think of a museum with walls on which to hang works of art. But if we pursue the medieval model, we realize that the art is placed in a building, with its already designated function to spread and sustain the larger belief system the building itself already embodies. The building, as it were, commissions and solicits art to support as iconographic supplement and illustration an underlying ideology. Without attributing any conscious intentions, these authors draw our attention to what visitors imaginatively experience as they are drawn into a

Figure 1.1   Frank Gehry, Frederick R. Weisman Art Museum, Minneapolis (1993). Photograph by Bob Firth, used with permission.

museum by its particular architectural devices for marking the separation of its special space from that of the street and the everyday. We either rise up steps, or seek out grand entrances in long blocks of blank wall. We may pass through glass panels into vast atria, and then take escalators to ascend to the specially planned suites of rooms through which we pass, aided by acousti-guides or new digital hand-sets, labels, and other orientation aids to the "story" of art which is on offer. This process is experienced, however, as a ritual. Site and Façade are followed by a reading of the Passage which Duncan and Wallach compare to ancient labyrinths – those specially constructed, disorienting ordeals that were associated in the ancient world with a psychologically transformative "spiritual" journey through spaces of archaic encounter with terror, abjection, and sexual difference, at the end of which the "initiate" who had endured the ordeal experiences enlightenment or release. At the heart of the ancient labyrinths of the mysteries was a feminine deity – either a terrifying Mother Goddess or what the authors call the Gorgon Whore – modern versions of which plotted out the hang of MoMA that ran from Picasso's monumental *Demoiselles d'Avignon* (1907) and other of his surrealist images to De Kooning's toothy-smiled *Woman* (1950–2), while more beneficent images of maternal plenitude await the visitor to the sculpture garden in the work of Renoir, Maillol, and Lachaise.

In this first reading of a museum hang as text, Duncan and Wallach argued that the recapitulation of ancient rituals and iconographies serviced a contemporary capitalist ideology, shaping the art-viewing subject for the modernist, competitive, and individualistic society (of Bertram Stone):

> The ritual clarifies social experience by recreating it imaginatively in symbolic form. In this way, the labyrinth nightmare exalts as positive values the competitive individualism and alienated human relations that characterize contemporary social experience; but rather than overcoming alienation, it simply stands alienation on its head. The ritual turns you into a celebrant of alienated experience. It reconciles you to pure subjectivity by equating pure subjectivity with the "human condition." The alienated social relations in which human powers are projected onto an inhuman scale are reproduced in the form of monsters (Gorgons) and overwhelming forces. Human and material needs are experienced here as something to be repressed and transcended before they can be satisfied.[15]

The Moderns closes its narrative of thwarted and re-found love with the institution of *the* museum of modern art, MoMA, with the creation of a formal logic for what otherwise appeared to be a contingency of relations of production and distribution, identities in play, and interests at work. Barr's originally creative logic became so utterly compelling that it remained until the turn of the twenty-first century the template for all museum engagements with the modern. Its institutionalization paradoxically rendered void Barr's initially experimental application of philosophical aesthetics and what was then the novelty of new German and Austrian constructions of a history for art from Riegl to Wölfflin to the chaos of modern art-making since the 1880s.

In his 1999 Walter Neurath Lecture, Nicholas Serota, Director of the Tate, London, explored what he called the "Dilemma of the Museums of Modern Art," which he suspended between "Experience or Interpretation."[16] Is the museum charged to deliver a history of art lesson to its visitors? Or should it be hung so that each visitor can experience the work unscripted by its place in such a narrative? Tracking tendencies in

curatorial strategies in displaying permanent collections and in new archi-
tectures for single artist or single collector displays, Serota is left with no
resolution. Thematic displays such as that adopted for the Tate Modern
avoid the canonical narratives of a narrowed view of what is important in
modern art (tending to exclude any but great white men). Displays of
single artists are also not the complete answer, since they deprive the
visitor of context, reference, and dialogue in the making of art as social
and communal process. The model forged so brilliantly by Alfred Barr in
1929 to bring intelligibility through plotting a chronological development
called the modern to the mess of contemporary art that was at that very
moment almost at the end of its own "moment" rapidly ossified into a
straitjacket. No other model has emerged to resolve the contradictions in
which that model was forged: a secularizing but still deeply religious
culture; art negotiating its own relations to life, society, and otherness;
market-led privatizing production, fostering radical individuality and
gambit-playing; the necessity for conditions of shared intelligibility and
critical interpretation; a perverse relation to the only possible sources of
financial support for this entrepreneurial artistic production – the moneyed
classes, who themselves relate in often contradictory fashion to the material
basis of their social and economic dominance by espousing liberalism in
the arts.

Yet Barr clearly planned MoMA as an active player in the culture which
it was created to curate: in the absence of existing frames of knowledge and
narratives for the understanding of what appeared to be a chaotic and
indecipherable rejection of the very concepts of culture that the newly
founded grand survey museums of the nineteenth century existed to
enshrine, Barr's concept for MoMA was innovative and trend-setting.
One of its most significant interventions was to place education – or
shall we say the creation of constituencies and communities for art –
onto a primary agenda, there being no widespread acceptance of, or
means of finding intelligible, "the outrageous art we all loved," in the
words of MoMA's three women founders. Yet this museum became the
paradigm for most modern art museums, and its exhibitionary and
discursive framing of modern art became the doctrinaire model for the
teaching of the subject throughout most art history institutions. MoMA
created the terms of intelligibility and dissemination of the new, while
having to consolidate art as always already known within its fixing definitions, preferred narratives, and ultimately selective canon. The museum
installed a racist, sexist, and Eurocentric conception of the modern against

which we are now obliged to agitate from the disqualified margins of race, class, gender, and sexuality, i.e. what was placed categorically outside what the museum defines alone as art worthy of being part of the canon.

The Moderns' scene in MoMA sets up the Eastern (effete, over-educated, Europeanized) connoisseur, who is taking young male initiates (suggestions of homosexuality and art appreciation as well as professional sexism) around the new cathedral of the modern – the art museum – where they stand in hushed silence to contemplate the genius of the masterpieces of modernism. Hart, standing behind, contemplates something else created for the viewer by the narrative that s/he has witnessed. The viewer sees the label *Nathalie de Ville Collection*; the viewer knows the history of the works; they are Hart's work. Does this make a fool of the connoisseur – unable to tell the forged from the authentic? Does it rather question the authentic itself, proposing instead, in a sense suggested by Mieke Bal, that meaning and effect in art are products of the framing: institutional, discursive, and fantasmatic?[17] We see what we desire to find. We see what the institution creates for us to desire. We accept the staggered relations of viewing that the film stages: the desiring art lover is the first rung: he speaks movingly of what these paintings do for him and performs the aestheticization of both art object and art subject. The students stand to be transformed from ignorance and insensitivity into art lovers: the blank pages onto which museum education writes its script. Hart, the unrecognized artist, stands behind these two first lines of viewing, learning himself through the talk of these mediating others, finding in their misrecognition, a (mis)representation of himself.

The film affirms both sexuality and desire in its more driven abstractions as the condition of the authentic that transcends the museal classification which is based on legalities: ownership as provenance. This reveals a tension, in a banal and otherwise not very significant way, between what we might call cultural value that derives from the site of making with its imperatives, purposes, histories, and singularities, however trivialized and conventionalized here as love, and what we can call the economic value conferred on the object that, through a variety of discursive and institutional frameworks, is remade as a repository of investments. These can only be expressed in monetary terms and consumed in religious ones. This confusion lies at the heart of any deliberation on the museum after modernism. The preservation and educational missions of the museum and the gallery are hooked on the impossible contradiction of these twin forces/possibilities within modern capitalist systems.

Tele-vision

"Know art! know life!" says the legend on this flyer for new books from the major art publisher Thames and Hudson (Figure 1.2) under a photograph by Nick Turpin of somewhat curious viewer behavior in London's National Gallery. Seated, a white middle-aged man, dressed more for

Thames & Hudson world of art   Spring 2002

Figure 1.2   Leaflet produced by Thames and Hudson. Photograph by Nick Turpin, 2002.

bird-watching in the country, takes his binoculars to a unseen painting, while other visitors perform the viewing ritual at a more standard proximity to the objects on display, arranging themselves around the edge of the room, moving to the instructional art-historical narrative of the hanging sequence that prevails in national museums and art galleries still working on the classic nineteenth-century model of the aristocratic palace with its series of rooms *enfilade*. Seeking to get optically close to the work from which he is physically distant, the seated gallery visitor enhances his vision with magnifying lenses that cut out even that movement.

The apparatus for telescoping vision across the real gap of space between viewer and painting obscures his eyes and brings the now virtualized image close, yet secretively so, allowing the man almost to incorporate it in cinematic close-up, hence privately: enhanced vision, suspended corporeality, an experience of losing oneself in the scopophilic fantasy of the magnified visual field. In a way, this viewer perfectly allegorizes the generic art book that this photograph is used to promote as a means both to *know art* – all art, art itself, art in general, art as a generality, art as knowable – and to *know life*, which is somehow offered also in its entirety and generality by knowing art. Knowing, seeing, visually mastering, leaves the viewer centered and disembodied in a perfect fantasy that the museum in its virtual form as book feeds: the art book is a product of museum consciousness. If knowing art and knowing life are synonymous, there is a short circuit to knowledge by means of the tele-technology of vision that can traverse all space and bring the distant close via representation. The art book is the purchasable, commodity form of the museum. Yet the art book is the museum without walls, hence without the apparent frames of either architectural layout or iconographic programming.

What was once located in space, and distantly so, so that we needed to travel here and there to see it in person, can now come into my home and into my library, and I can know it, but only through that technological translation from thing to image, from object to sight, from its singularity in time and space to a generic example of a category – art – whose meaning and purpose are predetermined by the infinite relations within which it is set, relations which reduce its living particularity as the product of concrete mental and manual labor within social relations of production to what Marx would call, speaking of the bourgeois subject, "its unreal universality."[18] Here the performance of commodity fetishism is visible, conjuring out of sight the very existence of the *labor* that produces what the museum and the book return to us only as the image of art, art as an image.[19]

It is now a truism that the creation of technologies of photographic reproduction transformed not only our relations to art, but in effect created art as that unreal universality. In the formulation of his idealist aesthetics that would be published as a three-volume psychology of art (1947–50) under the title *Les Voix de silence* (1935 and 1951), André Malraux coined the phrase "museum without walls" (Figure 1.3). But, as Rosalind Krauss has pointed out in her article on the "postmodern

Figure 1.3   André Malraux with illustrations for *Le Musée imaginaire*, 1950. © Maurice Jarnoux/Paris Match/Scoop.

museum without walls," this term is treacherous in such a translation. Malraux's "master conceit," *le musée imaginaire*, "better translated as the *imaginary museum*, addresses the space of the human faculties: imagination, cognition, judgement." In English, "museum without walls," however, still suggests a building, even one without definition and confinement.[20] For Malraux, the museum of the imagination is the modern historical situation of art, that is the product both of stage one – the creation of the public museum – and of stage two – its expansion through photographic reproduction that, by manipulations of scale, angle, and uniformity of surface, creates new objects entirely for a proximate lens-based visual appropriation, where, in effect, viewing becomes consumption and voyeurism. Hence the dissemination of our generic knowledge of things as "art" is structurally dependent on technologically expanded modern musealization itself. This effect, however, is not bound to architecture and place.

Thus expanded, Art makes that place – the museum – which still offers specific, if over-visualized, encounters, itself merely the already known guardian of the original of the image. The original must in many ways always disappoint because of the heightened expectation raised by reproduction of its exclusive visuality through a technology that intensifies luminosity and gloss in comparison to the solid, aging materiality of crafted things and painted surfaces. This paradox is what offers particular possibilities for current interventions via museum programming in the museum as site of a concrete embodied, social, and intellectually directed encounter, either through the exhibition or a different access to the collection itself.

Writing of nineteenth-century critics like Théophile Gautier, Edmond de Goncourt, and Charles Baudelaire, Malraux reminds us of our novel situation:

> What had they seen? What had been seen, until 1900, by all those writers whose views on art still impress us as revealing and important; whom we take to be speaking of the same works we know, and referring to the same *data* as those available to us? They had visited two or three galleries, and seen photographs, prints or copies of a scarce handful of masterpieces and their readers had seen even less.[21]

Taking a very different track from Duncan and Wallach, Malraux regrets the museum as desacralizing. He argues that the museum is the very sign of modernity's reclassification of objects from ritual, religious, architectural, and decorative uses. Implying a link between the category of art and modern secularization, he argues that museums created "art" by extracting crucifixes from churches and making them into sculpture or painting, and portraits from dynastic galleries and presenting them to us only as Titians or Rembrandts.

This radical decontextualization and translation was, in fact, a widespread complaint made most poignantly by the nineteenth-century art administrator Quatremère de Quincy. Talking of museums as warehouses of cultural debris, the once revolutionary minister of culture in France (1816–39) expressed what became a standard regret at its very foundations at the beginning of the nineteenth century. The museum was seen to wrench works from their vital sources in social and religious life to assemble only the material husk: "It is doubtful that you transferred the network of ideas and relations that made the works alive with interest. Their essential merit depended on the beliefs that created them, on the ideas to which they were tied, to the circumstances that explained the community of thoughts that gave them their unity."[22]

Thus the selected great works gathered in the museum of the viewer's mind become "art." Or shall we say, they are reduced from the vibrant cultural process and semantic activity that generated the work and created its meanings in a community of meaning-users when the museum – that legacy of covetousness and national piracy – first created the level and public playing field on which once diverse objects and artifacts, relics and monuments, fragments and traces, could become comparable, classifiable, and knowable in a form of knowledge that we call art history. Under what rubric is material, symbolic, ideological, temporal difference annulled and a new logic of relative difference – style, period, nation, school, master – created? The answer is the public collection, the assemblage and display, the isolation, and, in effect, the aestheticization of things made within aesthetico-symbolic practices as the Western concept of art that becomes identical with its own historicist histories. To say this at this stage is not to judge this historical change in the banal postmodern Manicheaism of good/bad. That is history. That is what we have to deal with. That is what we come "after." That was what determines the current debates and dilemmas. So the question is what to do with what cannot be undone through nostalgia, ethnography, or more ideological critique.

If Quatremère de Quincy bewailed the isolation of objects in the museum taken out of their original cultural contexts, there were other nineteenth-century analysts who would invert the nostalgic complaint that museums petrify and fossilize. In his reading of Hegel's *Phenomenology of Spirit*, published in 1807, one year after Quatremère de Quincy's *Considerations Morales*, Didier Maleuvre points out Hegel's initial agreement and then his volte-face, which leaves us with the alibi of the modern museum that is the enacted institutional foundation for what has become art history. Hegel dismisses the living garments of time and history of the artwork as ultimately incidental happenstance. He endorses the fact that the museum offers us access to art, like plucked fruit that is linked both to the tree where it grew and to the person to whom it is offered. The museum mediates between the necessary conditions of art's making and its rebirth in consciousness and reflection. What was once a mere fact, the relation of Michelangelo's *David* to the Signoria, known or realized through the museum, becomes inward. That acquired knowledge reveals that what was the artwork's context was always the product of the mind. It was always an intellectual and theoretical condition. Maleuvre concludes: "Only in cultural recollection does the true significance of culture emerge for Hegel. In that sense our recollection of antiquity is truer to the spirit of antiquity than antiquity was in itself. Antiquity is more genuinely itself in the British Museum than in the Temple at Paestum."[23]

Lest this seem merely the Eurocentric suprematism it probably contains, we might add that Hegel is simply refusing the lure of authenticity and essentialism to argue that meaning is always the effect of mediation. Historical consciousness is precisely the product of a lapse of time, of a gap. It shares in a psychoanalytical sense of desire with its constituting verso of loss or absence. In some ways, to grasp that there has been history as opposed to sequential segments of lived time, there must be reflection. Consciousness must be created of that which is no longer, or from which the reflecting subject stands apart. The museum is both an image of history and a historical image of the Hegelian, European moment of historically conscious subjectivity.

Maleuvre offers a political reading of these two poles of thinking: Quatremère de Quincy creates a dichotomy of theory versus praxis, abstracted from versus living within culture. This thesis, while appearing to stand for a cultural contextualization that many might now applaud, can easily become an apologia for fascist aesthetics, nationalist, and racist ideologies of relations between culture and land, blood and soil. "The drive for identity stands behind nationalism." Hegel's insistence that culture is always "a *theoria* of culture," always a mediated and reflective way of thinking about, analyzing, and understanding what is different and non-identical ensures a means of resistance.[24]

Maleuvre argues, using Novalis' phrase of "homeless conscience," that "[i]n offering an image of uprooted culture, the museum preserves the self-estranging drive of culture. The museum stands true to antiquity by doing to antiquity what it, *as culture*, did to itself."[25] Thus, in comparing these two founding philosophical discourses on the museum in modernity (or the museum as one face of the modern), we can locate the contradiction as indicative of modernity itself. On the one hand, modernity is subject to nostalgia for what it feels it has lost: tradition, connectivity, and self-identity. This nostalgia becomes dangerous if it falls into fascism. On the other hand, modernity is prey to its own inaugurating rootlessness in intellectual self-consciousness. Thus it oscillates, suspended between regressive conservatism and edgy estrangement as the drive of critical creativity itself.

Merleau-Ponty against Malraux: "Painting" versus Style

I want to return now to Malraux for one further moment before moving on with the question of posterity: the museum not *of* but *after* modernism as the Canadian museum programmer and cultural thinker Judith Mastai posed and practiced it. The use of photographic reproduction after 1900 and the dissemination not just of a museum's contents but the museal concept of art through reproductive technologies as art books enabled the playing field to become less institutionalized and more subjectivized. For Malraux, the great historical shift is this: the terrain on which art now functions is that of the human mind – imagination, cognition, and judgment. But in that mental museum, what is distilled is only what can be held in common within this cacophony of diversity: style. Instead of Hegelian difference, there is a classically humanist search for an internal identity between all objects: realized in what we call the dominant paradigm MoMA itself imposed and Alan Rudolph ironically held up for inspection in the person of the connoisseur in his film *The Moderns*.

Style for Malraux bears witness simply to the human spirit of creativity. Krauss summarizes Malraux thus: "These great fictions that the *musée imaginaire* makes visible are, then, so many stories about the collective spirit of human creativity, so many versions of the inventiveness evidenced by the Family of Man, like multiple documents of Man's Fate."[26] In his introduction to Merleau-Ponty's critique and review of *Les Voix de silence*, "Indirect Language and Voices of Silence," Galen A. Johnson elaborates this further:

> Malraux's museum without walls was an intentional isolation, *arrachement*, in order to present a history of human artistic creativity. The panorama enabled Malraux to establish his central theses about modern painting that engage Merleau-Ponty's essay: a critique of the limitations of the modern-day art museum, an individualism and subjectivism regarding modern painting as an expression of the painter's personal style or inner world, an objectivist Hegelian notion of a spirit of painting that controls the style of a historical epoch even across cultures, and a cult of genius regarding the heroes of modern art that approaches religious fervor. Influenced by Nietzsche and Gide, Malraux finds in modern painting a return to the worship of the sublime and exotic that characterized primitive religion. Consequent upon the death of God, Malraux was determined to ward off the death of culture and to establish the artist as a replacement of the divine.[27]

Read thus, Malraux's project exemplifies theoretically what Duncan and Wallach suggested: the appropriated and bourgeois recalibration of the ritual-religious model for its own constitutive ideology. The museum retrospectively flushes all art of the post-medieval era with the mourning colors of its post-religious exile, which is then disavowed by the substitution of the artist-genius and the cult of art distilled as style. Here lies not only the aestheticization of art but also its sacralization. Malraux writes: "What genius is not fascinated by the extremity of painting, by the appeal before which time itself vacillates? It is the moment of possession of the world. Let painting go no further, and Hans the Elder has become God."[28]

In his analysis of Merleau-Ponty's phenomenological opposition to Malraux's aesthetics, Galen A. Johnson focuses on the philosopher's commentary on a film of Henri Matisse at work, which showed the artist's pencil arrested and moving above the paper before he made his mark. In the documentary, Matisse expressed alarm when he saw this section of the footage. He felt naked and deeply exposed, and feared the gesture would be read as hesitation or uncertainty, which he vigorously disclaimed. Instead, he explained that he was "unconsciously establishing the relationship between the subject I was about to draw and the size of my paper." Galen comments: "Merleau-Ponty agrees with Matisse, that the slow-motion of the camera's 'eye' should not be taken as revealing the truth about Matisse's gesture as a painter, for Matisse acted in the world of human perception, gesture and time, and the film makes us believe that the painter's hand originated in the physical world of abstract scientific possibilities."[29] It is here that this question of the museum visitor with his binoculars can be situated, *here* being a complicated field of historical legacies, intertwining technologies of vision with institutional collection and isolation, display and presentation, and an effect that reifies the aesthetic simultaneously in the dual and possibly contradictory spaces of the utterly subjectivized interior world of an abstract spirituality and the rationally objectivized flow of the spirit that form the basic pedagogical premises of museal art history, whether in the gallery or the book, the university or the art college. The counter-position draws on Merleau-Ponty's reading of art, notably modern painting, for its sub-philosophical exploration of the becoming of phenomenological, embodied, and situated consciousness in the "intertwining of vision and movement."[30]

In his analysis of *Museum Memories: History, Technology, Art*, Didier Maleuvre reads Malraux's aesthetics as deeply indicative of its bourgeois moment:

> The history of museums reveals changing practices in the ways of presenting and apprehending art. From the cabinet of curiosities to the modern art gallery, the culture of aesthetic visuality undergirds an ideological production of the individual. The aestheticization of the artwork in the museum parallels the aestheticization – neutralization and autonomization – of the bourgeois subject in industrial society. The museum constitutes a formidable model of civic membership, a ritual of social identification, in short, a technology of the subject.[31]

Maleuvre rehearses the core argument of Duncan and Wallach's founding analyses of the "Museum of Modern Art as Late Capitalist Ritual," which plotted out the process of this refashioning of subjectivity through a choreographed encounter with that actual collection of images which further reveal a deeply gendered structuring of this alienated bourgeois subjectivity. He further argues that by tracking this integration of the ideology of art's presentation in the museum and its virtual extensions, the art book and its now digital dispersion in cyber-virtuality, with the ideology of autonomized bourgeois existence, we can begin to imagine its counterforce: namely the possibility of a museum and a museum subject attuned to the situated encounter with the emancipatory thrust of art-making itself. That works at all times against false, idealizing universalization on behalf of particular knowledges, specified subjectivities, and contested meanings – in a word, WORK. Perhaps it would do to recall here Merleau-Ponty's distinction between *peindre*, to paint, the artist's living work, and *la peinture*, the painting, as "the enshrined and abandoned artwork as a fetish of capital exchange."[32]

Rather than being an institution dedicated to the education of its publics in conformity and compliance to authority, Maleuvre argues that the museum could become cultural, in the Hegelian sense suggested by the work of art that is liberated from what is fixed and too often essentialized as "culture." What fails, therefore, in museum education that aims at recontextualization is often this difficult concept of art as the *theoria* of culture, when *theoria* means puzzling, taking a close look at, thinking about, reflecting upon. Instead, the dominant tropes of consumption, entertainment, cultural assimilation, commodification, and aestheticization, with their residual religiosity, prevail, and even the introduction of visual culture or anthropological approaches to art as culture find themselves in politically suspect company. We may decry art itself in our demonizing of its museal framing, reducing everything to the undifferentiated flow of representation and image which leaves little space for this encounter of work-thought. Further, there is a danger that, in the search for means of reintroducing those cultural voices and places that Barr's admittedly sexist and racist canonical modernism excluded, identity and related badges of cultural fixity become more than momentary tactics, necessary but dangerous. They can as easily trap some of us in "other cultures," rather than in the particularities of situated knowledges and located art-making, with all its complex discomforts and disidentificatory potentials of what modernism has made of art. To have the space from which one speaks acknowledged can, all too easily, become a new prison house in which all that such identity-based art is allowed to speak of is its geo-ethnic allocation.

These debates from the 1800s to the 1950s create a framework within which to situate Canadian thinker and educator Judith Mastai's practice as cultural work on the side of the emancipatory thrust of art as a living and unashamedly intellectual practice. Judith Mastai trained as an actor and participated in the new interdisciplinary art and extended experimental activist theatre of avant-garde London during the 1970s. Extending ideas of performance and participation, she undertook doctoral research into adult education, asking how people engage with knowledge outside the formal educational timetables and institutions. Long before "life-long learning," she researched relations of non-academic constituencies to discontinuously acquired social knowledge, empowerment, and change. Working on government projects such as public education programs on alcoholism, drugs, and violence against women, Mastai was then invited to enter a new field: public programming for a leading Canadian museum of modern art, the Vancouver Art Gallery.

Approaching the ethnography of the art world about which she knew little, applying research methodologies to identifying its varied constituencies – artists, curators, collectors, accountants, administrators, conservators, visitors of all ages and cultures – Mastai addressed the museum from outside its own self-framing (Oberhardt 1) and beyond even its counter-frames (Oberhardt 2) and even popular representations (Oberhardt 3). She was as independent of the art-historical paradigm as she was of new museology. She wondered about the apparent stand-off between modern art museums and artists in their home towns. She wondered why there was so much undirected "education." How were the gallery volunteers/docents being trained and in what knowledges? Only in the standard narrative interpretations of the canonical story? How could they learn about the new social, feminist, and postcolonial art histories being produced down the road in the University, which might mean something to varied gendered, classed, aged, cultured visitors/users?[33] Did museums conceived in nationalist terms really think about or know the needs of their highly diverse constituencies in the era of mass migration, asylum-seeking, and globalized postcoloniality? Was the museum a landmark of civic pride competing with the museums of other cities and countries in a supra-national but enclosed art dialogue? Or was it a public resource capable of making its contents as active forms for the life-long learning of resident artistic constituencies of the present and future – through younger people? What did a museum of Euro-American modern art, with its anthropological view of non-European *artifacts*, mean for people young and old from the vast range of cultures and nationalities of immigrant societies with displaced first nation and aboriginal peoples? Were they excluded? How would they find themselves in its spaces, stories, categories? How was the museum responding to the challenges of changing technologies and information systems that any ordinary citizen knew about, while social philosophers analyzed their meaning for society and subjectivity? (See the chapters by Bal, McMaster, and Phillips in this volume.)

Defeated by a too-early death before she could fully realize and be recognized for her growing interventions into these crucial debates about the museum, Judith Mastai's contribution can be grasped under three headings, which I have derived from a reading of her surviving papers and experience with working with her on many projects and events that reshaped my own understanding of my own projects.

First, Mastai was concerned with the question of the public art gallery – the title of a university course she proposed in 1992 and taught in several universities. This involved taking on the historical, hence modern, legacy of the museum, whose first post-revolutionary effect was to deprivatize collections of royal treasures and aristocratic trophies and offer them to public ownership and contribute to the creation of that new sphere and new experience: a democratic public. Given both the Habermasian emancipatory definition of the public sphere and Foucault's more de-pressing analysis of how, under bourgeois rule, the public sphere would inevitably fall prey to the material mechanisms of the economy and power, the media, etc., this project – to sustain or even reinvent the radical possibility of the instruments of colonized and appropriated public space and dominative rather than communicative reason – was no mean task.[34] It was profoundly political. Could the art museum, declared redundantly *mauseological*, become a forum of a reclaimed public project that could address the massive issues raised by postcoloni-ality, multicultural populations and the pressing issues of class, sexuality, and gender: difference?

Second, Mastai's work was unapologetically intellectual. Written on the original document for a summer institute in critical museology that we planned at the Art Gallery of Ontario in 1998 was the legend: "an invitation to intellectual play." What I did not understand then and am realizing only now, as I do this work in the painful and terrible absence of her extraordinary mind and person, is the full meaning of the phrase. What she had in mind to incite was intellectual, cognitive, thinking, reflecting activity directed at understanding, at difference in the Hegelian sense, at transformation not confirmation. Play in its post-structuralist sense includes both the ludic, and hence the dialectic of repetition that marks the path of the death drive and our release from its deadly drive to stasis, and the mechanical sense of "give" as in a loosened screw, some-thing not bolted rigid but allowing some room for movement. Where were we to play but in the museum? The museum can be used for its resources – from collections, to libraries, to docents, to registrars, to packers and porters, to conservators and managers. Judith Mastai, the sociologist and outsider, recognized non-hierarchically the entirety of the system of the museum, including the least visible forms of necessary labor. She assumed that all the workers had a take on what the museum did and what meaning it might have for others. The catalyst, the trickster figure in this anthropology of culture as knowledge-making and social change, was the educator. No longer the bearer or transmitter of formally disciplined information – the canonical story inducting the passive receptive visitor through the carefully rehearsed ideological script of masterpiece and genius – the educator becomes a facilitator of a way of working in the enlivened museum once the museum is itself redefined as a public space with responsibilities, not to some fetishized generality or fiction of the bourgeois mind called art or the public, but publics, specific, contesting constituencies with a variety of different competences, positions, needs, histories, and purposes in relating to this resource, to this site of provocation of debate and difference, of memory, amnesia and creative possibility. Judith Mastai's paper "There Is No Such Thing as a Visitor" is included in this volume.

I stress again this Hegelian notion of cultural work as dis-identification, rather than as the problematic medium for attempting to assimilate and hence reassert a selective hegemony. Think of the endless troops of schoolchildren brought to national museums of the West, there to be inducted, to learn how to become part of a national entity through its fossilized, fixed historical culture. If cultural institutions are used to manage cultural diversity through an unchanged model of the equation between conserved (rather than reread) cultures and identities, structural Western racism, sexism, homophobia, and class structures are paradoxically confirmed. An effective challenge to social relations of production, racism, sexism, and homophobia has to be produced as an effect of working, as a creation of changed understanding at the level of the interaction of geographically fluid, psychologically liquid subjectivities, with histories and geographies of difference that can be staged through the museum as an open and productive public institution.

It is here that Mastai's challenge to education or programming as the mere retailing and marketing of the essentially authoritative and in-house manufactured object-based narrative is most radical. It is here that the challenge to the commercialization of the museum as part of national heritage and municipal tourism becomes most acute. For, as I understand her project, Mastai wanted the very planning of exhibitions, the very structuring of the overall activities of the museum or gallery to be permeated by the questions generated from the education or programming department, itself theoretically recast by its real intellectual engagements with currents in all aspects of social and cultural analysis, including close working with artists as creative thinkers as well as with sociologists, anthropologists, historians, psychoanalysts, and scientists. The educator or public programmer must be the one who thinks outside either the adoring art-historical paradigm or the demonizing museological frame. In Oberhardt's model, the educator is in the fourth free frame, thinking in the changing world of ideas so as to deconstruct and reinvent what is conserved and exhibited in the museum as dynamic elements of living cultures.

Instead of inviting the educators in only after the art-historical paradigm-bearing curators have made their textual decisions, the educators should be part of the overall strategizing of the museum as a public resource. This department is the open passage that mediates between the conservatory and disciplinary operations of specialist curators and budget-minded museum managers and the concrete, non-unified publics, the incredibly varied (which is not the same as stratified or classified) constituencies of the museum that its works and its workers have to serve rather than service.

Finally, the third key point that I have deduced from my reflections of Judith Mastai's work and practice is the intimate relationship between the historically and theoretically informed critique of the origins and practices of the modern museum – modern in the sense of its revolutionary origins in the late eighteenth century – and the artistic practices that emerged in the late twentieth century that are now being rapidly curated and museally classified as conceptual art. This practice resumes a dropped stitch of that moment of the 1920s – something of Duchamp's eroticism and irreverent relation to the concrete and everyday lurks in Alan Rudolph's construction of Nick Hart's kitsch rewriting of the Sistine Madonna by Raphael, and its circulation in public as a "wet dream." Conceptual art reclaimed Duchamp's virulent resistance to what he dismissed, with Impressionism in mind, as "retinal art" – represented in *The Moderns* by the injunction to stand in silent awe observing the mystery of Cézanne's unique genius – as opposed to seeing art as a specific if unusual form of "thinking," or, in Merleau-Ponty's terms, "embodied," already engaged in philosophizing about conditions and relations of human consciousness and understanding.

Mastai's interests in the works of Lawrence Wiener, Terry Atkinson, Mary Kelly, Sutapa Biswas, and Sunil Gupta,[35] in the relations between art and language, New York and Vancouver conceptualism, and feminist theory and postcolonial interventions in practice and art history(ies) were not arbitrary. In her outline for a university course on "The Idea of a Public Art Gallery," Mastai identified the shift in the early twentieth century to a deepening relation between the museum of modern art and the art market, to focus on making reputations for artists which put the idea of the public art gallery under severe scrutiny. From whom? From contemporary artists whose practice performed an "institutional critique." The art gallery became the topic of work for many artists, such as Daniel Buren, Marcel Broodthaers, Hans Haacke, and Fred Wilson.[36] Such critique was a political facet of conceptual art. Far from being merely another "ism" to be curated into the standard chronological flow charts and floor plans, Mastai saw a specific kind of contemporary artistic practice – practice as critique – as itself part of the history of the museum/gallery. At the same time these practices strained the older distinctions and relations between making and curating, between market and authority. They tried to find a space in which art could work rather than merely satisfy the endless hunger of the commodity market with its value enhancers in the museum/market/studio circuits of NATO (the European-American Atlantic axis that dominated the modern art world). Finally Mastai discussed artists such as Anne Ramsden, Jamelie Hassan, and Irene Whittome, whose works address specifically the role of museums in positioning cultures and histories in relation to each other, within patterns of relativizing meaning that leave intact the core space of art for the NATO world.[37]

Judith Mastai's practice defied professional demarcations between art-historically trained curators and educators to curate two exhibitions that demonstrated her sense of art and exhibition both as a necessary provocation of debate and as a responsibility toward histories that are erased by official museums.[38] *Women and Paint* featured Jane Ash Poitras, Eleanor Bond, Allyson Clay, Miran Fukada, Pamela Golden, and Dorrit Yacoby. This remarkable intervention, at the Mendel Art Gallery in Saskatoon in 1995, exemplifies her process of thinking and working. There can be no doubt that painting as a central mode of modernist practice was radically displaced after the early 1960s, not only by what came to be called conceptual practice, but also by increasing engagement with lens-based media, photography, video, and, ultimately, more digital technologies. In 1989, as part of a preparation of the Vancouver art community and interested publics for an exhibition of work by Mary Kelly, Mastai ran first a series of reading groups and then invited me to do a week-long seminar on the extended artistic practices and theoretical frameworks within which Kelly's work was operating. The seminars were to enable Vancouver artists and art historians to have the resources and confidence with which to engage with Kelly's conceptual work when it was encountered, rather than find themselves excluded by a lack of keys or terms of analysis that formed the community of knowledge from which the work was generated. At the end of the seminar, a conversation was staged between myself and Mary Kelly, and published by the Vancouver Art Gallery as another element of Mastai's interventions.[39] During this conversation, the depressing state of feminist criticism was discussed. It was then being claimed that older feminists had proscribed paint in favor of "scripto-visual" media, as if artists were or could be authorities dictating what anyone else should use. Mary Kelly stressed that no one can dictate choice of media or what Terry Atkinson would call "resources of expression." She would, however, anticipate critical consciousness on the part of an artist in relation to systems of representation, to social conditions of distribution and reading and to semiotic potentialities. Alerted to a debate that served negatively to dichotomize and divide an already marginal community, in her exhibition conjoining "women" and "paint," therefore, Mastai explored contemporary practices by women who had chosen what in general was now a marginal, but still ideologically freighted, practice: painting, rather than the medium "paint." The small show selected artists from Canada's First Nations, from Japan, and from Israel. Claiming no comprehensiveness, the cases served as "research": here's a problem, so what is actually happening and what will be the outcome of enabling others to engage with such a range of intellectually and critically self-aware artists, for whom a non-unified practice of image-making that called upon computers, photographs, and all manner of media and objects was radically redefining "painting"?[40]

The second exhibition, *Social Process/Collaborative Action: Mary Kelly 1970–1975*, is discussed in chapter 11 of this volume, "Anxious Dust." It was of enormous historic importance, focusing on the little or unknown early work of Mary Kelly (writing here in chapter 7), resurrecting both the film *The Nightcleaners* (Marc Karlin and Berwick Street Film Collective, 1975), the most important political film since Slatan Dudow and Bertolt Brecht's *Kuhle Wampe* (1932) and the collaborative project of Margaret Harrison, Kay Hunt, and Mary Kelly, *Women and Work* (1975). Mastai established an archive of resources from which that work was itself formed in the British Women's Movement, the Artists' Union, and the flurry of magazines and reading groups which constituted the political singularity of the feminist movement in Britain in the 1970s. The accompanying publication was more than a catalogue. It provided a documentary history of a lost moment, reassembling the intellectual framings of that moment through a series of specially written and archive articles that made access-ible to contemporary publics the historical conditions of emergence of the radical alliance between feminist thought and politics and conceptual artistic practice in an intellectual community around 1970, which included the making of *The Nightcleaners*.

As a result of the art-historical adoration paradigm and the narrow, canonical story of even contemporary art, much of the art of that moment and its histories have not been curated. Excluded from the museum, they are effectively de-accessioned for the publics who, uninformed, are denied critical awareness of important and creative aspects of the histories of art in the later twentieth century. The museum is so significant and far-reaching in its effects precisely because it is cultural gate-keeper, judge, and executioner, as well as archeon: the home of cultural memory.[41] Political art happened; feminist interventions were made. Creative alli-ances were forged between film and art, class and conceptualism, gender and Marxism. Without curation or archivization, they disappear from our store – cultural archive – of possibilities. Without curation, visitors to art galleries and museums will never be prompted to seek out books or more information on artists they never encounter in the galleries, or events and practices to which they are never introduced. Thus the circle of our knowledge is effectively censored and regulated if the museum is exclu-sively directed by the insiders – the keepers of the art-historical paradigm, themselves trained inside its canons, and anxious to maintain "face" amongst that small insider community. As educator, traveling in transdis-ciplinary fashion across cultural disciplines and practices, with her own special sets of interests, Judith Mastai intervened by curating the exhib-itions no one else thought to conceive or situate. This was exemplary in terms of the idea of a public art gallery, the space in which knowledge is not to be managed, but produced and offered in equity and honesty as expanded histories.[42]

In 1995, John O'Brian, Hanif Jan Mohamed, and Judith Mastai founded and edited a journal for critical art theory, *Collapse*. From the late 1980s, Mastai had initiated and ran a series of educational programs and events at the Vancouver Art Gallery and the Art Gallery of Ontario that actively changed the terms of self-understanding as well as cultural placement of both the invited participants and the local publics who formed the audiences and co-participants. She believed one of the museum's/gallery's major responsibilities was to the continuing education of the artists of the community in which the gallery was situated. The concept of the public often excludes the primary constituency for an art museum – artists and art students. If the gallery, the market, and the magazine have been shown by artists, in their critique of the institutionalization of art, to be nugatory, venal, incorporated, and complicit, Mastai showed how else to use the public space for intellectual debate and the creation of a critical mirror in which to read contemporary cultural arguments provoked by the making of art. Artists are not merely the museum's obvious customer; the museum is responsible for continuous development and sustenance of a lively artistic community.

Mastai questioned the merely cosmetic change in museums that allowed some feminism, a little multiculturalism, and one or two shows about sexualities and identities, while framing them within the usual packaging as specials, as necessary concessions to new but still outsider interests. Responding to the commitments of contemporary artistic practice itself, she reframed the museum's liminal spaces. She opened its doorways to the world within and beyond its walls, as the site of interruption of business as usual, as the space of serious education that involved discussion, debate, and resulting mutual transformation of all parties invited in on terms that were never patronizing or irrelevant to what she called their own narratives.

Thus, in a brief paper, a fragment of which survives, in which the phrase from leading museological theorist Eileen Hooper-Greenhil, "museums after modernism," becomes the keystone of her reflections, Judith Mastai explains how she originally defined her work through the idea of a laboratory. The laboratory as paradigm for the workshop, the seminar, the reading group, the symposium, the day conference, the schools project, and the artist in residence did not serve cultural management, the administration of bourgeois ideologies of art as object before whose fetishized value the visitor is taught to genuflect. It served its opposite: it was a place of making and experimentation, whose impact was precisely on the subjectivity of the participant – the player, the investigator, the experimentalist, working with made things and making things whose significance was not their objecthood, but their capacity to incite meaning and activate thought.

From her reading of Amelia Jones on performance and subjectivity, Mastai cited the definition from Antonin Artaud of performance: "A direct communication will be established between the spectator and the spectacle, between the actor and the spectator, from the fact that the spectator, placed in the middle of the action, is engulfed and physically affected by it."[43] Mastai defined her project as performance: "Every day, in many ways, my colleagues and I are engaged in performing a continually emerging institutional subjectivity. Change is not an interlude, but a condition of our work."[44] Performance here evokes both her own theatrical history with its ability to enact and act upon, and the philosophical sense made popular by Judith Butler, in which certain kinds of statements implicate their sayer in an action, a realization of the thought. The museum is remade daily as the realized promise of art as work.

Museum work becomes both performativity and performance art. As art itself, it transforms the uses of space, the identity of the institution and the nature of the collections. It changes the concept of the public so they become participants in a cultural activity that is both a creation of involvement and the manufacture of the necessary distance of critical reflection and self-consciousness. This work involves, therefore, a changing and continuously transformative subjectivity – what Marx in his still Hegelian vocabulary would call "consciousness for itself." This is dialectics in action; this is reading and understanding Adorno's critique of capitalist society's administration of culture, his rejection of its nostalgic, essentializing, nationalist, racist, sexist, even fascist tendencies, protected from critique under the banner of the purity and autonomy of art as a secularized religious value.

This method is also profoundly Brechtian. Judith Mastai argued in a paper she gave at a conference in Leeds in 1999 that many who used the ideas of Brechtian distanciation often forgot that, for critical reflexivity to occur, the participant must first be attracted to and engaged by the play. The museum must, she argues, include "a pathway of desire." Those of us who make art, study its histories, and critically analyze it are the ones who like it, seek it out, wish to live with it. We also admire it and want to know it.

Judith Mastai's practice of education as performance/performativity shares with radical artistic practices of perpetual displacement, critique, and investigation of the conditions of subjectivity, knowing, and meaning from which it was nourished the question of what it is to be "after modernism." This does not mean simply swapping modernism for some new entity: postmodernism. Although Zygmunt Bauman's concept of liquid modernity had not matured before Judith Mastai died, I think she would have found the sociologist's sense of the radical instability of the new modernity both as depressing as it is, and as perceptive as it is of certain possibilities which critical artists are trying to negotiate with human-scaled responsibility. Mastai insisted that art may be playful, but it must offer something more than negativity and critique. There has to be pleasure in this too, an erotics even of the mind: intellectual play.

If we are to ask "what next?" we need to set the contenders that appear by our subtitling this collection "Strategies of Engagement" and placing these "after modernism" some difficult questions. "After modernism" might be taken as a circumlocution for the more mundane postmodernism, which claims succession and supervention while actually reifying some desultory aspects and delusions of now uncontested capitalist modernity itself. Yet I wonder what the relation of "after modernism" is to Adorno's chilling definition of our historical predicament as *after Auschwitz/nach Auschwitz*.

By labeling our epoch as AA rather than AD/CE, as *le différend* – that which cannot yet be phrased in Lyotard's terms – we are caught in a chronotope: a time/space relation.[45] Temporally, we come *after* Auschwitz as a location that stands for a terrifying historical event that we come chronologically after, but *toward* which our consciousness is forever turned. The German word *nach* contains both meanings of *after* and *toward*. But in the sense of following, coming *after Auschwitz* as an event places us always temporally *behind* something that has happened. Like gleaners, we must follow behind the reapers of history, haunted by the persistent affects of that trauma's belatedness, unable to transcend the past. After modernism – which implies both after *and* toward its destructive apogee at Auschwitz, which leaves us still saturated by unconscious traumatic affects – does not imply, therefore, supersession or emancipation from either modernity's aspirations for enlightenment, rationality, and democracy, or from its inevitable contradictions created by structural inequity and perversion of instrumental reason. Nor are we released from the burden of constant confrontation with capitalist modernity in its colonial, neo-colonial, fascist, and now global phases. Coming after implies that we are chained to a critical reflexivity of modernity's defining problematics and of its ideals. What happened at Auschwitz is, as Bauman has argued, both indexical of, and excessive to, the deep logics of modernity.[46] The museum *after* (modernity's cultural consciousness)

modernism is also the museum that falls prey to Adorno's unstable pro-
hibition of poetry after Auschwitz and his refusal of the compensations of
thoughtless consumption of aesthetic beauty created by the very culture of
which Auschwitz was an equally defining product. These reflections lead
us toward the problem of the museum and the representation of trauma
that will be addressed in several chapters in this collection – by Reesa
Greenberg and artists Vera Frenkel and Mary Kelly. Adorno relented on his
initial negation of the very possibility of art after Auschwitz by acknowledging its necessity but under forever changed circumstances: it being
"virtually in art alone that suffering can find its own voice, consolation,
without being immediately betrayed by it."[47] Put crudely, awareness of the
shadow of the Holocaust, and the shadow of all scenes of barbarity,
genocide, ethnic cleansing, torture, and persecution, and of all that
which would deny the commonality of that which bears a human face,
and all abrogations of human rights becomes an ethical imperative that
then shapes our choice of attention.

In the art world at the turn of the twentieth century, we seem caught
between necessity and opportunism. Traversing the disparate array of art
on offer, we are switch-backed violently between incompatible tendencies.
There is art of irresolute levity and playfulness that warmly embraces the
postmodern time-out on modernist seriousness. Then there is art made
often as an act of survival and of witnessing. This kind of art is driven to
deal with modernity's still deeply unfinished business that seems relent-
lessly to inhabit every fiber of being, every chain of thought, every sight of
the world. There are those for whom this business of modernity's atro-
cious outcomes is so personally present that it would constitute the
deepest immorality to accept the postmodern end of history that allows
all to play in a world of pastiche, mimesis, and forgetful recycling. Such
realities present the museum after modernism – after Auschwitz, after
Hiroshima, after Rwanda, after Bosnia, after Apartheid, and in the midst
of capitalism's rampant globalization – with real moral responsibilities.
Our cities are now homes to the refugees of these violations, our cultures
called upon to be permeable and responsive to sufferings that, as trauma,
have no time limit and are not confined in space to "over there" or in time
to "back then."

If, in its bourgeois incarnation, the museum is a creator of the image of
history, and if, in its potentially critical form, the museum can be the
perpetually changing creator of the necessary space of reflection in which
to know our histories in the thinking, political, and ethical mind, what

immorality is it to deny history in its living contradictions? To marginalize the historical events of the postcolonial movements, the legacies of slavery and persistent endemic racism, the feminist challenge and its intellectual revolution, to contain and package them like vaccinated, tamed doses of social poisons against which publics can be moderately inoculated by managed exposure to a spectacle of their alien otherness is a political act that is as violent as it is craven.

Looking Back from History

The legend in red and black, the new colors of Thames and Hudson after a major rebranding make-over, frames on the white ground of the lower half of the leaflet: Edward Lucie-Smith's new edition of *Movements in Art Since 1945*, with a lozenge-shaped detail of one-time refugee from an Eastern bloc culture, Gerhard Richter's painting of the girl with averted head. Based on a photograph that has been transformed into painting in such a way as to set up as an issue the difference between lens-based images and the materially manufactured, singular object, product of a hand–mind operation, Richter takes us back to Matisse and Merleau-Ponty one final time. To "Know art! know life!" now we add: "Know death! know suffering!" Photography was theorized by Roland Barthes as a death machine, always placing death, absence, the past, and the never-recuperable before us, making viewing a perpetual mourning, the viewer an endemic melancholic.[48] If the legacies of the horrific period of the modern that lies between 1789 and 1945 or 1989 or 1995 or Srebenica 1999 or September 11, 2001, or all sides of the continuing mutual nightmare in Israel/Palestine, are deadly and hard to bear, such that we too wish to look away, is the museum after modernism to be the site of perpetual mourning or are there artistic practices that offer a means of going on, working through, of encountering the uncanny anxiety necessary to stay awake?[49]

To my endless regret I was not able to take up Judith Mastai's invitation to participate in the program she created around the exhibition at the Art Gallery of Ontario of Charlotte Salomon's *Leben? oder Theater?* in 2001. Aware that there were many Canadian scholars already deeply involved with Salomon's work, and otherwise already committed despite working on a monograph on the artist, I failed to come to Toronto for this exhibition. Judith and I shared a sense of the grave danger of interring Charlotte Salomon and her work in the graveless space of Auschwitz where the artist was murdered in 1943 at the age of 26. Mastai wanted instead to bring to the public's attention another history of the extraordinary cultural activities of Jewish resistances in the fascist period from which this act of cultural defiance of many deaths was extracted in an unclassifiable opus combining image, text, and musicality. Far from working to integrate a newly discovered "genius" into the old story of German Expressionism or even a newish one of women in art, Mastai saw the exhibition as an occasion for changing perceptions of how one kind of artistic work hinged between trauma and narrative resisted the theatricalized aesthetics of the fascist state that mobilized its museums as part of a major cultural program of Nazification.

After modernism/after Auschwitz involves us in thinking about both history and trauma – about what we can remember, want to forget, dare to ask: how to represent. This is not to make art therapeutic. It is to conclude a consideration of the work and meanings of Judith Mastai's project with the recognition that what she was doing was an ethical work of profound political importance, based in a concrete and personally lived relation to history, and predicated not on the need for cure but for working through. Here, art and thought were the active and necessary processes, not isolated in the museum but opened into the world, while making sure that that world acknowledged the thinking of artists and the relevance of engaged art in and to our worlds. The museum/gallery after modernism is an opened public space that can become their stage, where they are investigated and performed. It is a brave vision; it was a real practice. It can move us on, after as we must come, beyond as we must wish to be, yet dialectically accepting that there is no elsewhere. There is nowhere else to go. Gathered in this volume are some of the people who worked with Judith Mastai. Others unknowingly share that larger interrogation of the museum, forging of new practices, archiving of significant histories from the margins. For Judith Mastai, there was no problem in the *and* between art *and* history, visual *and* culture. That was the brilliance. It is, however, the stumbling block for those barricaded behind the defensive walls of one or other of these entities. Bringing together artists, art historians, museum programmers, directors, and cultural theorists, this intervention argues that if we understand this possibility and its imperative to make the museum/gallery the living point of exchange and performance, the art-historical canons and subservience to bourgeois capitalist values must be shattered and the stand-off between the keepers of the selective tradition and the creative thinkers in culture must be won by the latter.

Notes

1 Suzanne Oberhardt, *Frames within Frames: The Art Museum as Cultural Artifact* (New York and Washington: Peter Lang, 2001).

2 Key texts in this critical genealogy include: Paul Vergo, ed., *The New Museology* (London: Reaktion Books, 1989); Eleanor Hooper-Greenhill, *Museums and the Shaping of Knowledge* (London: Routledge, 1992); Tony Bennett, *The Birth of the Museum: History, Theory, Politics* (London: Routledge, 1995); Mieke Bal, *Double Exposures: The Subject of Cultural Analysis* (New York: Routledge, 1996); Nick Pryor, *Museums and Modernity: Art Galleries and the Making of Modern Culture* (Oxford and New York: Berg, 2002). To this we should add a series of studies on the ways artists have intervened in analysis of the museum: James Putnam, *Art as Artifact: The Museum as Medium* (London: Thames and Hudson, 2001); Lisa Corrin, ed., *Fred Wilson's Mining the Museum* (New York: The New Press, 1994); Donna de Salvo, *Past Imperfect: A Museum Looks at Itself* (Southampton, NY: The Parrish Art Museum, 1993); Anna Harding, *Curating: The Contemporary Art Museum and Beyond* (London: Wiley Academy, 1997); Douglas Crimp, *On the Museum's Ruins* (Cambridge, MA: MIT Press, 1993). Immensely important are the essays collected and analyzed in Reesa Greenberg, Bruce Ferguson, and Sandy Nairne, eds., *Thinking about Exhibitions* (London and New York: Routledge, 1996). On nationalism and race, see especially Annie Coombes, "Museums and the Formation of National and Cultural Identities," *Oxford Art Journal* 11/2 (1988): 57–68.

3 Bennett, *The Birth of the Museum*. The phrase was the title of his article in *New Formations* 4 (1988): 73–102.

4 Oberhardt, *Frames within Frames*, p. 6.

5 Ibid., p. 2

6 The frame has been a topic in philosophy and deconstruction since Jacques Derrida's extensive analysis of the frame as "parergon," as "a supplement to the work that it is part of;...the link between work and world...however hard it tries to be that cut." The quotation is from Mieke Bal, "Framing," in *Travelling Concepts in the Humanities* (Toronto: University of Toronto Press, 2002), p. 140. Jacques Derrida, *The Truth in Painting* [1978], trans. G. Bennington and I. McLeod (Chicago: University of Chicago Press, 1987).

7 Zygmunt Bauman, *Liquid Modernity* (Cambridge: Polity, 2000).

8 Oberhardt, *Frames within Frames*, p. 1.

9 In fact MoMA did not have its own space until 1931. The opening show in 1929 was on the twelfth floor of the Hecksher Building. The Museum opened at 11 West 53rd Street only in May 1932.

10 See Russell Lynes, *Good Old Modern: An Intimate Portrait of the Museum of Modern Art* (New York: Atheneum, 1973).

11   Dwight Macdonald, profile of Alfred H. Barr, "Action on West 53rd Street," *The New Yorker* (1953); cited in Lynes, *Good Old Modern*, p. 251. Barr had used the phrase "three-ring circus" to Beaumont Newhall in 1935. Cited in Alice Goldfarb Marquis, *Alfred H. Barr, Jr.* (Chicago: Contemporary Books, 1989), p. 137.

12   Carol Duncan and Alan Wallach, "The Museum of Modern Art as Late Capitalist Ritual: An Iconographic Analysis," *Marxist Perspectives* 4 (1978): 28.

13   Architect Charles Jencks coined the phrase "postmodern." See C. Jencks, *The Language of Post-Modern Architecture* (New York: Rizzoli, 1977). His expanded analysis appears in *The New Paradigm in Architecture: The Language of Post-Modernism* (New Haven and London: Yale University Press, 2002).

14   Justin Henderson, *Museum Architecture* (London: Mitchell Beazley, 1998). Henderson titles each example. San Francisco Museum of Modern Art (Mario Botta) is "A Cathedral for Modern Art."

15   Carol Duncan and Alan Wallach, "MOMA: Ordeal and Triumph on 53rd Street," *Studio International* 1 (1978): 57.

16   Nicholas Serota, *Experience or Interpretation: The Dilemma of Museums of Modern Art*, The Walter Neurath Memorial Lecture (London: Thames and Hudson, 2000).

17   Mieke Bal, "Reading Art?" in *Generations and Geographies in the Visual Arts: Feminist Readings* (London: Routledge, 1996).

18   Karl Marx, "On the Jewish Question" [1843], in *Early Writings* (London: Penguin Books, 1975), p. 220.

19   The classic argument about this is Walter Benjamin's "The Work of Art in the Age of Mechanical Reproduction" [1936], in *Illuminations*, ed. Hannah Arendt, trans. Harry Zohn (London: Fontana, 1973), pp. 219–54. The simplified account of the loss of aura through reproduction was taken by John Berger in his famous intervention, *Ways of Seeing* (London: Penguin Books, 1971), which influenced a whole generation.

20   Rosalind Krauss, "Postmodernism's Museum without Walls," in Greenberg et al., *Thinking about Exhibitions*, pp. 340–8.

21   André Malraux, *Le Musée imaginaire* (Paris: Gallimard, 1965), p. 11.

22   Didier Maleuvre, *Museum Memories: History, Technology, Art* (Stanford: Stanford University Press, 1999), p. 15. In what follows I am indebted to the work of Didier Maleuvre, especially his opening chapter, "Museum Times."

23   Ibid., p. 28.

24   Ibid., p. 29.

25   Ibid.; italics in the original.

26   Krauss, "Postmodernism's Museum without Walls," p. 345.

27 Galen A. Johnson, "Structures and Painting: 'Indirect Language and Voices of Silence'," in *The Merleau-Ponty Aesthetics Reader: Philosophy and Painting*, ed. Galen A. Johnson, trans. Michael B. Smith (Evanston: Northwestern University Press, 1993), p. 20.

28 André Malraux, *The Voices of Silence*, trans. Stuart Gilbert (Princeton: Princeton University Press, 1978), p. 356.

29 Johnson, "Structures and Painting," p. 21.

30 Maurice Merleau-Ponty, "Eye and Mind," in *The Merleau-Ponty Aesthetics Reader*, pp. 121–50.

31 Maleuvre, *Museum Memories*, p. 15.

32 Johnson, "Structures and Painting," p. 24.

33 One of the projects in which I was involved was a video of my readings of the Art Gallery of Ontario's nineteenth-century art collections, which was then used by Judith Mastai to explore with docents other forms of knowledge of these paintings than the modernist-formalist or heroic artist stories.

34 Jürgen Habemas, *The Structural Transformation of the Public Sphere* (Cambridge, MA: MIT Press, 1989); Michel Foucault, "The Eye of Power," in Colin Gordon, ed., *Power/Knowledge: Selected Interviews 1972–1977* (New York: Pantheon Books, 1972), pp. 146–65.

35 In 1989 Judith Mastai brought to Vancouver the exhibition *Fabled Territories: New Asian Photography*, organized by Nigel Walsh and curated by Sunil Gupta at the Leeds City Art Gallery, which included British/Asian artists working in photography, such as Zarina Bhimji, Chila Burman, Sutapa Biswas, Pratibha Parma, and Sunil Gupta. Sutapa Biswas was invited to lead a workshop for women of color in Vancouver. The workshop met for a month three to four times a week and produced its own exhibition, *Eleven Women of Culture*, which led to the purchase of one work for the Vancouver Art Gallery, other exhibitions, and a higher visibility of the issues around gender and ethnicity in the art world. Nonetheless, the event stirred up controversy in Vancouver. In surviving notes on this affair, we find the following introduction to the paper by Judith Mastai:

> *Fabled Territories*
> - exploration of the sociology of art institutions
> - how structural racism operates
> - why an institution such as an art gallery would seek to change this
> - why it is imperative that cultural institutions should take a lead in doing this.

36 Mary Kelly, "Reviewing Modernist Criticism," *Screen* 22/3 (1981): 41–2, repr. in Mary Kelly, *Imaging Desire* (Cambridge, MA: MIT Press, 1996), pp. 82–108. This remains a major analysis of the temporary exhibition in the circulation

and definition of post-war art in which she defines the triple axes of analysis: materiality (of the practice), sociality (institutional contexts), and sexuality (at the level of representation).

37   For an engagement with a critical remapping enacted in the five platforms of *documenta 11* (2002) curated by Okwui Enwezor, see Griselda Pollock and Alison Rowley, *Now and Then: Feminism/Art/History – A Reading of documenta 11*, CATH Documents, no. 3 (2006); also on <www.leeds.ac.uk/cath/documenta11/aah.html>.

38   For another aspect of this struggle see my "A History of Absence Belatedly Addressed: Impressionism With and Without Mary Cassatt," in Charles W. Haxthausen, ed., *The Two Art Histories: The Museum and the University* (New Haven: Yale University Press, 2002), pp. 123–42. Judith Mastai also commissioned me to do a lecture when the Courtauld Collection was exhibited at the Art Gallery of Ontario in 1999, analyzing the effect of there being no women artists included in this most accessible and influential representation of Impressionism in Britain.

39   Mary Kelly in conversation with Griselda Pollock at the Vancouver Art Gallery, June 1989, *VAG Document I*, introduction Margaret Iverson, Vancouver Art Gallery, 1989.

40   Judith Mastai, *Women and Paint*, Saskatoon, Mendel Art Gallery, 1995.

41   For discussion of the double sense of *arche* in the word "archive" as both the home of the record-keepers and the source of knowledge, as commandment and commencement, see Jacques Derrida, *Archive Fever: A Freudian Impression*, trans. Eric Prenowitz (Chicago: Chicago University Press, 1996).

42   Judith Mastai, ed., *Social Process/Collaborative Action: Mary Kelly 1970–1975* (Vancouver: Charles H. Scott Gallery, Emily Carr School of Art and Design, 1997). The exhibition traveled to Edmonton Art Gallery, Leeds City Art Gallery, Agnes Etherington Art Centre, Queen's University, Kingston, Ontario, and Norwich Gallery.

43   Antonin Artaud, *The Theatre and its Double* [1938], trans. M. C. Richards (New York: Grove Weidenfeld, 1958), p. 96; Amelia Jones, *Body Art: Performing the Subject* (Minneapolis: University of Minnesota Press, 1998), p. 1.

44   Judith Mastai, "Performing the Museum: Education, Negotiation, Art Galleries and their Publics" (unfinished manuscript), cited in the epigraph to the Preface to this volume.

45   Jean François Lyotard, *The Differend: Phrases in Dispute* (Minneapolis: University of Minnesota Press, 1989).

46   Zygmunt Bauman, *Modernity and the Holocaust* (Cambridge: Polity, 1989).

47   Theodor Adorno, "Commitment" [1962], in Andrea Arato and Eike Gebhardt, eds., *The Essential Frankfurt School Reader* (Oxford: Basil Blackwell, 1978), p. 312.

48 Roland Barthes, *Camera Lucida*, trans. Richard Howard (London: Fontana, 1982).

49 I draw this idea from Andrew Hebard's reading of Jean Cayrol's final words in Alain Resnais's *Night and Fog* (1955): see Andrew Hebard, "Disruptive Histories: Toward a Radical Politics of Remembrance in Alain Resnais's *Night and Fog*," *New German Critique: An Interdisciplinary Journal of German Studies* 71 (Spring–Summer 1997): 87–113.

2

Women's Rembrandt

Mieke Bal

Figure 2.1   Rembrandt van Rijn, *Adam and Eve*, 1638, etching touched in black chalk, grey wash and pen and brown ink, 16.2 × 11.6 cm. London, British Museum (inv. no. 1852-12-11-42). Photo © The Trustees of the British Museum.

Figure 2.2   Rembrandt van Rijn, *A Portrait of a Young Woman*, 1632, oil on canvas, 92 × 71 cm. Gemaldegalerie der Akademie der Bildenden Künste Wien.

What's in a Name?

"Rembrandt's women": here are two of them (Figures 2.1 and 2.2). What are they? They are images made by one of the greatest artists of the Western tradition. But what does it mean to say they are "Rembrandt's women"? What does it mean to look at an exhibition entitled "Rembrandt's Women"?[1]

"Rembrandt's women": make no mistake about it, they constitute a profoundly enjoyable corpus of great art. We were happy to have the opportunity to see such a large number of great artworks together, works that are seldom all in one place. I do not wish to spoil that fun. Nor do I wish to disclaim my own participation in that visual feast, my own complicity in what I will also criticize. I hope that instead of annoying you, my critique will enhance your pleasure by making the images richer and more complex, and your own experience of what they mean, more exciting.

The title suggests a standard thematic exhibition about a canonical artist. It sounds so "natural," so normal, that you wouldn't think twice about it. It promises an exhibition with Rembrandt's depictions of women in it: paintings, drawings, etchings, in which we see how the great artist represented, and hence – we assume – looked upon, the females of the human race as they lived in his world. I will stop to look at some of these works. But I will also argue that the title indicates a lot more, namely the presuppositions underlying the art-historical underpinnings of this exhibition and others like it. Precisely because the title seems immediately clear, it contributes to naturalizing how our culture deals with its heritage. Therefore, I take the title and its implications as seriously as I take "Rembrandt" himself, or rather, the Rembrandt corpus itself.

The axioms of art history derive from four central concepts: history, intention, "work of art," and oeuvre. To train as an art historian means to examine bodies of art using those terms. I will suggest that these concepts are problematic and can be modified. To denaturalize them – to show what they hide, and expose what they entail – I offer the following supplementary concepts:

- for "history," as the reconstruction of the past, I propose "*preposterous* history," an inquiry into the present and the meaning of the past in and for it;
- for "intention," as the authority of the individual artist, I suggest visual interaction, the meaning of art for the present viewer;

- for the "work of art," as masterpiece, I focus on "the work this work does," actively;
- for "oeuvre," as the collection of masterpieces authenticated by connoisseurial skills, like stylistic and iconographic appreciation, I suggest "the meaning of the artist as a cultural figure today";
- and, lastly, to "Rembrandt the genius," I add "Rembrandt" the cultural construction.

These are not oppositional concepts. I will not replace the axioms of art history with my alternatives. Instead, I will try to persuade you that the latter complicate but also enrich the former, without necessarily replacing them. For art history, too, is a cultural construction. To simply reject it is ineffective. My attempt to take a slightly different look at the representations of women in the Rembrandt corpus can be considered as a case of the alternative conception of the study of visual art as it is currently being proposed – namely, as visual culture studies.

Specifically, by complicating the axioms, I aim to argue that as a discipline, art history, including the kind of exhibitions it generates, is bound up with deeply patriarchal presuppositions. As a result, when taken at face value, the title of the exhibition exposes the patriarchal nature of these four axioms. My agenda in reversing the title is to offer an alternative view to these patriarchal implications through a closer look at some of the pictures. For I don't think that these implications do justice to Rembrandt's representations of women: not to the profound understanding of the Genesis story as evidence of woman's wisdom to accept the human condition, including time, evidenced by Adam's aging body (Figure 2.1); not to this beautiful portrait of a young woman ready to leave her fixed place as her husband's other half, to shed the uncertainty in her eyes, and to become an active person (Figure 2.2); not to this woman with the generic, beloved, Saskia face, who is holding the image of Medusa, the femme fatale, in an attempt to ward off the men who come too close (Figure 2.3).

From Rembrandt's Women to Women's Rembrandt

"Rembrandt's women": do these women belong to Rembrandt (Figure 2.4)? He "made" them, depicted them. But what exactly did he depict? Figures he owned, figures he created, or figures through which he visually

Figure 2.3 Rembrandt van Rijn, *Bellona*, 1633, oil on canvas, 127 × 97.5 cm. New York, Metropolitan Museum of Art, The Friedsam Collection, Bequest of Michael Friedsam, 1931 (inv. no. 32.100.23).

"argued" with his culture? Some images depict women as sacrificial victims of patriarchy-gone-berserk. Iphigenia, sacrificed for politics – in fact, for war. Lucretia, stolen by one man from another, killed, and then

Figure 2.4   Rembrandt van Rijn, *Lucretia*, 1666, oil on canvas, 105.1 × 92.3 cm. Minneapolis, The Minneapolis Institute of Arts, The William Dunwoody Fund.

used for politics. You can read about Lucretia in many texts, including in a superb long poem by Shakespeare of the same name.[2] There, Lucretia's husband Brutus was the first to use the dead Lucretia, when he displayed her lifeless body on the forum and thereby successfully triggered the Roman revolution. She was raped and killed in her function as the foundation of democracy. Cultural history subsequently followed suit, using her death to work through the dilemma of chastity versus suicide, "forgetting" that rape was what killed Lucretia. Cultural history used this story not to indict rape, but to establish an allegory for liberation from tyranny, to instill allegorical reading as a cultural practice that distracts from what we actually see.

So, no, such women do *not* belong to Rembrandt. He depicted them as he saw them, including his response to what cultural history had done to them. But I submit that he depicted them not by endorsing their stories but, on the contrary, in ways that foreground the troubled relationships between women and men that permeate patriarchal culture. I am not claiming he was a feminist. But I am claiming that, for reasons unknown and unknowable, many – not all – of the images of women in the Rembrandt corpus show an astonishingly sympathetic and critical vision of male/female relationships. I am claiming, in other words, that Rembrandt's women constitute a "Rembrandt" (not a man, but an oeuvre, in a slightly revised sense) supportive of women: a *"women's* Rembrandt."

Who is this "Rembrandt"? Is he the one we can read from today's vantage point, as a figure of preposterous history, a history that endorses the impossibility of suspending everything between the seventeenth and twenty-first centuries as a positive opportunity for reflection rather than an inevitable predicament? Who – what kind of an artist – is "women's Rembrandt"? Let me give you a preposterous description of one of his early self-portraits (Figure 2.5). This very early self-portrait, from 1629, evokes uncertainty. The face features the symptoms of vanity that make one want to categorize the painting as idealized. As if moustache and mouth, arrogant eyebrows, and straight nose alone are not telling enough, the hairstyle and hat, gown and light leave little room for doubt that the painting is idealized. On the other hand, this feature of self-idealization signals insecurity, as does the hesitant eye, directed almost, but not quite, at the viewer.

Of what, however, does the self consist in the case of a young artist?[3] The idealization of self and the insecurity about it also refer to what this subject wants to be: a subject making objects, a subject whose identity is *in* the work. The painting has the features not only of the presentation of a proud and insecure young man, but also of the masterpiece as required by the guilds or, more likely in the case of this artist, by the urban patrons or the court. Consider the carefully accomplished strokes that display

Figure 2.5   Rembrandt van Rijn, *Self-Portrait*, 1629, oil on panel, 89.7 × 73.5 cm. © Boston, Isabella Stewart Gardner Museum, Bridgeman Art Library.

the artist's craft: the varied surface/substances of the hair, the feather, the scarf, the chain, the velvet, the jewel, the tender wrinkles, and the slightly shiny reflection on the nose. It also offers the features through which this painter will create his own painterly image: the empty background, the decentered light, and the almost monochrome palette. The proud and insecure young painter aspires through this work to the status and identity of a master.

The self is represented as both conforming to the standards of quality (it is both handsome as a face and skilled as a painting) and as being different (it is insecure as a face and original as a painting). It positions the artist as a disclosing subject, talented yet inexperienced, still with a soft moustache yet eager to gain a place in relation to the world, to others, as the overly skillful details betray. As such, the portrait contains the contradictions of narcissism itself. It constitutes the relationship with the self in otherness.

This image is all we have. Nothing more. The art-historical desire to "reconstruct" the "real" Rembrandt would not accept this "preposterous" discourse of self and identity, of narcissism, a discourse that smacks of psychoanalysis. But I offer it as meaningful for today in a variety of ways. It gives, for example, an understanding of individual self-presentation to an age suspicious of both individualism and romantic visions of artistic genius. It does justice to a preposterous view of history: one in which an endorsement of the present helps us understand the past, not just on its own terms or just on ours, but as an interaction. I also offer it as a description that meaningfully connects to the painting. Visually, the description is not "off the wall." Does it cover the artist's intention? Certainly not. No documentation exists that could even approximate that intention.

Let me then juxtapose this description to a quote from the most authoritative, properly historical, and, indeed, most descriptive account of this painting, in Volume I of the three-volume *Corpus* by the Rembrandt Research Project:

> [W]orldly finery is *retained* in the cap with ostrich plume [feather], the colourful cloak and the chain, but a more emphatic allusion to the transitoriness of things is missing. Bearing in mind Rembrandt's tendency...to eliminate express symbols or attributes...one can *assume* that in this case too the idea of vanity is not, or not entirely, abandoned.[4]

This passage comes from the chapter on style. Since the premise of *Corpus* is that stylistic analysis constitutes the most reliable method for understanding the corpus historically and for authenticating the works, it can be assumed that it is also a reliable key to appreciating, if not all the results, at least the way these are achieved. In view of this, and to make my claim about the four axioms of art history a bit more concrete, I contend that in this passage the authors of *Corpus* overrule their own premise. The obvious vanity of the self-presentation is translated from style into iconography, to mean not personal ambition but the culturally sanctioned theme of the vanity of earthly things in the face of unrelenting death – Protestant austerity. Rembrandt's specific self-image is subordinated to a cultural cliché. This is the research team's twentieth-century vision of Rembrandt's place in his culture, not a historically valid reconstruction. Nor is it grounded in visual evidence. On the contrary. And this countering of visual evidence is explicitly stated.

However, in this distraction from the image, more is at stake than just a disavowed projection. The negative discourse ("not entirely abandoned") points to a willful overruling of the artist's intention insofar as that intention is seen as inscribed in the corpus. This is implied in the reference to his express "tendency." According to the authors of *Corpus*, "Rembrandt" has a visible tendency, which goes against the grain of this kind of flat iconography. But instead of that tendency being heeded, it is alleged as a reason to ignore it. The passage implies: if Rembrandt did not want to incorporate the kind of "express symbols or attributes" that inform iconography, then he should have; since we know better than him, we will still pin the work down as a case of a traditional vanity picture. Moreover, the appeal to the most general subject (vanity) demonstrates the tendency of iconography to overrule specificity as well as intention. The meaning of the image is not grounded in the present, or in the depiction, or in the subject (self-portraiture), but in something that this painting is not: a vanity, most frequently a still life with a skull or some such object.

So far, I have done two things. I have set up my case for "women's Rembrandt" by complicating the historical claim with the need to acknowledge the inevitability of a *preposterous* position. I based that claim on the unavowable but undeniable preposterousness of even the most solid and self-aware historicist account. I have also suspended the possibility of appealing to the artist's intention by showing that such an appeal is self-serving, and that it obscures the blatant overruling of that intention in a preposterous bossiness. Not the seventeenth-century artist but the twentieth-century critic rules supreme. And what he overrules – with the same sweep that overrules historical argumentation, inscribed intention, and visual specificity – is the avowed vulnerability of the self. For me, it is this subject that opens the door to a glimpse of "women's Rembrandt." For it is this vulnerable subject that is liable to align himself with those people who are structurally vulnerable: women. In other words, the critic over-rules women's Rembrandt.

Women's Rembrandt at Work

Let us now look at one of those women who are not "his," but whom he visually supported. The desire to purify each work from the dust of earlier readings is another of the research team's claims. I will argue that the "purity" of the work is untenable.[5] What is more, it is also a way of limiting what the work can do. I propose that, rather than giving ourselves over to the sanctified object, we can look at the work as picture, which solicits us to interact with it. This is the work's work. In the face of that work, the act of viewing is an accountable cultural act performed by each of us in the present.

Bathsheba with King David's Letter (Figure 2.6) was not included in the exhibition *Rembrandt's Women*, but it is discussed in the catalogue, by Eric Jan Sluijter, the only author who shows a sensitivity to the possibility that "the nude" need not be, by definition, semi-pornographic, that what we see is a painting, not a woman, and that the viewer is part of the work of that painting.[6] It is a complex work in terms of the various modes of reading it elicits. It can be read biographically, as moderately voyeuristic, or in another way altogether. A first approach, a biographical reading, will appeal to viewers who are familiar with "Rembrandt's" work and life, and who are interested in the connections between them. They may see in this painting a portrait of his common-law wife Hendrickje Stoffels, "Rembrandt's woman" in a more pedestrian sense as discussed in the catalogue by Dudok van Heel, who represents the view of Rembrandt's women as "the women he owned." This is evidenced by his embarrassing title: "Rembrandt: his life, his wife, the nursemaid and the servant."

The second mode of reading this work is genre-based. It consists of considering it as a traditional nude, and can be seen as turning it into a potentially but ultimately not really voyeuristic work. First, it exhibits the woman's body without representing the voyeuristic gaze either for identi-fication or for ridicule. Second, it does not thematize any contact between the naked woman and the viewer, proposing neither an appeal for help nor acquiescence. Third, this link with the question of voyeurism brings iconography into the picture, and leads, hence, to a third reading. The pre-textual story in the Hebrew Bible, in II Samuel 11, itself implies the woman's nakedness, the enticing effect it has on the voyeur, and the subsequent rape. There is surely a connection between the verbal story, the pre-text in which voyeuristic vision determines the events, and the popularity of the subject in painting in general.[7]

This iconographic reading – which travels from the text, via the preceding images that interpret and reinterpret it, to the image at hand – will help to identify the subject relatively easily, if the reader is familiar enough with the tradition. The naked woman, the vague suggestion of a roof in the background, the servant busy with the woman's toilet, and the letter in the woman's hand are all firmly established in the pictorial tradition. This letter suggests a fourth way of reading the work. Let me call it "literal," punning on the letter but also on the need to take literally, seriously, what we see.[8] The fact that the woman is naked, and that her toilet is being attended to, seems to be enough to suggest she is being prepared – "made beautiful" – for a man, and this connection seems to suggest that the image be interpreted in terms of the doxa or commonplace concerning Bathsheba and her story. Out of reach for a critical response, the power of this implied viewer hovers over the woman's visual existence. This is not "Rembrandt's woman," however, but our contemporary construction.

We cannot attribute to Rembrandt the desire to construct a narrative. For what story would result? Elderly woman cleans nails of naked woman's foot? Woman holds letter just received? Yet there is a sense of focalization in the woman's pose; her body, not her gaze, is slightly turned toward the viewer.[9] True, the woman's look is remarkable. She is undeniably melancholic and reflective. The reflectiveness is enhanced by the fact that her head turns away from the viewer while her body does not. Although the image clearly makes sense as a whole, what sense it makes cannot easily be determined. We are left with a sense of narrativity that is not fulfilled; with a sense of wholeness that does not satisfy; with a frustrated need to position ourselves in relation to a viewing situation that the narrative should bring forth but doesn't. If one looks for a letter in II Samuel 11, one will indeed find it; but Bathsheba never sees it. It is not linked to her "infidelity," but to her husband's murder. For it is the letter that David writes to the leader of his army, in which he orders the latter to expose the bearer, Uriah, Bathsheba's husband, to mortal danger. The letter is, literally, the harbinger of death.[10]

But let us now suspend the pre-text and simply look at the letter as a *visual* sign. It covers Bathsheba's knees. Her legs are crossed, and their

Figure 2.6   Rembrandt van Rijn, *Bathsheba with King David's Letter*, 1654, oil on canvas, 142 × 142 cm. Paris, Musée du Louvre. Photo: Réunion des musées nationaux, © Hervé Lewandowski.

crossing, pointed at by the letter that partly covers it, is the locus of a distortion. It is there that narrative and ideology collide and collude. Realistically and narratively speaking, the legs are crossed so that the servant/procuress can fulfill her duty and prepare the woman for royal rape. At the same time, rhetorically speaking the body is turned toward the viewer, who stands in for the king as the voyeur whose act of vision prepares him for the rape. Thus, the much-criticized "fat" belly becomes a "natural" consequence of her distorted, twisted body. The idea of distortion, meaningfully inserted in the painting, is covered but also foregrounded by the letter. It crosses two patriarchal ways of looking at this image. The distortion comes to preclude this smooth appropriation. Here is how this distortion becomes visually conceptualized: if coherent and unproblematic voyeurism were the point, crossing the figure's legs the other way would have been much more convenient. Although the figure's right leg is crossed over her left leg, the right foot remains to the right of the knees. Had the figure crossed her legs the other way, no awkward twisting would have been necessary. But then the body would not have been turned so much toward the viewer. This is women's Rembrandt's rhetorical figure of disfiguration: a disfiguration of the patriarchal representations of women in the nude, and of this biblical figure in particular, so frequently used as an alibi for pornographic painting.

This reading becomes, in fact, quite plausible in the face of the letter. First, in the middle of the diagonal line leading from Bathsheba's melancholic look to her foot held by the servant's hand, there is a text: the letter, that thus draws attention to its function of cover-up. Second, it also foregrounds the iconographically anchored meaning of "decency": this woman does not "look back" to the viewer. But neither does she look at her partner in the narrative. For, third, the line from Bathsheba to the servant only emphasizes the fact that she does not look where her eyes are directed. Her inward look goes nowhere, rigidified as it is in melancholy. Is she already mourning her murdered husband? or her appropriated body? "Women's Rembrandt" – not the intention of the artistic genius, but the collection of images left for us to deal with under the name of "Rembrandt" – does not decide. He, or rather, it, this image, solicits our reflection.

Patriarchy's Women and Rembrandt's Discontent

"Women's Rembrandt" consists of a body of such *working* works. That body we call corpus – the word for a dead body. So far, I have argued for its life: its live presence for us today; its interactive liveliness that entices us to work with it; its cultural position as both custodian and critic of the cultural legacy of, mostly, patriarchal gender relations. In the remainder of this chapter, I will challenge the dead quality of art history's concept of the oeuvre. I will expose "oeuvre" as a fixated, increasingly purified, closed, and autonomous collection of equally dead works – objects whose meanings are fixed, once and for all, by critics claiming to speak for history and the artist's intention.

To that effect, I will mobilize – in the double sense of that verb – two sets of works in which women are struggling with the powers that confine and harm them. The first consists of the likes of Bathsheba: figures who carry the burden of allegorical stories in which they are twice victimized. Susanna, Lucretia, and the innumerable anonymous women caught in art's "double exposure" as "The Nude." The second consists of women who take power over men – Judith, Delilah, Yael, Potiphar's wife – and are demonized for it. "Women's Rembrandt" probes and questions these relations in works that belong to the culture in which they were conceived, made, and made to work, but which also criticize that culture. The two "types" of women and their allegorically erased stories constitute the self-defense of patriarchy; women's Rembrandt will have none of it.

Two paintings: *Lucretia*, from 1664, in Washington, DC, and *Susanna Surprised by the Elders*, from *ca.* 1645, in Berlin, the latter not in the show but discussed in the catalogue together with nr. 110 (Figures 2.7 and 2.8). Both are works from "women's Rembrandt" in that they present deeply sympathetic, compassionate representations of women who embody abuse. This is what binds these works together, while they are different in almost every other respect. The one is a glorious work, the other somewhat modest in its small format, its dark state, and its lack of monumentality. The one is a single-figure painting, almost a historicized portrait, the other a dynamic narrative. I contend both are equally narrative, if considered within a story different from the pre-textual one in the Roman and biblical traditions respectively. The story they act out is that of voyeurism as an abuse coextensive with rape.

The subject of the chaste Roman Lucretia, who stabbed herself in the presence of her husband and father after she had been raped by her husband's fellow-soldier, was familiar in Rembrandt's time.[11] My very first impressions of the 1664 painting (which I got to see in the workshop where it had just finished being cleaned) were Lucretia's movement away from my gaze and the deadly color of her face. But, as Arthur Wheelock, the curator of the department in Washington rightly remarked, despite her deadly pallor, the cleaning had actually brought her back to life. Her hands had come forward, emphasizing the force and the surprise of her act of suicide – literally, self-killing. I was immediately struck by the earring on Lucretia's left ear: it does not hang straight. This suggests movement of both her head and her hands. In an iconographic reading, this averted gaze would simply indicate her "decency," her refusal to return the gaze of the viewer, and thus to acknowledge the latter's naturalized right to witness

Figure 2.7   Rembrandt van Rijn, *Lucretia*, 1664, oil on canvas, 120 × 101 cm. Washington DC, National Gallery of Art, Andrew W. Mellon Collection. Photo © 2005, Board of Trustees, National Gallery of Art, Washington.

her plight by visually taking her in. Reading the painting narratively, "for the plot," we would interpret Lucretia's movement as a consequence of the presence of the men. Father and husband are trying to comfort her when suddenly she kills herself.[12] The frontal light becomes significant. The woman – the subject, or, rather, the object, of the representation – stands right in the middle of the canvas. Her body is turned directly toward the spectators.[13] The chaste Lucretia has become public property through her rape. The visual representation of the woman at the moment of her self-killing partakes of this "publication." In accordance with the culture, Lucretia is put on display for the eyes of the indiscreet onlookers. Critiquing that same culture, she turns her head away in order to break contact with the spectators, preferring isolation to remaining an object of their voyeuristic gaze.

Her raised left hand, then, comes to signify resistance to that gaze, a request to the viewer to turn away. Denying contact with others, in this final moment of death at her own hand, she seems to say that she alone can perform it. Even in pitying, the sympathizing onlookers are, at this moment, indiscreet and superfluous. This interpretation is, of course, preposterous. It is not premised on the historical reconstruction of the work, allegedly as the artist intended it, nor on the autonomy of the work of art from its messy embeddedness in the web of cultural signification, including its after-effect, its work. But, unlike iconographic readings, which would explain it through the pre-texts and the pre-images, this reading forcefully explains one tiny detail, which, for me, constitutes its secret as a "*women's* Rembrandt." It is the earring that does not hang straight. Its oblique position accounts for the sense I had when it was, literally, unveiled to me: that Lucretia actually moved, that she was still alive, and that she swiftly turned her head away from me. It was the work's *work*: its power to strike over four centuries and reach us today, compelling us to ask questions that have routinely been smoothed over. The narrativity of this work is played out between the painting and today's viewers.

Rembrandt has the reputation of an exceptionally narrative painter, at a time when Dutch painting distinguished itself as more descriptive in comparison with narrative Italian painting.[14] This opposition may be too stark, but I find it helpful to focus on the small signs of narrativity Rembrandt inserts in largely still paintings, like portraits or other single-figure paintings such as this one. The sweep of the earring, tiny as it is, turns the painting into a narrative, but not a simple "third-person" narrative that tells someone's story. Rather, it turns the work into a "second-person" narrative, implicating the viewer as an agent or even "character."[15]

The narrative in the *Susanna* painting is different in rhetoric, in narrative style, and mode of representation. Yet here, too, the critique of visual abuse as continuous with rape is central. In the painting *Susanna* (Figure 2.8) the position of the Elders is split into the two aspects of the complex

Figure 2.8   Rembrandt van Rijn, *Susanna Surprised by the Elders*, ca. 1645, oil on canvas, 102 × 84 cm. Berlin, Stattliche Museen zu Berlin – Gemäldegalerie. Photo Joerg P. Anders.

of voyeurism: looking and touching.[16] The Elder on the right side of the painting is not only looking on; he is recumbent in the seat of justice. His left hand is holding a stick, the staff that symbolizes power as conventionally as the phallus represents power through male sexuality. His right hand holds on to his seat, perhaps suggesting how little there is that holds him back from acting, while at the same time emphasizing the power this seat bestows to him. If we follow the eyes of this figure, however, we notice that he is not just watching Susanna; he is also watching his colleague.[17] Thus, we are offered this Elder as a possibility for identification, but this identification is not imposed. Instead, it is offered for reflection. For there is no continuous movement from the internal to the external onlooker. This virtual circle is broken by Susanna's direct address to the external viewer. I contend it is the extent to which she participates in the structure of looking, and specifically connects the internal visual event to the outside, which determines that the painting cannot be dismissed as a voyeuristic work.

This is also clear from another detail, which binds this work to the earlier *Susanna* (Figure 2.9). When considered on the flat surface,

Figure 2.9 Rembrandt van Rijn, *Susanna Surprised by the Elders, ca.* 1636, oil on panel, 472 × 38.6 cm. Mauritshaus, The Hague, Royal Cabinet of Paintings.

Susanna's left hand is an iconographic allusion to the Venus tradition, hence, to eroticism. But when also considered in depth, it pushes backwards, thereby raising the question of the function of such allusions. For her hand does not merely allude to that tradition. It also wards off that same eroticism through its defensive attempt to push aside the threat that comes from behind. Through that slight shift the gesture comes to life: it is narrativized, and thus loses its fixity of meaning as pure iconographic allusion. In the earlier painting, this gesture stands out even more emphatically. This is due to the red color of her hands. These red hands indicate both class – the model is a working woman – and a sharp sense of nakedness: she just took off her clothes. The clumsily twisted legs, the knees pressed together, they all point to this woman's painful position between a rock and a hard place, to a potentially voyeuristic viewer and the voyeurs threatening her with rape.

Similarly, in the later work the second Elder's gesture of undressing Susanna, if viewed in isolation, could work for voyeurism. Semantically, it represents what the voyeur, enticed by the visual experience, would like to do: take the next step, from looking to touching. Yet, in combination with Susanna's appeal to the viewer to turn his eyes away if the undressing eventually occurs, it can simultaneously be seen as criticizing the gesture. It says: the body may be naked in a moment, but please don't look.

Let me pause at this juncture to reiterate the central concepts of art history and the supplementary concepts I am proposing in the name of visual culture. My interpretations of the *Bathsheba*, the *Lucretia*, and now the *Susanna* paintings neither contradict nor endorse alleged historical evidence. They exceed it, to include, within the sense of history, the effect the paintings may have for contemporary viewers – for you and me. As such, these paintings are not immutable works of art, but instead art that works. It works that way not because of the artist's intention, although, again, I see no evidence that on some doubtlessly unreflected level these effects could not have been intended. It just seems futile and self-serving to speculate on his intentions.

"Women's Rembrandt," symmetrical to "Rembrandt's Women," is ours, not to "own," to appropriate through projection of our own desires, but to "create," self-reflexively to construct, with the help of these paintings. That construction takes place not in enslavement to an illusory history, but in a dialogue between the seventeenth century and the twenty-first century. The seventeenth century can, to all intents and purposes, be considered largely – but not and never wholly – patriarchal, whereas we like to think that in the twenty-first century we are a little more critical of, if not quite "beyond," such social structures. But part of my agenda here is to argue that such stark oppositions between the two historical moments are questioned when we consider together, on the one hand, "women's Rembrandt," and, on the other, an endeavor to reconstruct "Rembrandt's Women" as a section of a corpus, or oeuvre.

In order to complicate the notion of "oeuvre" as a collection of masterpieces authenticated by connoisseurial skills such as stylistic and iconographic appreciation, I will now elaborate the meaning that the artist as a cultural figure has today, through the juxtaposition of two relatively early paintings, both from 1636 and neither in the show, although *Danae* is discussed in the catalogue.[18] While these paintings appear to perpetuate age-old stories of male domination, I hope to show that they *work* – as responsible visual agents, soliciting our accountability as contemporary visual citizens – to question those meanings. The two final cases address – rather than reiterate – the two legacies on which our culture has been built: biblical and classical antiquity respectively. In the same way as I began by setting up the figure of women's Rembrandt through a double interpretation of his early self-portrait, I will juxtapose the discourse of the reconstruction of the oeuvre in *Corpus* with the preposterous discourse of the construction of the cultural figure of "women's Rembrandt," a figure not confined to his "dead body."

Upon entering the small, shallow room in the Städelsches Kunstinstitut in Frankfurt am Main, the striking force of *The Blinding of Samson* makes you press your body against the wall opposite but too close to the painting (Figure 2.10). In a brilliant curatorial act, the museum thus facilitates the work's performance of horror in the face of violence. The confinement in the room that is almost too small makes the viewer aware of a feeling that needs to be reflected on. For that horror reaches out over four centuries, indeed, over two and a half millennia, during which the story of Samson's betrayal has continually captured the popular imagination. For the old rabbis and Church fathers, for Milton and other poets, for preachers of various denominations, for many painters and sculptors, the story has meant a case of the femme fatale, the danger women represent for men as objects of their desire.[19] Many mythical stories result from this inexplicable fear, and my two final cases stand here as probing that fear.

I juxtapose these two paintings because they have similar compositions. This helps us see how they complement and comment on each other.

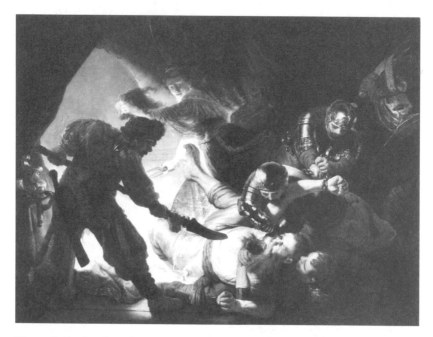

Figure 2.10   Rembrandt van Rijn, *The Blinding of Samson*, 1636, oil on canvas, 205 × 272 cm. Frankfurt am Main, Städelsches Kunstinstitut.

In comparison, the woman in the *Danae* (Figure 2.11) exudes a power that the figure of Delilah does not visually match. The comparison suggests we suspend the story as we know it and, instead, look at the story as we see it here. The centre of the *Samson* is quite emphatically Samson's face and body – which is why the work of this painting is to transfer horror onto the viewer. In the *Samson*, the archaic experience burdens the subject, both painter and onlooker, with the trace of absolute effort: everyone but Delilah is engaged in the effort, which accumulates in Samson's right foot.

The importance of this work for the present argument rests in the way it can illuminate not only the tradition of representations of this mythical story up to Rembrandt's time, but also the continuation of that tradition today. In excess of the work as historical, intentional object, its treatment also reveals the fear for women that compels even twentieth-century experts to take that fear for granted and to perpetuate the attribution of it to the object of desire: the figure of Delilah, guilty by projection.

Figure 2.11 Rembrandt van Rijn, *Danae*, 1636, oil on canvas, 185 × 202.5 cm. St Petersburg, The State Hermitage Museum.

To make this case for a deconstruction of the oeuvre, I quote from and summarize the interpretation of the Rembrandt Research Project. The interpretive part of the commentary begins with a description that is both visually convincing and heavily reliant on dogmatic, mythical meanings: Delilah "who *as the victrix* is placed highest up in the picture area."[20] True, she stands at the top of the triangular composition; not true, that place does not make her "high" in the sense conveyed by the solemn Latin word "*victrix*," of central importance. The picture's focus is lower, on the area where the point of one soldier's weapon covers Samson's breast, and the dagger of another puts out his eyes. Rather than standing victorious, Delilah is on her way out of this scene of horror.

The text continues with a characterization of the picture's style: "a typical product of the influence of the Italian early baroque," that is, baroque in terms of spatial diagonal composition and lighting, which is true. This may well be Rembrandt's most "Caravaggesque" painting. But the following wording betrays a pre-established interpretation not warranted by the painting: "the dramatic contrast between *the* physical suffering and brutality on the one hand, and *feminine* triumph on the other." The textual "symptom" that betrays the beginning of another attempt to overrule the painting is the choice of "the," a depersonalized generalization of suffering and brutality, which contrasts with the attributed "feminine" and the "triumph" imported from interpretations exterior to the painting. A rephrasing that brings this linguistic symptom to light would be: "the dramatic contrast between *male* physical suffering *and* male brutality on the one hand, and *feminine* disengagement with it on the other." In other words, Delilah, standing not so much higher but primarily farther away, is on her way out of the scene of horror. Although in the story she did betray Samson's secret to her fellow tribesmen, the painting "comments" that she had nothing to do with the horrible consequences, of which nothing indicates that she was informed.

Further, if we look at her face in the painting, her bulging eyes suggest a horrified response to what they see, a horror that mirrors that of the painting's viewers, locked into the small gallery in Frankfurt and just as fascinated yet eager to escape as this figure herself appears to be. Rather than dismissing the reading in *Corpus* in favor of my alternative one, however, I propose to suspend both, recognizing that, ultimately, the face is unscrutinizable, unreadable, and through that unreadability solicits reflection on visual meaning and cultural acts of meaning production.

Regarding the moment depicted, the authors of *Corpus* rightly comment that horror was aesthetically considered positive at the time. But they then, again wrongly, attempt to overrule the painting: "*yet* the choice of moment shown *does not alter the meaning of the picture – it has to be seen as* an exemplar of the power of woman, such as was popular especially in the 16th century."[21] On the one hand, they place the work's work within the baroque aesthetic of the time, on the other, by means of the contrastive "yet," they betray an awareness that this aesthetic is in blatant contradiction to the meaning they had already decided, and for which no viewing of the painting is necessary, namely the cultural cliché of the power of women, generalized into "woman." This cultural cliché, especially popular in the sixteenth century, is not only utterly uninteresting for a savvy and complex artist; it is also literally outdated. Wouldn't a critical response to, rather than an uncritical reiteration of, this old cliché be a more plausible enterprise for a recalcitrant painter like our – or at least, women's – Rembrandt?

Not only does this argument of the oeuvre-builders overrule the work qua image, as well as neutralize its work, the horror; it also oversteps the carefully defended boundaries of the oeuvre, by placing the painting somewhere else, in Italy, and in another time, a century earlier. With something bordering on contempt for art, the authors underwrite the autographic authenticity of the painting as made by Rembrandt's hand, but not by his mind, his vision, or his cultural agency.

Let me end on a brighter note. A climactic moment in the construction of the oeuvre is *Corpus*'s celebration of the *Danae* as an uncontested masterpiece, a work that stands for the oeuvre as its *pars pro toto*, or synecdoche (Figure 2.11). Jubilantly, the authors write: "both pictorially and psychologically the work is a masterpiece that bears the characteristic features of Rembrandt's style and techniques, albeit from different periods."[22] Gary Schwartz builds the corpus on the relation between the artist and his patrons but does not fail to respond to the paintings in his argumentation. He describes *Danae*, in a phrase that goes a long way to explain why the authors of *Corpus* are so happy here, as: "Rembrandt's most succulent painting of a female nude."[23] Sluijter, in his catalogue essay, calls it "one of the most sensual nudes in European art."[24] Another gentleman is less happy; what some celebrate, others find offensive.[25] The most relevant comments for my argument are those that betray a deep ambivalence. Here is Sir Kenneth Clark's appraisal of the *Danae*:

> The closest Rembrandt came to a statement of his ideal was the Danae in the Hermitage, where he certainly wished to make the figure as beautiful as he could. But his love of truth got the better of him. She is sensuous and desirable, but beautiful is not the word that comes to one's mind.[26]

In these reactions we see the typical conflation of representation and object that comes with the eroticization of viewing. In *Corpus* this conflation remains implicit, although a bit later it will show its hand. Schwartz bases an important but not otherwise plausible revision of the corpus on this conflation. Sluijter's analysis, by far the most detailed and sensitive, turns it into the artist's program. He makes a convincing case but fails to see what the artist does within that program. Clark may not be a Rembrandt scholar with the same scientific pretensions as the others but he is perhaps even more important here for his position as a cultural mediator. In Great Britain in particular, but also elsewhere, more people have absorbed this "knowledge" than that of the academic scholars.

The structure of these discourses is most blatant in Clark's text. If the body constructed for the mind's eye inspires lust, the painting is praised; if it does not, the painting or drawing is criticized. In these reactions, with the exception of Sluijter's, the work of representation itself is ignored, so that the work of art disappears behind the object represented. This attitude reflects the notion that what is seen is the "real" thing. If that thing is a woman, the one conventionally responsible for inspiring desire through her beauty, then the work of art is judged according to how successfully that end is achieved. The work is elided. And seeing and perception are thus radically separated in this approach to art.

Let me first note that the naked woman looks away from the viewer. The painting thematizes and problematizes voyeurism; it does not cater to it. Even the plainest iconographic reading ought to acknowledge that Danae is thus made legible as a "decent" woman, not as acquiescing to voyeurism. The woman is represented as naked in her most private space, on her bed. But her nakedness does not make her a passive object for visual appropriation. Where Bathsheba was represented in her emphatic passivity, this woman derives power from her body by the very fact that it is almost exposed offensively. Her beauty, desired by both the pre-textual, desiring Zeus and the viewer, is not an object for possession-taking. She emphatically disposes of it herself.

The hand she raises directs us. Together with the look of the servant (an internal focalizer) behind the curtain, the hand dismisses gaze.[27] The implied onlooker is compelled to follow the narrative structure of focalization and look, with the servant, with the woman, somewhere else. Had the internal focalizer not been represented, the gesture would have been deprived of its narrative status and have become empty, a pretext for a better look at the body. For the powerful arm, which makes us aware of this woman's self-disposal, certainly does not preclude the viewing of her body. But it does encourage awareness of that act of viewing.

The *Danae* can be seen as *about* seeing, about the transgression of the taboo on access to the woman's body, and about the interdiction against seeing. Seeing, this painting proposes, is not the same as desiring to see something (else). It thus makes a statement about the two issues that our commentators so happily conflate: the body and its representations in a visual culture ambivalent about gender and sexuality, on the one hand, and the question of visual representation itself, in a visual culture ambivalent about visual depiction, on the other. It asks how these two problematics are intertwined, how that entanglement may have informed the taboo on visual depiction in fundamentalist, text-based cultures dominated by a male deity, and how a more, let's say, artistic approach to the act of looking can reassure those who fear – and not wrongly, if our commentators are any indication – that seeing is too easily believing; or desiring, appropriating, consuming for that matter.

In an ultimate attempt to subordinate the oeuvre they are so painstakingly busy constructing, the authors of *Corpus* become sublimely self-deconstructive when they conflate this allegedly succulent nude with the wicked triumphant femme fatale: "There has never been any doubt that the picture shows a woman waiting for her lover.... It has even been seen as 'Potiphar's wife offering herself to Joseph'."[28] That scene seems quite different, and its aftermath leaves the woman rather miserable.[29] Schwartz acknowledges that no particular source story can be established beyond doubt. Yet, the universal interpretation ("never") based on the alleged pre-text of the painting, as a representation of sexual anticipation and woman's eagerness to be penetrated, is made to stand under the sign of the danger of male sexual desire. The contrast Schwartz established between the horrible *Samson* and the attractive *Danae* is thus neutralized when the power of beauty ascribed to the female body is turned into seduction for the demise of male heroes.

The question of the oeuvre – so easily alleged for interpretations that are obviously based on the critic's, not the artist's, vision – thus recedes into the background. "Rembrandt's women" is not a section from the "oeuvre." Rembrandt, for one, never conceived or considered "his" women together, his representations of women as a meaningful grouping. He never took them to meet a standard of "beauty," nor as a cliché of the deadliness or sheer power of women. "Women" is not a genre, for example. "Women's Rembrandt" would, I submit, turn in his grave if he were to see, presumably with sadness, how his interventions, which made his artwork, continue to be neutralized into an seemingly innocuous, but not so innocent, aesthetic of works of art. An aesthetic of ethical indifference, of misogyny, and a perpetuation of men's privileges.[30] "Rembrandt's women" are the critics' women, attributed to a "men's Rembrandt." They are subjected and dead. "Women's Rembrandt" is alive, today, helping us to cope with a visual culture that is often violent but also a dynamic culture of pluralism and debate.

Notes

1 *Rembrandt's Women*, ed. Julia Lloyd Williams (Edinburgh: The National Gallery of Scotland, 2001).
2 On this poem, see my article "The Rape of Lucrece and The Story of W," in A. J. Hoenselaars, ed., *Reclamations of Shakespeare* (Amsterdam: Rodopi, 1994), pp. 75–104.
3 This and the following two paragraphs were taken from my book *Reading "Rembrandt": Beyond the Word–Image Opposition* (New York and Cambridge: Cambridge University Press, 1991), pp. 209–10, slightly modified.
4 Josua Bruyn, Bob Haak, Simon Levie, et al., *A Corpus of Rembrandt Paintings*, Stichting Rembrandt Research Project, 3 vols. (The Hague, Boston, London: Martinus Nijhoff Publishers, 1982, 1986, 1989), vol. I, p. 223; emphasis added.
5 See Gary Schwartz, "Rembrandt Research After the Age of Connoisseurship," *Annals of Scholarship* 10/3–4 (1993): 313–35, for an excellent critique of this aspect of *Corpus*.
6 Sluijter, "Horrible Nature, Incomparable Art," in Williams, ed., *Rembrandt's Women*, pp. 43–5. Sluijter calls it "probably the most impressive" of Rembrandt's female nudes (p. 43). Demonstrating an awareness of "women's Rembrandt" and pointing out the complexities of viewing, he writes: "Here Bathsheba is no longer the ignoble seductress she was in earlier depictions, but rather the victim of her own beauty, a beauty no one can resist, least of all the viewer of the painting" (p. 45).
7 In the history of Western art, the theme of Bathsheba's bath is as often depicted as Susanna's bath, and, I am afraid, for the same reason. Although – and in some sense because – viewing is represented in these stories as disturbing, they both lend themselves to voyeuristic purposes as well as to a critique of voyeurism.
8 The letter's function depends on the reader's knowledge of the story and the mode of reading adopted. But, in fact, recognition of the subject rests more probably on a somewhat uncomfortable logic, which reverses the relationship between the visual text and its pre-text.
9 While this serves the voyeuristic purpose, it does not connect to an alternative story that would thus be focalized. Only when the viewer identifies with King David the voyeur – when, in other words, the body is offered to both the

king and the customer – can a *fabula* be constructed, but that would put the viewer in an uncomfortable position.

10   After Bathsheba's appropriation by the king, the letter ushers us into the second, grimmer part of the story. Assigning that sinister function to it, then, is a problematic way of dealing with the biblical images. Elements of the story get rearranged, and motifs striking in their dramatic function are combined with motifs that have a stark effect on visual imagination.

11   In a very broad sense, we can speak of Dutch culture in the seventeenth century as a *textual community*, to use Brian Stock's terms: see his *The Implications of Literacy: Written Language and Models for Interpretation in the Eleventh and Twelfth Centuries* (Princeton: Princeton University Press, 1983), pp. 90–1. Simon Schama's *The Embarrassment of Riches* (London: Collins, 1997) provides a description of this community. The *visual* culture of that community as analyzed by Svetlana Alpers can best be imagined as partly overlapping with Schama's description; see Alpers, *The Art of Describing* (Chicago: Chicago University Press, 1983). Hence, its visual culture forms that part of the *textual* community that is concerned with visuality. To confront my analyses in this book with historical evidence, a similar analysis of the culture's textual base would be needed: what did people read, and about which texts did they talk, not only the burgher elite but also the larger community? Sermons held in churches are a powerful source for such an inquiry. Although this is for the time being only an idea for a project, its relevance could be demonstrated by the sheer number of scholars who base their claims on unexamined assumptions about this textual community. Several examples can be found in Gary Schwartz, *Rembrandt: His Life and His Paintings* (London: Viking Press, 1985), e.g. his assumptions about the Samson myth.

12   For she has to act swiftly before they can restrain her. Such a reading is realistic in its argument. It is an explanation of the detail in terms of the "real" story, taking the motivations from the story rather than from the scene as it is depicted. It is also verbal in the traditional sense, since it superimposes on the painting an "underlying" verbal story that the painting is then supposed to "illustrate." The appeal to such a realistic reading demonstrates how much even traditional art interpretation owes to the relations between visual and verbal texts.

13   So is her bodice which, closed beneath the bosom, has an opened "lock." This opened closure refers rhetorically to the violent opening of Lucretia, to her simultaneous rape and her display, with the latter coming to stand for the former.

14   Alpers, *The Art of Describing*.

15   On "second-person" narrative in painting, see chapter 6 of my book *Quoting Caravaggio: Contemporary Art, Preposterous History* (Chicago: Chicago University Press, 1999).

16 For Freud, looking is derived from touching, the former being an inferior and preparatory version of the latter.

17 The line of sight moves from his eyes to the other man, from the latter's eyes to Susanna, from her eyes to the external viewer. This line of *sight* is related to the distribution of *light*. The brightness of the looking Elder's face makes it plausible to begin reading this visual narrative through him. Reading brightness as relevant is part of the cultural construction of "Rembrandt": the distribution of light is one of our cultural assumptions about this art.

18 *Danae* is discussed by Sluijter (in Williams, ed., *Rembrandt's Women*, pp. 41–3).

19 This meaning, lest we forget, is a clear case of projection: it is the desire of the male for the female that frightens the subject of desire. As a result, he construes the object as dangerous.

20 *Corpus*, vol. III, p. 190; emphasis added.

21 Ibid., p. 191; emphasis added.

22 Ibid., p. 215.

23 Schwartz, *Rembrandt: His Life and His Paintings*, p. 129.

24 Sluijter, in Williams, ed., *Rembrandt's Women*, p. 43.

25 I find Schama, in his recent book *Rembrandt's Eyes* (London: Allen Lane, 1999), embarrassingly in collusion with the "projectionists" whom I am critiquing in this chapter. So much so that I refrain from quoting his semi-pornographic discourse, lest I reiterate what I find utterly objectionable.

26 *Feminine Beauty* (London: Weidenfeld and Nicholson, 1980), p. 23; emphasis added. This passage incidentally provides a good case for my point about projection: words like "wished" and "love of truth" prove it. Clark's response, whatever it is, is attributed to the artist: *he* wanted to make a statement on beauty, but *he* was too honest to disregard truth. A variety of implications become clear when we try to sort out this statement. The net result is that the artist will always be a clone of the critic: a woman lover, a connoisseur of female beauty, an honest person, and all for clinging to the "truth" of women's deficient beauty without reflecting on the standards by which her beauty is measured; sensitive to the visual appeal to the senses and aware of the difference between artistic beauty and sexual attraction. An astonishingly modern "Rembrandt" and a surprisingly self-centered and simple man emerge from this picture.

27 The term "focalizer" comes from narrative theory to indicate, here, the represented subject of looking. For the narratological term, see Bal, *Narratology: Introduction to the Theory of Narrative*, 2nd edn. (Toronto and Buffalo: University of Toronto Press, 1997). The necessary transformation of the concept for use in visual art analysis has been explained in Bal, *Reading*

"Rembrandt": Beyond the Word–Image Opposition (Cambridge: Cambridge University Press, 1991), pp. 158–61.

28 *Corpus*, vol. III, p. 220.

29 For this unhappy aftermath, see Rembrandt's painting in the exhibition: cat. nr. 120. See also Williams, ed., *Rembrandt's Women.*

30 As an indispensable antidote to this indifference I have proposed the concept of "ethical non-indifference": see Mieke Bal, "Religious Canon and Literary Identity," *Lectio Difficilior* 2 (2000); available online at <www.lectio.unibe.ch/00_2/r.htm>; repr. in *The Mieke Bal Reader* (Chicago: University of Chicago Press, 2006).

3

Museums and the Native Voice

Gerald McMaster

Introduction

He lies back on a bed of cool sand and closes his eyes. He hears people around him, many who are talking about him. He remains very still, however, not wanting to give away that he hears them. He doesn't acknowledge them; instead continues to keep his eyes closed. He lies there for some time, pissed off at what some people say about him, yet he remains unresponsive. Finally he wakes after having fallen asleep, his back aching, he opens his eyes. He decides to get up and move around. He surprises those who are near; they gasp; he shocks them; he leaves.

This is James Luna's, now well-documented and well-quoted work, *The Artifact Piece*, performed at the San Diego Museum of Man in 1987 (Figure 3.1). Luna has gone on to do many more performance pieces, but this one stands out as his most brilliant work. On one hand, it represents the new type of Native artist using performance art and Native voice to challenge the representation, authority, perspective, and visuality of Native peoples in museums; and on the other, it puts up a mirror for us to look into and question these received ideas.

For nearly a century the institutional space of the museum has been so far removed from aboriginal communities that the museum visitor, upon seeing old artifacts, must have sensed that aboriginal people were long extinct. Indeed, museological discourse was about the past verging on necromancy. As anthropologist Michael Ames has pointed out: "Museums

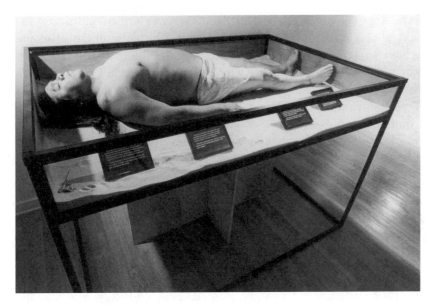

Figure 3.1 James Luna, *Artifact Piece*, 1987. Courtesy of the artist.

are cannibalistic in appropriating other peoples' material for their own study and interpretation, and they confine their representations to glass box display cases."[1]

In reaction to such techniques of exposition, aboriginal contemporary artists began a critical discourse about the space that constituted them as their subject. They disliked the inference that their work could only be regarded as ethnographic because quality was valued less than identity. Though some artists maintained strong connections with museums, there came a generation whose members were not so forgiving. Instead, they took every opportunity to bring attention to museal practices through their art.

For example, several years ago, I asked my old friend and colleague Edward Poitras his views about showing in and having his work collected by a human history/ethnographic museum (one similar to that where Luna performed his piece). I was working at the Canadian Museum of Civilization in Ottawa. At the time it was the only institution that took aboriginal contemporary artists seriously, since ethnologists are generally empathetic to Native peoples. Poitras said to me that he did not mind; that he felt at home with his ancestors. (During my days at the Canadian Museum of Civilization, I had managed to secure a gallery devoted to exhibiting the works of aboriginal contemporary artists; and since 1989 several very successful exhibitions, presenting the works of Canadian and American artists, have been mounted. The position of the artists has changed over the years; many have had successful exhibitions in mainstream art galleries. Their work, of course, speaks the same language as most contemporary artists; yet they remain connected to various Native communities.[2]) Poitras's response about feeling at home with his ancestors was less about acquiescing to an ethnographic identity, than about referencing the collection's content.

For me this was an intellectual breakthrough. It told me that not only had Native artists gone beyond worrying about where they were exhibiting; they were now saying that ethnologists and anthropologists did not have a monopoly on collecting and interpreting the past of Native peoples. The fact that most ethnologists were unconcerned about Native aesthetic systems is a clue to institutional detachment. To this end, I want to frame this chapter around the idea of *Native voice*, defined not merely as Native people talking, but in terms of representation, authority, perspective, and visuality, using the interventionist works of James Luna, Rebecca Belmore, Joane Cardinal-Schubert, and Jane Ash Poitras as reference points.

James Luna: Museums as Site For Conflict and Negotiation Over Meaning

In southern California, museum-goers came across an intriguing work, centered on the body of the aboriginal artist challenging everyone's ethic of the aesthetic; at the same time it was a critique of museums' representation of Native Americans. James Luna's *The Artifact Piece* confounded viewers by thoroughly implicating them and completely deferring subjecthood to the viewer (Figure 3.1).

Luna, of Luiseño descent, was born in Orange, California in 1950, and currently lives on the La Jolla Reservation, Valley Center, California. His spectacular performances, complemented by installation pieces, often find him as the central figure. Like many other artists, his experiences of being aboriginal motivate his work. In particular, he targets a society that gives little regard to aboriginal people and a museological discourse that has long referenced Indians in the past tense.

The Artifact Piece plays on presentation/representation, presence/absence, subject/object, and observer/observed. Artist Jimmie Durham says: "[Its] outrageous Indian humor…has been so valuable to our survival,"[3] a humor that catches viewers in a "candid camera"[4] situation before they realize they are the victims of a duplicitous joke.

Luna introduced the work at San Diego's Museum of Man in the midst of its permanent exhibitions. Lying on a bed of sand, with various personal artifacts around him, arranged in quasi-museum display, Luna was, as British art critic Jean Fisher describes, the "undead Indian of colonialism."

The Artifact Piece prompted diverse reactions from the observers, who stared at the "body-as-artifact," as representation and thus synecdoche. Viewers were attracted to the body because of its reality effect. The occasional movement in the belly belied the "body-as-object," and evidenced its identity as living being. The semiotic effect of this piece lies in the viewer's treatment of it. The museal discourse compelled viewers to treat it as object. It is likely that museum-goers, in this southern California state where the Indian is both fiction (of Hollywood) and artifact (of the museum), did not know the historical underpinnings of this piece. In some ways, this is the attractive aspect of it, in that it caught viewers completely by surprise, Luna, the artist, is rendered powerless and excluded, until, of course, he decides to get up off the table. At that point he renders viewers suddenly self-conscious as they realize that they are now the spectacle: "This 'being seen' is precipitated in the voyeur by what Sartre calls '*le regard*'."[5] The observer is now on view and becomes "other." For a moment, the artifact piece is alive, giving the artist/aboriginal person control over his identity and subject position.

This piece's force is not unlike female strippers who play with their male observers; there the power relation is always tenuous, the play/tease power relation is inverted. The body as eavesdropper waits for the moment when to disarm the gaze. I recall Luna telling how outraged he felt because of the comments he had overheard during his position as eavesdropper. He could not believe the kinds of ideas people continued to hold true about Indians. Sometimes it is worthwhile not knowing what people think, otherwise, we might live in constant paranoia.

There is little evidence that Luna's critique of museal exposition and his exposure ("performance") changed individual viewers' attitudes, though it may have clarified the public's identification of Indians as past and savage. Luna *has*, however, influenced the discursive space of ethnographic museums, which in their presentations now must consider their power relations.

Rebecca Belmore: Critique of Authority

In the late 1980s, a pivotal exhibition brought attention to itself by raising profoundly disturbing issues in aboriginal re/presentations. This exhibition, *The Spirit Sings: Artistic Traditions of Canada's First Peoples*, was organized by the Glenbow Museum (Calgary, Alberta) in conjunction with the 1988 Winter Olympics.[6] Aboriginal contemporary artists like Rebecca Belmore were moved to address the issue of authority.

In *Artifact #671B* (1988) Belmore, best known for her performance and installation works, presented herself in a display case outside the Thunder Bay Art Gallery, a Shell Oil logo on her chest and a Canadian flag upside down on her back. In the performance, she sat by the wintry road along which the Olympic torch passed through Thunder Bay; the temperature was sub-zero. Several signs surrounded her: "Artifact #671B 1988," "Glenbow Museum presents," "The Spirit Sings Sponsored by Shell Oil," and a very large "Share the Sham" sign. Small prayer-like flags hung on a rope, perhaps as petition to the objects in the exhibition. This may be the first work explicitly critiquing a particular museum. In addition, several aboriginal people supported her; indeed, many of Belmore's later works have received very public displays of aboriginal support. Though it does not take much reading to see the intended target, the evidence of strong support makes the work more powerful. Such is the nature of her work: it requires the participation of others.

The number, "671B," may reference Belmore's Indian status, which, like a museum's catalogue number, objectifies. This performatory act, in part, brought attention to the role played/not played by aboriginal people in the production of the exhibition, not as active participants but as "artifacts." Aboriginal people, she points out, continue to be treated as artifacts by governments, cultural institutions, and multinationals, especially during the production of this project. Shell Oil was the official sponsor for the exhibition and the government of Canada was criticized for not settling land claim disputes with the Lubicon Cree, on whose land Shell was drilling. For its duplicitous role in "sharing the sham," the Glenbow Museum suffered in its public relations as people began to take notice of the issue. Aboriginal people, for their part, strategically used the Calgary Winter Olympics to call attention to economic, social, and historical injustices. They no longer wanted to be treated as passive objects, "dead or alive." Museums and corporations, they say, can no longer have total control over the aestheticization of their image, using aboriginal people as cultural dupes.

Belmore's performance is theatre – political theatre. Aesthetic considerations are minimized; but the production is highly constructed. All the elements of protest are here. While the institution and corporation wanted to use aboriginal artifacts to enhance their institutional and corporate images, they fully expected that the consumer would endow them with value by attendance. The artist and aboriginal people, on the other hand, harnessed performance art as an effective strategy to create a conscious sense of self and agency while critiquing authority.

Joane Cardinal-Schubert: Power and Authority

Alberta curator-turned-artist, Joane Cardinal-Schubert, had witnessed the way museums handled historic Indian artifacts and recognized how museums had long controlled their message. After having visited the research collections of the Canadian Museum of Civilization to research the museum's collection of the Blood First Nation War Shirts, she began work on a large installation called *Preservation of the Species*, which became a critique of museal power and authority, and which included the work *Is This My Grandmother's?* (1988). "I thought," she says, "what kind of possessions do Native people have of their grandparents, and great-grandparents? None. They're all in Ottawa in the [museum] drawers."[7]

Cardinal-Schubert had seen before how aboriginal material culture was handled and so it didn't surprise her when she saw in the museum's storage vaults many objects stuffed into clear plastic bags. The practice of cellophaning, or putting objects into plastic bags, was considered preventive care, since many of the objects are made of organic material, and storing them this way prevented insect infestation. Cardinal-Schubert's focus on the physical and discursive distance between museum artifacts and their originating communities is the crux of the issue addressed by all the artists whose work I am considering. For several decades now, aboriginal peoples have become much more aware of the historical circumstances that led to the removal of hundreds of thousands of objects from their communities – objects which have sat lifeless in storage facilities around the world.

The question for both communities is: How can life be brought back to these objects? Though in works like these there are no answers, only more questions, the artist *can* give voice to the issues. Inevitably, the more questions that are raised, the more responses follow. Unfortunately, these artists are often seen as agitators and not as intellectuals who ask difficult questions. To this end, many artists have understood full well the strategies of resistance, articulation, and empowerment, of connecting art with the social and political. Cardinal-Schubert, like others, felt anger and searched for a strategy of response and found it in her work, which, she says, is part of her ongoing life practice.

Cardinal-Schubert was first struck by the beauty of the historic objects, but consideration of their treatment in the museum generated horror, fear, and helplessness. Horror in seeing the objectification of her heritage; fear in the reverential sense that many of these objects were sacred and she could do little to rescue them; and helplessness in that she knew little of the appropriate address to be made to the object as a traditional way of entering into dialogue. Some of these impressions led her to ask: Is this my grandmother's? The question may seem rhetorical, but clearly it has been on the minds of aboriginal people for some time, and Cardinal-Schubert was brave enough to ask it.

In *Is This My Grandmother's?*, a dress, as synecdoche, leaves us to ponder its many implications. The dress, created by the artist, is encased in plastic and hangs on a wooden cruciform support; it appears as it might when worn. The metaphor of the cross is not so much about Christianity as it is about an ancient indigenous directional symbol; yet it leads us in several directions. First, in the idea of the encased dress, Cardinal-Schubert presents it as an object, under wraps, for examination in its artifactuality, appearing displaced, desanctified, and devalued; yet it is a symbol of repatriation. Its outstretched necrotic, death-like arrangement, as if on a rack, is quite the opposite; as the artist suggests, it is how it would appear in a ceremonial dance. We cannot, however, dismiss how visitors might read the wooden support, as a kind of cross or tree, as an instrument of torture, persecution, or ridicule, which for Christ later came to represent sacrifice. Cardinal-Schubert makes a similar pronouncement in that the dress is condemned to suffer and never to return to its original purpose, to remain forever an artifact, and always "other." The question she asks of visitors and institutions is being answered by a new generation of vitally and socially conscious indigenous peoples.

Jane Ash Poitras: Visuality and Display

Jane Ash Poitras does not share the same museological polemic as the other artists discussed here, though she utilizes similar critical strategies. Instead of criticizing the (ab)use of the object, her subject is the Indian body politic as a casualty of modernity. Against modernity she positions the spirituality of the shaman as salvation for aboriginal culture. Begun in the late 1980s, her *Shaman Never Die* series has expressed the shaman's subject position of healer for many of the social ills aboriginal people experienced during the reservation period (from approximately the 1880s to the 1950s). The shaman as metaphor is traditionally positioned as magician, priest, mystic, poet, and master of ecstasy.[8]

Though a prolific painter, in *Transformation, Assimilated Indian, Hudson's Bay Lure* (1992), Poitras used installation to explore new questions. Employing three museological display cases (arranged in the style of a conventional museum exhibition) as metaphors for seduction, change, and conversion, she reflects on a personal journey of discovery, from birth to death and back to rebirth.

The first display case, titled *Hudson's Bay Lure*, is framed around materialism, commodification, and wonder; The Hudson Bay Company has long had a colonial presence. Of the three vitrines, this one has the look and feel of an early-twentieth-century showroom – the other two are modern – and it is filled to capacity. This case performs at least two functions: the first is to entice customers to consumer goods made by Indians; the second is an ethnographic trap, displaying objects salvaged from aboriginal cultures as a cabinet of curiosities. The display is designed to entice and seduce viewers, to interpellate them within a dominant ideology as they look upon their "other." The viewer is to look upon these objects with fascination; yet, the artist discourages our desires as we move to the next case.

The second case, *Assimilated Indian*, presents the dangers of habits and addiction, an unbearable lightness of being, in which addiction signifies death. A skeleton, hovers over a field of cigarette butts, reaching for a can of beer. Drinking among aboriginal people has long been a sign of resistance, to counter the pain of existence and the conditions of poverty. Furthermore, the idea of assimilation has also always been part of the anthropological discourse describing the aboriginal state of affairs: a kind of longing for the past while, at the same time, aboriginal cultures are absorbed into the great body politic of the West. Assimilation is to make similar, to change identity. In this case, Poitras's skeletal figure is the final signifier of this idea. In the end, we all become the same. However, there is a subtle twist, for this work is also about museal practices, beginning with the exposition of aboriginal people as artifact and ending with the intense interest in their remains.

In the last case, *Transformation*, we sense freedom, self-control, resistance, and rebirth. The vitrine is completely empty, an anathema for museums that need objects for display. The relationship is transformed. There is a sense that museums can no longer (ab)use aboriginal people for museal purposes. The transformation is a shift from subjection to sovereignty.

Conclusion

These artists reflect a larger movement that critiques both museological and anthropological practices and discourses. Luna's critique of representation; Rebecca Belmore's critique of authority; Joane Cardinal-Schubert's critique of power and authority; and Jane Ash Poitras's use of museological strategies to show the Indian body politic as a casualty of modernity. Each interrogates museum practice through *Native voice* in a complex game of rhetoric that many ethnographic museums never expected to be articulated by their subject and object of study.

Notes

1   Michael Ames, *Cannibal Tours and Glass Boxes: The Anthropology of Museums* (Vancouver: University of British Columbia Press, 1994), p. 3.
2   *Reservation X* (1998); *Edward Poitras: The Venice Project* (1996); *Indigena: Indigenous Perspectives on 500 Years* (1992); and *In the Shadow of the Sun* (1989).
3   Jimmie Durham, "A Central Margin," in Kinshasha Conwill, Nilda Peraza, and Marcia Tucker, eds., *The Decade Show: Frameworks of Identity in the 1980s* (New York: Museum of Contemporary Hispanic Art, The New Museum of Contemporary Art, and The Studio Museum in Harlem, 1990), p. 172.
4   The idea of a "candid camera" comes from the name of a well-known American television show in which the show's host would surreptitiously trick ordinary people into doing skits usually set up by the program. The

person(s) would be filmed doing and saying funny things. We, the audience, are the observers. Only at the end did the host finally tell the victim: "Smile! You're on Candid Camera!"

5   Quoted in Kaja Silverman, *The Threshold of the Visible World* (London and New York: Routledge, 1996), p. 164.

6   Since *The Spirit Sings* exhibition of 1988, (re)presentation of aboriginal material culture has developed into a burgeoning critical discourse. Curators who routinely collected or exhibited such objects are now asking serious questions about their practice. Indeed, *The Spirit Sings* became a watershed in Canadian museology. With the subsequent release of the *Task Force Report on Museum and First Peoples* (1992), many museums are now taking greater pains to work with aboriginal peoples on what/what not to exhibit and collect. As an example, at the Head-Smashed-In site, near Lethbridge, Alberta, curators negotiated with the local aboriginal community on how to exhibit medicine bundles. A compromise resulted in which simulations were created. The simulated experience of the exhibition, however, served as a reminder to viewers of the great respect accorded these sacred objects, thus establishing a principle that sanctity has little or no place in museums, that sacredness does transcend museum realities. This is but one example, but it's a quantum leap made from just a short while ago.

7   Karen Duffek, "Beyond History," in Karen Duffek and Tom Hill, eds., *Beyond History* (Vancouver: Vancouver Art Gallery, 1989), p. 36.

8   These are some of the terms used by Eliade to describe the shaman, which he argues is primarily a religious phenomenon of Siberia and Central Asia. "The word [shaman] comes to us, through the Russian, from the Tungusic *Šaman*": Mircea Eliade, *Shamanism: Archaic Techniques of Ecstasy* (Princeton: Princeton University Press, 1964), p. 4.

4

Exhibiting Africa after Modernism: Globalization, Pluralism, and the Persistent Paradigms of Art and Artifact

Ruth B. Phillips

Change must be brought into your museums, especially in the way you collect, exhibit and interpret African works of art. Tear down your old-fashioned exhibitions and let the voice of Africa and African artists be heard in our museums.

Emmanuel Arinze[1]

Introduction: In the Modernist Moment

In 1959 the Museum of Primitive Art in New York City organized a series of lectures by prominent anthropologists on "aspects of primitive art."[2] Robert Redfield used the occasion to explore the different kinds of access to African objects provided by the two display paradigms that had developed in Western museums during the previous half century. In his talk, published under the title "Art and Icon," he defined the art display as promoting the appreciation of the "immanent" formal qualities of the object in order to maximize the viewer's visual and aesthetic experience.[3] This is typically accomplished by spatially isolating and carefully lighting the object and minimizing texts and other distracting accompaniments. In contrast, the ethnographic display directs attention to the object's iconic or "transcendent" meanings in order to favor the visitor's cognitive understanding. Immanent meanings are drawn out through the use of extended texts, photographs, maps, dioramas, mannequins, and other didactic materials. In the best traditions of liberal humanism and modernist universalism, Redfield argued that although notions of art and icon are invoked by different kinds of museums and separate academic disciplines, they are neither antithetical nor mutually exclusive. Rather, he urged, they offer complementary paths to understanding and can never be completely separated. "Whether we come to see the artifact as a creative mastery of form, or see it as a sign or symbol of a traditional way of life," he concluded, "we are discovering, for ourselves, new territory of our common humanity."[4] Redfield's lecture was published two years after Britain granted independence to Ghana, an event that set in motion a chain reaction of African political decolonization. During the following decades, a body of post-structuralist and postcolonial theory emerged that exposed to critique the notions of culture, art, and scientific objectivity that underlay modernist primitivism in both art-historical and anthropological discourse. Yet 25 years later, when the Museum of Modern Art opened its 1984 blockbuster exhibition, *"Primitivism" in 20th-Century Art: Affinity of the Tribal and the Modern*, the central premises of its curator, William Rubin, were seen to have shifted barely at all from those that had been articulated by Redfield.[5] The show's narrative was formalist, contained no contemporary African work, and made no effort to bring African perspectives to bear on the objects. It reinscribed the modernist dialectical opposition between small-scale societies, seen as bounded, homogeneous, immobile, and local, and great civilizations, seen as open, cosmopolitan, mobile, and global.

The MoMA show was the catalyst for a heated debate about the appropriative role of the museum not only in terms of the physical removal of objects from originating communities, but also in overwriting indigenous systems of expressive culture with Eurocentric and essentializing notions of *both* art and artifact. The immediate responses and subsequent reflections of Clifford, McEvilley, Foster, Price, Vogel et al., Errington, and others have become required reading for a generation of students.[6] Two subsequent African exhibitions proved nearly as controversial. The boycott of the Royal Ontario Museum's 1989 *Into the Heart of Africa* and the unprecedented number of revisions made to the London Royal Academy's 1995 *Africa: Art of a Continent* when it traveled to the Guggenheim in New York in 1996, showed that the issues opened up in 1984 were far from resolved.[7] These more recent debates both drew on and fed theorizations of globalization and culture, specifically in relation to the representation of diasporic and Creole groups, the histories of agency and travel of the West's "others," and contemporary art from Africa.

It was against this history of debate that four prominent museums in the United States and Great Britain undertook reinstallations of their African collections that opened to the public between 1995 and 2001. The resulting exhibits provide an opportunity to assess the impact of two decades of critique on modernist constructs of art and artifact. The earliest of these projects was the Metropolitan Museum of Art's reinstallation of one of the African galleries in its Michael C. Rockefeller Wing, beginning in 1995. In 1999 London's Horniman Museum opened *African Worlds*, a new exhibition that replaced a previous exhibition devoted to world ethnography.[8] Also in 1999 the Smithsonian Institution's US Museum of Natural History opened its new *African Voices* exhibition in galleries previously occupied by a conventional mid-twentieth-century ethnographic display on Africa. And in 2000 the British Museum opened the Sainsbury African Galleries in new space created underneath its restored Great Court.

All these exhibitions involved the rethinking of curatorial approaches and – except for the Metropolitan – a complete redesign of architectural space and exhibition furniture. To varying degrees, the installations that were replaced had represented Africa as distant from and prior to the space and time of Western modernity. At the Metropolitan, in the Horniman's universal survey exhibition of world ethnology, and in the Smithsonian's 1960s Hall of African Peoples the geographical space of "Africa" was confined to regions south of the Sahara and, disproportionately, to West and Central Africa, while the time of Africa was the fictive ethnographic present.[9] The immediate predecessors of the British Museum's Sainsbury Galleries were a series of rotating, temporary, special topic exhibits staged at the Museum of Mankind, the British Museum's former off-site ethnographic branch in London's Burlington Gardens. While these exhibits contextualized objects more fully than had the main building's earlier typological displays, overall they continued to represent Africa as a set of distanced, localized cultures.

As numerous analyses have demonstrated, such constructs of time and space are tied to discredited ideologies of primitivism and cultural evolutionism.[10] They inscribe essentialized notions of race and implicitly deny the modernity of Africa and the authenticity of diasporic African cultures.[11] In the discussion that follows I will use Redfield's formulation as a baseline against which to measure the impacts of postmodernist disciplinary reflexivity and postcolonial museum politics on the late twentieth-century exhibition projects that replaced these early and mid-twentieth-century displays. I approach this large task in two ways, both through a discussion of overall themes and narrative structure and by looking more closely at two specific kinds of objects. Where Redfield used Dogon sculpture to anchors his analysis, I will look at the ways that Benin brasses and Mende Sande Society masks are displayed in each of the exhibitions. The installations of these objects are useful diagnostics because both have become "canonical" genres in Western displays of African art, the brasses because of their historical importance and generally acknowledged quality of craftsmanship and artistry, and the Mende Sande Society masks because they are regularly used by museums to illustrate the role of African art in initiation. In addition, the Benin material raises central issues around colonialism, appropriation, and power, while the Mende masks do so because they have been the focus of feminist rereadings of African art.[12]

Reinstalling the Rockefeller Wing

Opened in 1982, the Metropolitan's Rockefeller Wing brings together the collections that Nelson Rockefeller had originally given to its predecessor, the Museum of Primitive Art, with other objects from Africa, Oceania, and the Americas acquired by the Metropolitan through purchase and donation (Figure 4.1). The modern architectural design of the wing contrasts with the neo-classical design of the adjacent galleries devoted to Greek and Roman art. Nevertheless, the aura of temporal remoteness, loss, and fragmentation that surrounds these displays seemed also to inform the initial African installations – an impression that the minimal tombstone labels did nothing to contradict.

Figure 4.1   African Galleries, Michael C. Rockefeller Wing, Metropolitan Museum of Art.

Unlike anthropology museums, most art galleries change their exhibits at regular intervals to rotate the permanent collections, feature new acquisitions, and accommodate new curatorial approaches.[13] Although the immediate cause of the Metropolitan's 1995 reinstallation was the integration of a major gift of 100 Benin works by Klaus G. Perls, the project was part of a rolling schedule of change in its African galleries. The new installations of the late 1990s are continuous in many ways with the Rockefeller Wing's earlier exhibits, as well as with the Museum's institutional traditions. The original geographical grouping of the African objects was maintained, the new objects were installed to "stand visually on their own," and to give primacy to the visitor's visual experience.[14] The masterpiece (understood either as an outstanding rendering of a classic object type or an important innovation) is privileged. Rather than creating dramatic ruptures with these traditions, the changes that were introduced between 1995 and 2000 intervened in them more subtly. Most noticeable is the greater contextualization of the objects supplied by new labels that incorporate maps and images. Extended texts provide detailed explanations of historical and cultural context and specific iconographic features. Curator Alisa Lagamma had to fight hard for these labels, but, once adopted, they stimulated similar innovations elsewhere in the Museum.[15] The Mende and Benin displays illustrate both the continuing emphasis on aesthetic quality and singularity and the new stress on iconicity. The single Mende Sande Society mask is an extraordinarily beautiful example of its genre (Figure 4.2). The impact of the exceptional carving and the inventive, complex iconography is heightened because the mask is displayed on its own in a pedestal case. The accompanying label provides information about the sixteenth-century origins of the Mende, the uses of masks in initiation, and the specific iconographic meanings of individual motifs.

Similarly, in the next room, the label accompanying the display of "Benin Palace Plaques" incorporates a reproduction of an early engraving showing the masks in situ and provides four dense paragraphs containing historical accounts of the palace and discussions of the court rituals and regalia depicted on the plaques. The text panel concludes: "Apparently, sometime before the end of the seventeenth century, the plaques were removed from the pillars of the palace and put in storage, where they were consulted on matters of court etiquette, costume, and ceremony. About nine hundred of these plaques survive today." The Metropolitan omits any mention of the confiscation of these plaques and other palace treasures by the British after its invasion of Benin in 1897 or of the path they traveled to reach New York.[16]

Rather than engaging with the politics of postcolonialism or restitution, the Museum has opted to foreground the rigorous art-historical scholarship on African art that has emerged during recent decades that barely existed in the time of Redfield and the Museum of Primitive Art. The fieldwork-based methods that have transformed African art history – and the prominence of Africans among its practitioners – are also reflected in the new installation approach used for the Baga mask in the exhibit. In keeping with the modernists' privileging of formalism in African art, the mask's raffia and cloth costume had long been removed, and it had been oriented vertically in order to maximize its sculptural qualities. In the reinstallation, priority has been given to suggesting how the mask would have been seen in performance. Working with an art historian specializing in Baga art, the Metropolitan's curators commissioned a reproduction of the traditional costume to be made in New York and remounted the mask horizontally, as it would be seen in Africa in performance. The new approach breaks not only with the formalist tradition, but also with modernist notions of authenticity.[17]

Figure 4.2 Mende Sande Society mask. Gift of Robert and Nancy Nooter, Metropolitan Museum of Art, 1982.489.

Another way in which changes are being introduced in the Rockefeller Wing is through new acquisitions which broaden the canon of African art beyond that associated with modernist primitivism. Recent purchases have included a fifteenth-century Ethiopian illuminated Gospel and a monumental silk woven mantle from Madagascar made in 1998 by Martin Rakotoarimanana, as part of a revival of a precolonial weaving tradition.[18] While such acquisitions conform to the traditional emphasis on aesthetic quality and rarity, they depart from the past preferences for sculpture, the arts of West and Central Africa, age, and pagan ritual contexts of use.[19] Because the changes that are being made at the Metropolitan are incremental, gradually altering from within a familiar installation, they may not be noticeable to the average visitor. They are moving, however, in the same direction as the far more radical innovations that are evident in the other new installations.

The British Museum's Sainsbury Galleries of African Art

Few would have predicted the dramatic change in installation approach that has occurred in the new Sainsbury Galleries of African Art at the British Museum. Funded by a gift from renowned collectors Robert and Lisa Sainsbury, the galleries are dedicated to the British sculptor Henry Moore. The lengthy text panel placed just outside the entrance for the opening of the Galleries included Sir Robert's statement that: " 'What I am is someone who liked artists who liked primitive and were influenced by primitive. . . . I liked Henry Moore's carving – Henry Moore liked primitive.' " The anonymous curatorial voice hastily intervened to explain that: "Primitive in this context is shorthand. As Moore himself remarked, 'primitive' is misleading if it is taken to imply crudeness or incompetence." Yet, the notion of the primitive imprinted itself through its multiple repetitions and framed the value of the African objects in exhibition in terms of the "wealth of experience and inspiration" (to further quote the text panel) they have provided for modern Western artists. This panel has since been changed and now contains a brief account of Moore's admiration for African art and his role in introducing Sir Robert Sainsbury to African art; the word "primitive" no longer appears.[20]

The introductory space presents large and dramatic examples of contemporary African art by artists from Egypt and North, South, East, and West Africa.[21] Their prominence strongly signals the exhibition's acceptance both of the revisionist "whole Africa" approach and of the authenticity of contemporary modernist African art. The 600-plus objects displayed in the four large rooms that lead off this space are grouped into seven categories based on media, technology, and function: Woodcarving, Pottery, Forged Metal, Masquerade, Brasscasting, Personal Adornment, and Textiles.

The curators, Christopher Spring, Nigel Barley, and Julie Hudson, who consulted extensively with more than 50 African artists, curators, and other experts, have written that this rather startlingly Eurocentric and old-fashioned material culture classification "is less arbitrary than it might at first seem, as a whole philosophy often underlies each different material and technology, and this can be used as a means of shedding light on African history and social life."[22] In this context, they argue, Benin brasscasting can, for example, "be seen to be about the strength and durability of kingship."[23] The main text panel for the Benin section, however, reveals the problematic politics of this imposed, etic, thematic structure and the objective curatorial voice through which the public is addressed. It reads:

> In 1897, following an attack on a British consular mission, a British punitive expedition took Benin City and sent the King, Oba Oronramwen, into exile. Many of the brass objects from Benin City fell to the troops and others were sold abroad to defray the costs of the expedition and compensate the victims. Benin brasswork was totally unknown in the West as it had been confined almost entirely to the royal palace and it so confounded current ideas about Africa that some refused to believe that it could be of exclusively Benin origin.

In this narrative the "victims" are white, the soldiers are guiltless, the Victorian rationale for the sale and dispersal of the kingdom's treasures is repeated uncritically, and the tropes of wonder and curiosity are exploited. Although the panel concludes with a statement about modern Benin and the restoration of court ritual, it makes no reference to compelling recent art-historical research on the objects' entanglement in histories of violence, colonial power, and racist discourses about art – or the British Museum's own central role in these histories.[24] The curators stress their new installation's recreation of the original sightlines for the mounted plaques, but the highly decorative and aestheticized installations overwhelm this worthy achievement, and act, rather, to anesthetize and efface the other history of imperialism and appropriation (Figure 4.3).

Figure 4.3 Installation of Benin brass plaques, Sainsbury African Galleries, British Museum. © The Trustees of The British Museum.

The curators have evocatively described the Sainsbury Galleries as, "highly aesthetic – white walls, open displays, enormous but very light cases, a clear plastic cliff of throwing knives frozen in mid-flight, a steel tree of pots that spirals up from floor to ceiling, and a whole wall of Benin plaques floating on slim poles." The new "house style," they explain, results from the "move from a simply ethnographic museum to a more catholic institution," and from the fact that "curators and [the] public are nowadays much more aware of the peculiarities of the museum gallery as a particular kind of space."[25] The Mende Sande Society mask on display tests this proposition. It is displayed in the Masquerade section amidst numerous other examples of canonical mask genres (Figure 4.4). The overall curatorial intent is to provide a level of ethnographic context within the aesthetic envelope and to amplify basic information through strategic juxtapositions with videos, striking installations, and contemporary works. In the present case, while proximity to the Sokari Douglas Camp figure of a Kalabari masquerader at the far end of the room might possibly "lead [the visitor] to question what a mask might be," it cannot provide understandings culturally specific to the Mende. The caption reads: "The Mende have one of the few African masking traditions

Figure 4.4 Installation of masks with Mende Sande Society mask in lower center. Sainsbury African Galleries, British Museum. Photo: Ruth Phillips.

where masks are worn and performed by women, as events of the Sande Society. It may be that this is because male and female initiation groups here operate in parallel." This brief text not only contains factual errors, but also ignores a substantial body of recent feminist scholarship on Sande.[26] It also employs the "ethnographic present," an ahistorical discursive convention that freezes the anthropological subject in a fictive past time of unacculturated authenticity.[27] This is particularly problematic given the horrific violence Mende people were suffering in Sierra Leone even as the label was being written. The underlying art installation paradigm assumes a prior exercise of taste and connoisseurship, yet the mask chosen is unexceptional in relation to the British Museum's fine collection of Mende masks – and also remains only partially realized because the crowded case makes it difficult to see individual pieces clearly. As elsewhere in the Sainsbury Galleries, the elegance of the design recalls the glossy displays of a superior department store, privileging the impression of quantity and variety over both ethnographic specificity and aesthetic singularity.

African Worlds at the Horniman Museum

The Horniman Museum's *African Worlds* is also an object-centered exhibition that borrows aspects of its installation approach from the art museum, and, like the Sainsbury Galleries, it, too, introduced a radical shift in design.[28] However, while the British Museum's curators had to fit into a predetermined institutional style, Anthony Shelton, who was then the Horniman's chief curator, worked with hand-picked designer Michael Cameron to create a "new visual language."[29] This takes the form of a modernist installation designed to sit uneasily within the classical vaulted space of the gallery. The materials are aggressively industrial and the cases incorporate asymmetrical, cubist, jarring, and disruptive elements. "It was...considered essential," Shelton has written, "to convey a sense of alienation in the gallery: alienation in the sense that these objects were displaced, far removed from the conditions of their usage and original signification."[30]

Shelton's curatorial approach also presents a sharp contrast to that of the British Museum team. Inspired by recent collaborative models developed by North American museums working with indigenous peoples, he created a curatorial committee of African and British professionals. They identified eight themes that reflect both European and African social, political, and epistemological categories: Patronage; Different Natures; Men/Women; Ancestors and Morality; Royalty and Power; Text, Image, History; Cycles of Life; and Parody and Humor. In parallel, Shelton initiated the *African Voices* project to collect interpretive statements from people of African and Caribbean descent living in London. These are given pride of place on the object labels – even though some criticize or express sadness about museum treatment and ownership of African objects.

The postcolonial historical sensibility and post-structuralist multivocality of *African Worlds* are evident in the exhibition's approach to the display of Benin brasses. These are installed in cases that suggest wall-safes, designed to maintain clear visibility while conveying both the value associated with the plaques and ambivalence about their presence in contemporary Britain. The main text panel gives a detailed history of the kingdom of Benin from 900 CE and the destruction wrought by the British expedition in 1897. It explicitly problematizes the issue of ownership, highlighting the comments of two prominent Nigerian co-curators, Joseph Eboreime and Emmanuel Arinze, who developed the historical interpretation that is presented and who, as the panel states, have also appealed "to the conscience of the world for a meaningful dialogue for a peaceful resolution of this shame of history."

A local, diasporic reality informs the Horniman's presentation of its Mende masks (Figure 4.5). They are interpreted by Mrs Beatrice Wusi, a Mende "wife and community worker" living in London. "It's supposed to be a mythical being that comes and teaches the children, the initiates, how to behave, how to sit properly," she states. "She teaches them how to dance. You see how they do her hair, her neck. Everything that we consider beauty... it's in there. It is something that personifies excellence. Anything that is good is in this. Really beautiful. You can see the culture in it. It's the leader, it's the mistress. That's what sowie [*sic*] is." Mrs Wusi's statement breaks down the exoticism of African female initiation through its presentation of the mask as the embodiment of an aesthetic and moral ideal, and of Sande as an institution of contemporary validity invested with important social responsibility. Because the expert speaking voice belongs to a woman living in London, the label conveys contemporaneity and proximity and works to collapse the distance between Europe and Africa.

Figure 4.5 Mende Sande Society mask installation with commentary by Mrs Beatrice Wusi, *African Worlds* exhibition, Horniman Museum, London. Photo: Ruth Phillips.

African Voices at the US National Museum of Natural History

The Smithsonian's decision to reinstall its African exhibits was directly stimulated by complaints from Africans and African Americans about racist and offensive aspects of the earlier 1960s displays. The curators, Mary Jo Arnoldi, Christine Kreamer, and Michael Mason, thus had a clear mandate to respond to contemporary critiques and new historical constructs of Africa and the diaspora.[31] As in the Horniman exhibition, the curators of *African Worlds* collaborated closely with Africans both in Africa and in Washington. The exhibition is organized along a central historical time line that opens onto sections addressing contemporary African life and cultures. These sections are grouped under three broad themes, Living in Africa, Working in Africa, and Wealth in Africa, each interpreted by means of large photo murals, interactive modules, and a mixture of historic and contemporary artifacts. The curators' desire "to increase understanding of the continent's modernity and its contemporary relevance" is manifested in the fact that nearly 70 percent of the objects they chose or acquired especially for the new exhibit were made after 1960.

The curators finalized their specific exhibition design only after testing a prototype exhibit module on typical Washington visitors. As a result, they abandoned an initial "poetic" relationship of text and object for a more unambiguous and didactic approach – rejecting, that is, the kind of reliance on the visitor's ability to infer meaning that is characteristic of art galleries and that was adopted by the Sainsbury Galleries and, to some extent, by the Horniman. The Benin display, which is part of the Living in Africa section, exemplifies the exhibition's overall privileging of colonial histories, contemporary life, and the voices of Africans. The main case features a poster created by Benin authorities for the centenary of the Punitive Expedition (Figure 4.6). It gives a detailed account of the 1897 invasion, reproduces a famous photo of the British soldiers with their loot, and includes a statement from the current Oba honoring "all our gallant heroes who fell during the British invasion." The installation thus foregrounds an artifact which is itself an historical/commemorative representation generated by contemporary Africans, causing the Benin brasses in the case to lose their meaning as art objects and to become illustrative adjuncts to the poster.

The Mende mask in *African Voices* is subordinated to a thematic message that is cultural rather than historical. It appears in the "Wealth in Africa" section, where it is juxtaposed with a modern Luba king's staff,

Figure 4.6 Benin installation, *African Voices* exhibition, US Museum of Natural History, Smithsonian Institution, Washington, DC. Photo: Ruth Phillips.

an Ethiopian graduation robe and diploma, and a fantasy coffin from Ghana (Figure 4.7). This eclectic assemblage challenges Western understandings of "wealth" with the notion that in Africa, "Wealth takes various forms: money, knowledge, and connections between people." Although the mask's association with initiation and its iconographic meanings are given in the object label, as elsewhere in *African Voices* the visual experience of the objects – which are often difficult to see because of crowding and bad lighting – is secondary to the historical and ethnographic texts. In the case of the Mende mask, the sense of bustling, contemporary vitality projected by the section of which it is a part elides the war, anarchy, and tragedy experienced by the Mende during the 1990s. This was a conscious design on the part of the curators, who wanted the exhibition to counter "media coverage that tends to emphasize 'Africa's problems'."[32]

"Modernity at Large" in the Museum

In "Art and Icon," Redfield constructed an imaginary dialogue between himself and a "common [female] viewer" whom he sets up as a kind of

Figure 4.7   Mende Sande Society mask, *African Voices* exhibition, US Museum of Natural History, Smithsonian Institution, Washington, DC. Photo: Ruth Phillips.

alter ego. This common viewer asks how it is that outsiders can acquire the right to judge objects made by members of other cultures, for, "perhaps the values they see in the work, the aesthetic values, are quite different from what you outsiders see."[33] Redfield, the anthropologist, answers that the artist is too far away to respond to such questions, may no longer make these types of objects, and probably lacks a tradition of critical discourse about art.[34] The common viewer is still not satisfied, and objects that "this exclusion of the artist and his own audience from the discussions seem[s] ... somehow not quite right – a great power decision on the aesthetic affairs of little peoples." At this point in his internal dialogue Redfield finally pulls out his big guns:

> There is no one in any better position to attempt to find reasons for the artistic success of the primitive artist than we modern Western outsiders for the reason that no one else has as much experience with many kinds of art.... The great civilizations of wide influence represent a coming together of various traditions. They are a mixing, a stimulating, a comparing of one traditional way with another. In these the habit develops of putting one meaning or value beside another. Western civilization is such a civilization.[35]

The ideology of high modernism that suffused both mid-twentieth-century anthropology and art criticism comes through clearly in these passages. The worlds of the West and the other are separated by real and conceptual distances that can be bridged only with great difficulty. Modernity, travel, and cosmopolitanism are prerogatives of the West. In Redfield's discussion, furthermore, the category of the aesthetic is assumed and the museum project is infused with nostalgia for lost authenticity. Although his lecture provides an insightful discussion of the different capacities of art and artifactual installations, it ends by reinscribing the spatial and temporal distances that high modernist discourses of both art and anthropology constructed between the bounded and local cultures of Africa and the mobile and cosmopolitan societies of the West.

Conclusion

Public perceptions of Africa as distant in time and space began to change in the late twentieth century, as the reality of globalization made itself felt through seemingly ubiquitous forms of cultural exchange and fusion. Today's dual consciousness was evoked by Holland Cotter in his 2002 review of an exhibition of contemporary African art: "Africa, whatever it is, is everywhere," he wrote. "It's far more than just a continent. It's a global diaspora, an international culture and a metaphor with fantastical associations for the West: gold, savages, 'darkest,' 'deepest,' liberation, devastation."[36] The distance between Redfield's moment of high modernism and the present moment of global/post/modernism can be seen in the way that all four of the exhibitions I have discussed seek to refute the dichotomies of there and here, then and now which characterized older museum representations of Africa and the West. All assert the equivalent cosmopolitanism of an Africa constructed as inclusive of the diaspora, and as mixed, hybrid, and contemporary as the West.

Yet modernist display paradigms of art and artifact seem to have only gained in rhetorical strength now that they are no longer so strictly tied to the discipline-specific museums that bred them. Unchallenged, they continue to invite primitivist fantasies. A further question logically follows. Why, in the light of three decades of post-structuralist and postcolonial critique, do these object-centered and objectifying modes of installation continue to retain their exclusive holds on museum display? The answer, I think, is both simple and complicated. It has to do, on the one hand, with a profound desire, deeply rooted in Western cultures, for the experiences of "resonance" and "wonder" that are produced by the presentation of objects as artifact and art.[37] The modern museum is a physical and spatial environment purpose-built to be a container for objects thus displayed. The "museum effect" is a function of the Western tradition of ocular centrism and it creates its objects as signs for knowledge and cognition and/or as points of access to spiritual and aesthetic experience.[38]

Whatever issues the postcolonial academic critic may raise regarding art installation such as those of the Metropolitan or the Sainsbury Galleries, many museum visitors of African heritage appreciate the recognition of their civilizations' achievements that is implicit in their beautifully designed displays. In an eloquent and searching discussion of the Sainsbury African Galleries, British-Ghanaian ethnographic curator Augustus Casely-Hayford reviewed what he terms the "battle for the soul of African art."[39] Although he does not cite it, his essay addresses many of the same issues as had Redfield's lecture a half century earlier. Casely-Hayford, however, argues that a middle path between art and artifact *is* possible and that projects like the Sainsbury Galleries are beginning to locate it:

> A chorus of people has asked how do we as Westerners get close to these objects, gain any kind of useful understanding of these things? Is this an art gallery or a museum? Two disciplines, different and rival sets of terms, different objectives and histories, yet the same objects. These have always been difficult questions to answer. But increasingly as knowledge of African

aesthetic traditions and the web of cultural and intellectual practice has grown in the West, art historians and ethnographers have begun to develop a language with which to holistically deal with our objects.[40]

It is striking that Casely-Hayford identifies himself in this passage as a Westerner. His remark is emblematic both of the increasing global extension of museum culture, of the diasporic interpenetration of Western and non-Western traditions of representation, and of the new hybridities that are beginning to emerge as museums adopt collaborative curatorial strategies and seek to address more diverse audiences. What has happened at the British Museum and the Metropolitan is not the rejection of the art paradigm, but a broadening of its parameters and movement toward inclusivity. At the Horniman and the Smithsonian, on the other hand, there has been an effort to loosen fixed relationships between certain signifiers and signifieds that had been established under modernist ideologies of progress and linked constructs of time and space. The African mask is no longer only "primitive" or "art," Benin brasses are no longer only curiosity or "loot." As multivocal curatorial processes do their work, these objects are being tied to new and different meanings attributed to them by people who have long lived within Western nations or who are now more closely connected through travel, media, and capital flows, but whose understandings of these objects have not before been reflected by the museums that own them.

As Arjun Appadurai has phrased it, globalization *is* "modernity at large."[41] Under colonialism, and even more after its formal ending, the West has been exporting museums and their technologies of representation as integral parts of modernity's archiving, memorializing, and nation-building practices.[42] What these four exhibitions also show, then, is how successfully museological conventions have been translating, so that now, in the era of globalization, museum savvy can be reimported to the "mother countries" through collaborative curatorial processes. As illustrated by both *African Worlds* and *African Voices*, such processes typically engage both Western-trained African museum professionals and non-professional community members who are mentored into the conventions of Western museological practice – and often come to constitute in after years a cadre of regular museum collaborators adept at manipulating the museum's conventions and characteristic technologies. Just as modernist ceramics by Magdalene Odundo, sculptures of masquerade figures by Sokari Douglas Camp, or Somali and Egyptian ethnographic artifacts have become part of the new, revised museum canon of African art and artifact, so has collaborative curation become the new museum practice that expresses contemporary pluralist ideology.[43] Equally, diasporic movements, educational systems, and multicultural policies in the arts are producing new, 'non-traditional' visitors who are socialized to understand the hierarchy of value inscribed by the Western art and culture system.[44] Yet despite the continuing allegiance to Eurocentric installation paradigms, when we compare the new exhibits to those they replaced there can be no doubt that the impacts of globalization on Western museums are no less important for the circular path they have been traveling around the globe.

Notes

1   Emmanuel Nnakenyi Arinze, "Glimpses of Africa: Museums, Scholarship and Popular Culture," *Journal of Museum Ethnography* 12 (2000): 3.

2   See Ruth Phillips, " 'Where is Africa?': Reviewing Art and Artifact in the Age of Globalisation," *American Anthropologist* 104/3 (2002): 11–19, for the review essay of which the current chapter is an expansion. Both are based primarily on visits to the museums discussed in 2000 and 2001. I have tried to accommodate changes observed during further visits to the Horniman's *African Worlds* in 2002, the Smithsonian's *African Voices* in 2003, and the British Museum's Sainsbury Galleries in May 2005, but my discussion does not reflect changes that may have been made since those visits.

3   Robert Redfield, "Art and Icon," in *Aspects of Primitive Art* (New York: Museum of Primitive Art, 1959). The other lectures in the series were by Melville Herskovits and Gordon Eckholm. The preface was written by Robert Goldwater.

4   Ibid., p. 38. Redfield's essay must be read against the political context of the McCarthy era and in relation to projects such as the Museum of Modern Art's major 1955 photographic exhibit, *The Family of Man.*

5   See William R. Rubin, "Modernist Primitivism: An Introduction," in William Rubin, ed., *"Primitivism" in 20th-Century Art: Affinity of the Tribal and the Modern*, 2 vols. (New York: Museum of Modern Art 1984), vol. I, pp. 1–84. Rubin was a student and colleague of Robert Goldwater, author of the classic work on modernist *Primitivism* (1939), and the intellectual mentor of the Museum of Primitive Art.

6   James Clifford, "Histories of the Tribal and the Modern," in *The Predicament of Culture: Twentieth-Century Ethnography, Literature, and Art* (Cambridge, MA: Harvard University Press, 1988); Thomas McEvilley, *Art and Otherness: Crisis in Cultural Identity* (Kingston, NY: Documentext, 1992); Hal Foster,

"The 'Primitive' Unconscious of Modern Art, or White Skin, Black Masks," in Foster, *Recodings: Art, Spectacle, Cultural Politics* (Seattle, WA: Bay Press, 1985); Sally Price, *Primitive Art in Civilized Places* (Chicago: University of Chicago Press, 1989); Susan Vogel et al., *Art/Artifact: African Art in Anthropology Museums* (New York: The Centre for African Art, 1988); Shelley Errington, *The Death of Authentic Primitive Art and Other Tales of Progress* (Berkeley: University of California Press, 1998).

7   For an exhaustive case study of *Into the Heart of Africa* with comprehensive bibliography, see Shelley Ruth Butler, *Contested Representations: Into the Heart of Africa* (London and New York: Routledge, 1999); for a useful introduction to the debates around "Africa: Art of a Continent," see Christa Clarke, "Africa: Art of a Continent" (exhibition review), *Art Journal* 56/1 (1997): 82–7; and Elsbeth Court, "Africa on Display: Exhibiting Art by Africans," in Emma Barker, ed., *Contemporary Cultures of Display* (New Haven: Yale University Press, 1999), pp. 147–73.

8   On the history of the Horniman and its ethnographic exhibitions, see essays in Anthony Shelton, ed., *Collectors: Expressions of Self and Other* (London: The Horniman Museum and Gardens, 2001) and Anthony Shelton, ed., *Collectors: Individuals and Institutions* (London: The Horniman Museum and Gardens, 2001).

9   Johannes Fabian, *Time and the Other* (New York: Columbia University Press, 1983).

10   See George W. Stocking, Jr., ed., *Objects and Others: Essays on Museums and Material Culture* (Madison: University of Wisconsin Press, 1985); Susan Hiller, ed., *The Myth of Primitivism: Perspectives on Art* (New York: Routledge, 1991); Vogel et al., *Art/Artifact*; Price, *Primitive Art*; and Errington, *The Death of Authentic Primitive Art*.

11   On diaspora, pluralism, and their implications for curatorial work, see James Clifford, *Routes: Travel and Translation in the Late Twentieth Century* (Cambridge, MA: Harvard University Press, 1997), esp. chs. 1, 7, and 10; and two useful edited volumes: Jean Fisher, ed., *Global Visions: Towards a New Internationalism in the Visual Arts* (London: Kala Press, 1994) and Nicholas Mirzoeff, ed., *Diaspora and Visual Culture: Representing Africans and Jews* (New York: Routledge, 2000).

12   Mende Sande masks were the subject of my 1979 doctoral dissertation. See Ruth B. Phillips, *Representing Woman: Sande Masquerades of the Mende of Sierra Leone* (Los Angeles: Fowler Museum of Cultural History, 1995).

13   This distinction is, of course, a matter of degree. Normally, however, objects in permanent anthropology exhibits are rotated for conservation reasons rather than to develop curatorial premises, which are embedded didactically in the overall narrative and thematic structure. Any analysis, however, is necessarily based on the particulars of a display studied at a particular moment in time.

The observations in this chapter were made during visits to the Metropolitan in 2001, to the Horniman in 2000 and 2002, to the British Museum in 2000, 2002, and 2005, and to the Smithsonian in 2001 and 2003.

14 Personal communication, New York City, December 3, 2001.

15 Personal communication, New York City, December 3, 2001.

16 Annie Coombes, *Reinventing Africa: Museums, Material Culture and Popular Imagination* (New Haven: Yale University Press, 1994). Like all Benin brasses outside Nigeria, those in the Metropolitan's collection originate from the British sale of the court treasures and changed hands many times before being donated to the Museum.

17 The project was initiated by Metropolitan Museum curator Julie Jones. Art historian and Baga specialist Fred Lamp oversaw the restoration.

18 Alisa LaGamma, "New Acquisitions: The Metropolitan Museum of Art, New York," *African Arts* 34/2 (2001): 72–3.

19 The Metropolitan's rigid departmental structure both facilitates and inhibits such shifts in focus. On the one hand, the support of the Medieval Department facilitated the purchase of the Bible, while, on the other, the Rockefeller Wing curators are prevented from acquiring contemporary African art because it falls within the province of the Modern Painting Department.

20 The passage reads, in part: "The links between the Sainsbury family and Henry Moore, and between both and the British Museum's Ethnography collections are especially close. . . . To an extent their interests developed in tandem. Moore is reported to have been influential in introducing Sir Robert to the British Museum collections, and especially to those from Africa and the Pacific. He once said, 'To discover, as a young student, that the African carvers could interpret a human figure to this degree, but still keep and intensify the expression, encouraged me to be more adventurous and experimental.' "

21 As of spring 2005, a new group of equally strong contemporary works had replaced the original group.

22 The results of the consultations are incorporated both into text panels and videos in the exhibition and also in the book published in conjunction with the opening of the Sainsbury Galleries. See John Mack, ed., *Africa: Arts and Cultures* (London: British Museum Press, 2000).

23 Christopher Spring, Nigel Barley, and Julie Hudson, "The Sainsbury African Galleries at the British Museum," *African Arts* 34/3 (2001): 21.

24 See Coombes, *Reinventing Africa*.

25 Ibid., p. 37.

26 See Sylvia Ardyn Boone, *Radiance from the Waters: Ideals of Feminine Beauty in Mende Art* (New Haven: Yale University Press, 1986); Carol P. MacCormack, "Nature, Culture, and Gender: A Critique," in Carol P. MacCormack and Marilyn Strathern, eds., *Nature, Culture and Gender* (Cambridge: Cambridge University Press, 1980); and Phillips, *Representing Woman*.

27   See Fabian, *Time and the Other.*

28   See Karel Arnaut, ed., *Re-Visions: New Perspectives on the African Collections of the Horniman Museum* (London: The Horniman Museum and Gardens, 2000) for a collection of essays exploring many aspects of the project.

29   Anthony Shelton, "Curating African Worlds," *Journal of Museum Ethnography* 12 (2000): 5.

30   Ibid., p. 13.

31   Mary Jo Arnoldi, Christine Mullen Kreamer, and Michael Atwood Mason, "Reflections on 'African Voices' at the Smithsonian's National Museum of Natural History," *African Arts* 34 (2001): 17–19.

32   Ibid., p. 20.

33   Redfield, "Art and Icon," p. 31.

34   Ibid.

35   Ibid, p. 34.

36   Holland Cotter, "From the Ferment of Liberation Comes a Revolution in African Art," *New York Times*, Sunday, February 17, 2002, Section 2, pp. 1, 40–2.

37   Stephen Greenblatt, "Resonance and Wonder," in Ivan Karp and Steven D. Lavine, eds., *Exhibiting Cultures: The Poetics and Politics of Museum Display* (Washington, DC: Smithsonian Institution Press, 1991).

38   Svetlana Alpers, "The Museum as a Way of Seeing," in Ivan Karp and Steven D. Lavine, eds., *Exhibiting Cultures: The Poetics and Politics of Museum Display* (Washington, DC: Smithsonian Institution Press 1991).

39   Augustus Casely-Hayford, "A Way of Being: Some Reflections on the Sainsbury African Galleries," *Journal of Museum Ethnography* 14 (2002): 126.

40   Ibid.

41   Arjun Appadurai, *Modernity at Large: Cultural Dimensions of Globalization* (Minneapolis: University of Minnesota Press, 1996).

42   See Benedict Anderson, *Imagined Communities: Reflections on the Origin and Spread of Nationalism*, rev. and extended edn. (London: Verso 1991); Virginia Dominguez, "Invoking Culture: The Messy Side of 'Cultural Politics'," *South Atlantic Quarterly* 91/1 (1992): 19–42; Barbara Kirshenblatt-Gimblett, *Destination Culture: Tourism, Museums, and Heritage* (Berkeley: University of California Press, 1998).

43   For further examples and discussion of the new canon, see Court, "Africa on Display." For further discussion of collaborative models in general, see Michael M. Ames, *Cannibal Tours and Glass Boxes: The Anthropology of Museums* (Vancouver: University of British Columbia Press, 1992); for an earlier example of the model used in an African exhibition, see Sidney Littlefield Kasfir, "Field Notes: Reimagining Africa," *Museum Anthropology* 12/1 (1995): 45–53.

44   Clifford, "Histories of the Tribal and the Modern," pp. 215–52.

5

Mirroring Evil, Evil Mirrored: Timing, Trauma, and Temporary Exhibitions

Reesa Greenberg

Setting the Stage

On March 17, 2002, *Mirroring Evil: Nazi Imagery/Recent Art* opened at the Jewish Museum in New York (Figure 5.1). The exhibition was unlike any exhibition in a Jewish Museum to date about art and the Holocaust. Before, imagery focused on victims of the Holocaust and the overall feeling tone was one of mourning. In *Mirroring Evil,* viewers were surrounded by Nazi imagery and left without any sense of certainty about how to respond to hitherto taboo images of Hitler, games about the Holocaust, and the sexual tugs of Fascism. As they struggled between states of voyeurism, repugnance, humor, engagement, and fear, as well as their assumptions of what to expect in a Jewish Museum, many viewers reacted negatively to the exhibition.

The museum understood that the premises of the exhibition were controversial, but believed that it had a responsibility to present the ways younger artists with links to either victims or perpetrators of the Holocaust were grappling with their respective legacies. In doing so, the Jewish Museum sought to expand debates and dialogues about how museums represent the Holocaust. Even if the art was difficult, the Jewish

Figure 5.1 Installation view: *Mirroring Evil: Nazi Imagery/Recent Art,* Jewish Museum, New York, March 17 – June 30, 2002, with warning signs and Alain Séchas, *Les Enfants Gâtés;* Tom Sachs, *Giftgas Giftset;* and Rudolf Herz, *Zugzwang.* Courtesy The Jewish Museum/Art Resource, New York.

Museum believed that it was important to exhibit artworks that portrayed a different range of responses, both as a source of information and as a catalyst for reconsidering Jewish museum Holocaust exhibition practice.

Mirroring Evil consisted of 19 works by 13 artists, some of whom are Jewish. All were under the age of 40. They came from eight countries, including Israel, the USA, Austria, Germany, and Poland. Most of the work had been exhibited in museums elsewhere but this was the first time the art was shown in a group exhibition. Norman Kleeblatt, curator of the exhibition, had identified a generation of artists using the ideas and cool language of conceptual art to create art about the roles of commercialization and the mass media, play, and sexual fantasy in relation to Nazi imagery and the ways the Holocaust functions in Western societies today. The very density of so many provocative works displayed together augmented the sense that artists were grappling with a variety of distinctive ways of coming to terms with their current relationships to a horrific history. The museum's installation, with its dramatic presentation and crisp choreography, played a major role in constructing an exhibition environment which simultaneously mimicked and deconstructed the aesthetic language of Nazi displays.   Kleeblatt based *Mirroring Evil* on a number of premises about representation and reality. To paraphrase:

- The Holocaust continues to play a major role in our lives. For example, Jewish identity today is linked inextricably to the Holocaust and German refugee law is a response to that country's role in the Holocaust.
- Younger generations have no direct experience of the Holocaust and know it only through images. Usually, these are filmic. In March 2003, Roman Polanski's docu-drama, *The Pianist*, based on an autobiographical account of Wladyslaw Szpilman's survival in Nazi Poland, and Menno Meyjes' fictional *Max*, which portrays Hitler as a young man seeking his destiny in art or politics, played simultaneously and prominently in North American cities.
- Images of Nazis are pervasive and glamorized in our society. Gorgeous, well-dressed Nazi officers are cultural icons.
- When faced with evil, our responses may not be adequate. Put another way, not everyone is a hero, or not a hero all of the time. In *The Pianist*, Szpilman risks his life when asking for his brother's release and when carrying guns into the Warsaw ghetto, but does not remain to fight in the uprising.
- Everyone has a moral responsibility when confronted with evil, but translating that responsibility into effective action does not always occur.
- Sometimes the line between moral certainty and moral ambiguity is not clear.

My Roles

I was involved with the exhibition at various stages and in four different ways: as an advisor, a consultant, an author, and moderator of a public program. Because of my previous writings on trauma and the representation of the Holocaust in Jewish historical museums, I was invited to be a member of the Scholars Advisory Committee established by the museum for the exhibition. The Committee was asked to comment on the advisability and viability of the exhibition concept during the initial planning stages. Its members included Ernst Van Alphen, author of *Caught by History: Holocaust Effects in Contemporary Art, Literature and*

Theory; Sidra Esrahi, author of *By Words Alone: The Holocaust in Litera-ture*; Lisa Saltzman, author of *Anselm Kiefer and Art After Auschwitz*; Ellen Handler Spitz, author of *Museums of the Mind: Magritte's Labyrinth and Other Essays in the Arts*; and James Young, author of *The Texture of Memory: Holocaust Memorials and Meaning* and *At Memory's Edge: After Images of the Holocaust in Contemporary Art*. Later, I was hired as a consultant to advise on strategies the museum could utilize to minimize the inevitable discomfort and controversies the exhibition would provoke in Holocaust survivor communities. My official involvement with plan-ning the exhibition ended in July 2000.

I also wrote an essay for the catalogue. "Playing it Safe: The Display of Transgressive Art in the Museum" charts recent art world controversies, suggests a psychoanalytic interpretation of visitor anger when notions of Eros and Thanatos are destabilized in the safe space of the museum and links feelings of abandonment in this regard to the museum as D. W. Winnicott's "not good enough mother." Lastly, with art critic Eleanor Heartney, I moderated a public debate about the exhibition on April 11, 2002. My long-term, long-distance association with the museum and the exhibition allows me an insider/outsider perspective.

Reception of the Exhibition

Mirroring Evil was the first group exhibition in North America of con-temporary artists using "imagery from the Nazi era to explore the nature of evil."[1] Even before the exhibition opened, art critics and Holocaust survivors decided that the exhibition was "wrong" and, for the most part, maintained that opinion after seeing the exhibition itself. In what follows, I want to look closely at the criticism by each group, to restage the content and tone of their arguments. Then, I would like to offer some interpret-ations for understanding the vehemence of those who spoke so stridently against *Mirroring Evil*. I will link the negative reception of *Mirroring Evil* to concepts of timing and trauma and, then, to the innovative typology used to install the exhibition.

Every aspect of *Mirroring Evil* was criticized, both before and during the exhibition. Its title was picked apart. The thesis – an exhibition portraying perpetrators, not victims – was castigated. The museum was chastised for even having contemplated mounting the exhibition. The selection of artists was maligned. The art was denigrated as juvenile or pornographic.

The style of the art was declared unworthy because it was perceived as late, late, out-of-date conceptualism. Individual pieces – and they vary from reviewer to reviewer – were vilified. The extent of the didactic material was disparaged and the exhibition was accused of being overly framed. The curator and writers for the catalogue were taken to task for, in the words of Ron Rosenbaum, author of *Explaining Hitler,* smothering the art, shackling it to a straitjacket of jargon and substituting "a simplistic moral relativism for engagement with the issues."[2]

The museum expected criticism from Holocaust survivors. Some protested to the press and the museum before the exhibition opened. Others picketed for an hour on the opening day. Elie Wiesel, Auschwitz and Buchenwald survivor and Nobel Laureate, called the exhibition "a betrayal." Menachem Z. Rosensaft, head of the International Network of Children of Holocaust Survivors, labeled it "trivializing" and "a desecration."[3] Darren Marks, Chairman of Young Americans for Freedom, declared the exhibition "disgusting" and "a mockery."[4]

Daring to suggest not all people image or imagine the Holocaust as a narrative of victimhood or a forum for mourning was deemed unacceptable. One explanation for their dissension is that *Mirroring Evil* offered a different set of images from those already familiar from Holocaust museums and memorials, Jewish museums, and previous art exhibitions in North America about the Holocaust. For many Holocaust survivors, the questions and concerns raised in a number of studies and in *Mirroring Evil* about "Shoah business," the commodification of the Holocaust, the eroticism of Fascism, and the construction of Jewish identity as inextricable from the Holocaust simply were not relevant.

Timing

One of the main arguments brought by Holocaust survivors was the question of timing. The museum was accused of not respecting survivors and their children, of unnecessarily reopening the wounds of trauma, of inflicting additional pain, all the more reprehensibly because it was a Jewish museum, one of their own, causing such grief. Timing is always a concern when confronting and working through trauma. For some, the sooner trauma is addressed the better. For most, trauma is encountered layer by layer, unfolding over time, never completely healed, more or less worked through. Working through trauma, by necessity, is painful. To mask trauma, to paper it over, to avoid elements or layers of traumatic events also produces pain, perhaps of a different kind, but the possibility that those who have been traumatized will become less fixated or free from acting out diminishes.

There are those who believe it essential to tell and retell the narrative of their trauma. Many build Holocaust museums and mount Holocaust exhibitions in an effort to bear witness and to memorialize the murdered as well as construct a pedagogic instrument in an effort to deter future genocides. They are tenacious in their belief that the Holocaust and its evils are represented from a perspective of victimhood. Perhaps too tenacious, for they disallow any alternatives. The museum's question, "Who can speak for the Holocaust?" – placed on one of the wall text panels and in advertisements for the exhibition – is frightening to those who believe that no one but survivors can say anything meaningful about what happened.

Somewhat unexpectedly, the attacks were extraordinarily widespread from within the sophisticated New York art community. Peter Schjeldahl, in his *New Yorker* review, "The Hitler Show" (April 1, 2002) called the exhibition "trivial shock," "dilettantish sado-masochism," "solemn smut," and "toxic narcissism." Michael Kimmelman of the *New York Times*, both before and after *Mirroring Evil* opened, declared the exhibition disrespectful and condescending, and called it "cheap and obvious." He ended his March 15 review commenting on *It's the Real Thing – Self Portrait at Buchenwald*, 1993, where Alan Schechner, the artist, inserts an image of himself holding a coke can into the famous Margaret Bourke-White photograph of concentration camp survivors. Kimmelman states: "Really it's just another twist on Duchamp's painted moustache on the Mona Lisa, a work of mischievous irreverence, nothing original, with the psychological ante upped by connection to Hitler."[5] Kimmelman dismissed Schechner's explanation of the work functioning in relation to issues of identity and identification, refused to acknowledge any commentary on concentration camp tourism, and ignored how viewers' manipulation of the digital work in time echoes the subtle changes over time we bring to history when looking back from a different place or context.

Art Spiegelman, creator of the 1992 Pulitzer prize-winning *Maus*, also cited Duchamp as a negative source for work in the exhibition. In the first five frames of his back-page cartoon published in the March 25 *New Yorker* entitled "Duchamp is our Misfortune," Spiegelman portrayed a skinhead (a male thug wearing a sleeveless, black undershirt with a skull at the sternum) in the act of painting a red swastika on a pale blue stone wall.[6] The final frame shows the swastika wall exhibited as art on the white walls of *Mirroring Evil* with the artist and admirers, drinks in hand, in front of it.

Spiegelman's swipe referred to a number of works in the exhibition using Duchamp as a source. One is Rudolf Herz's 1995 *Zugzwang*, another work dismissed in Kimmelman's review. Herz's title refers to the chess term that applies whenever a player's move becomes compromised or dangerous. In *Zugzwang*, Herz papers a room chessboard style with alternating, seemingly neutral, photographic portraits of Adolf Hitler, murderer of millions of Jews, and Marcel Duchamp, murderer of the traditional art often found in Jewish museums. The very presence of images of Hitler and Duchamp in a Jewish museum provokes questions about what forms of representation are allowed when and where.

Both Hitler and Duchamp were photographed 20 years apart by Heinrich Hoffmann, Hitler's official photographer. Herz conceived *Zugzwang* for the Kunstverein Ruhr in Essen after his well-received 1994 Munich Stadtmuseum exhibition, *Hitler and Hoffmann*, investigating the role of photography in glamorizing Hitler, had been cancelled in Berlin and Saarbrücken. To quote Norman Kleeblatt: "Even the rather aesthetically conservative director of Essen's Jewish Historical Museum, a space housed directly above Essen's Kunstverein, approved of the artistic and moral ambiguities central to *Zugzwang*."[7] Exhibiting *Zugzwang* under or in a Jewish Museum questions the recuperative and commemorative double project of post-Holocaust Jewish museums. Exhibiting *Zugzwang* at Berlin's National Gallery in 1999 challenged the post-Holocaust transparency of the post-war German state embodied in Mies van der Rohe's 1963 glass-wall building as well as German laws prohibiting the public display of material associated with the Nazis.

Spiegelman's cartoon refers specifically to Tom Sachs's 1998 *Giftgas* set, in which battered tins of "gas" decorated/wrapped with Tiffany, Hermes, and Chanel packaging are placed on a glass display shelf, framed in white and mounted on the wall. Spiegelman's caption suggests that artists in the exhibition are louts who give no thought to what they do and take no time doing it. Granted, Tom Sachs's comments in a March 10 *New York Times* magazine interview referring to fashion, like Fascism, as being about loss of identity, and his remarks on the "amazing German engineering and design" of the death camps, are provocative. Spiegelman's response, however, is reductive. Sachs's irreverence may well be a caustic comment on

Holocaust displays such as the one at the Imperial War Museum, London, which incorporate aged cans of Zyklon B gas and display them as relics. The artists in *Mirroring Evil*, with the possible exception of Sachs, who relishes his "bad boy" image, are not Spiegelman's louts or thugs. Spiegelman's rabid responses to the exhibition are, in my opinion, too rapid and are linked to another aspect of timing and trauma.

Trauma

Mirroring Evil is an exhibition about trauma that opened for viewing in a recently traumatized New York. The timing of the exhibition, March 2002, may well have been too soon after the September 11, 2001 mass murders at the Twin Towers and the futile, prolonged attempts to recover survivors. *Mirroring Evil* is an exhibition about evil men who dehumanize and commit mass murder. Even if nothing overtly linked the exhibition to recent events, those events may well be behind the hysteria with which the exhibition was received. Trauma specialists believe that the second wave of post-traumatic responses occurs about six months after the initial trauma. *Mirroring Evil* opened precisely at that time. In addition, the exhibition took place in the midst of other, related, ongoing traumas – during Operation Enduring Freedom, suicide bombings in Israel, Operation Protective Wall, and escalating, institutionalized, and individual acts of anti-Semitism throughout the world. All these events seem to have precluded a more balanced reception of art that examines our response to evil and mass murder in a not-so-distant past and its relation to evil now.

Often, when anger is so strong, there is also fear, denial, and displacement. The more vehement responses do not even attempt to offer alternative theories for why so much current art about the Holocaust is so ironic and distanced. Nor are there insights offered into how artists or curators might meaningfully portray the Holocaust now – aside from suggesting humor, a modality that proved contentious for Roberto Benigni in his 1998 film, *Life is Beautiful*. Little was said by the critics about how the exhibition keeps debates about the ethics of Holocaust representations alive, and expands its participants in a time when many would prefer to forget or believe the Holocaust and its repercussions are behind them.

Mirroring Evil fueled the argument for those who call for the end of ironic and pedagogic art and a return to beauty. In wartime, the call for art to elevate and distract is common: the conjuncture of *Mirroring Evil* and the events following September 11, 2001 may make it the tombstone exhibition for group shows that challenge orthodox imagery in relation to genocide and ask viewers to contemplate a personal position in relation to the issues raised by the works on display. There are more balanced reviews of *Mirroring Evil*, but these are not the ones heard. For example, Leslie Cahmi's article, "Peering Under the Skin of Monsters" in the *New York Times* compared *Mirroring Evil*, the Gerhard Richter retrospective at the Museum of Modern Art, and *Same Difference* at the Ydessa Hendeles Foundation in Toronto.[8] Interestingly, the reviews of the exhibition by women are far more tempered, and, at times, as in Eunice Lipton's essay for the *Guardian* where she calls the exhibition brave and brilliant, more enthusiastic, suggesting that there may be gendered differences in responses to recent trauma.[9]

There is another aspect of timing related to the traumatized responses to the exhibition. Originally scheduled to open in March 2001, it was delayed a full year, in part because the museum received a grant from the Animating Democracy Lab.[10] The catalogue/book, already in press, was released in December 2001, three months before the exhibition opened. *Mirroring Evil* was judged initially and primarily on the catalogue presentation of the works, an intellectual enterprise when compared to the more visceral experience of the exhibition, where the installation was carefully choreographed so that works worked together in three-dimensional space. Unfortunately for *Mirroring Evil*, its innovations in installation and their significance for constructing new meanings about art and the Holocaust got lost in debates about timing and trauma and appropriateness of style and subject. I suspect that the perceived sacrilege caused by the slippage between two genres, the contemporary, group, art exhibition, and exhibitions about the Holocaust, is another key element contributing to the anger the exhibition evoked. In *Mirroring Evil*, this slippage of display modes was destabilizing, working against notions of art as redemptive or art and beauty.

Typology

Mirroring Evil was a hybrid exhibition. It combined the white walls, bright lighting and uncluttered installation of a museal, contemporary art exhibition with installation devices found in Holocaust museums. Norman

Kleeblatt, the curator, and Dan Kershaw, the designer, borrowed, knowingly or not, a number of tropes from the Holocaust museum installation genre. These include a liminal introductory space, changes in lighting and floor coverings to shift mood and sensory perceptions, protective devices, extensive text, a tight narrative structure with a carefully plotted route, and a decompressing room before the exit.

In *Mirroring Evil*, each of these devices was incorporated into the exhibition. As viewers entered the exhibition space, they left the brightly lit, smallish, often noisy lobby of the Jewish Museum for a dark, relatively empty room that acted as a transition from the world outside and an introduction to what would follow. In *Mirroring Evil*, the introductory space was divided into two zones: one for text, one for images. The first and larger area contained descriptive panels about the exhibition. Directly across from the entrance door, there was a large, white, rectangular panel with the curator's statement, and close beside it, to the right, a smaller, black, square panel with white lettering warning visitors about the art they would see. The Director's message hung on a floor to ceiling, free-standing oval drape suspended mid-room to the visitors' left. The screen on the backside of the drape was used for a seven-minute loop consisting of excerpts from humorous or cautionary films and television programs in which the Holocaust figured, notably *The Producers* or *The Twilight Zone*. These were curated by art historian Maurice Berger, author of *White Lies: Race and the Myths of Whiteness* and creator of context areas for exhibitions like the *American Century Part II: Art and Culture* at the Whitney Museum of American Art, 1999–2000.

Unlike other art exhibitions, the context room in *Mirroring Evil* was not an aside, nor was it located mid-way through the exhibition space. Instead, it resembled the darkened rooms in Holocaust museums with minimal displays used to prepare visitors for what they are to see. This device is used at the Holocaust Memorial Museum in Washington and the Museum of Jewish Heritage in New York. In *Mirroring Evil*, the first room was a screening room, in more than one sense, empty enough to hold groups of visitors, preparing them for what was to come, warning them, establishing an inquisitive state of mind and providing examples of earlier media work with similar themes.

The artworks in the exhibition were reached through a second set of heavy glass doors. Beyond this point, the walls were white and *Mirroring Evil* appeared to resemble a contemporary art exhibition. The darkened spaces toward the beginning of the exhibition for Mischa Kuball, Maciej

Toporowicz, and Boaz Arad's video projections relating to Hitler's use of mass media seemed to be determined by the medium's needs for optimal visibility. Soon it became apparent that the exhibition route had been deliberately structured for maximum expressive effect, and lighting was instrumental in producing a sense of shifting sensations. Using a lighting schema for drama and narrative and to minimize viewer fixation and fatigue is closely related to devices found in Holocaust museums.

In the first two-thirds of the exhibition, viewers walked through alternating brightly lit and murky areas. Their trajectory moved from the dark introductory space to Piotr Uklański's white, lit, 1998 *The Nazis* C-prints, to Kuball's shadowy *Hitler's Cabinet*, 1990, then to the almost black side room with Toporowicz's *Eternity #14*, 1991, to the vibrant white and brilliant orange space of Alain Séchas's *Enfants Gâtés*, 1997, to a low, light room with Sach's and Schechner's works, Arad's *Hebrew Lesson*, 2000, and Zbigniew Libera's *Lego Concentration Camp Set*, 1996 (Figure 5.2). Herz's black-and-white *Zugzwang* followed on the same axis and opened into a white room with Christine Borland's *L'Homme Double*,

Figure 5.2 Installation view: *Mirroring Evil: Nazi Imagery/Recent Art*, Jewish Museum, New York, March 17 – June 30, 2002, with works by Zbigniew Libera, Boaz Arad, Rudolf Herz, and Christine Borland. Courtesy The Jewish Museum/Art Resource, New York.

where the brightness at the end of the sequence was amplified by a frosted window on the back wall of the enfilade. The carefully orchestrated, contrapuntal lighting from area to area disrupted any sense of corporeal stability a viewer might have felt. At the same time, the constantly shifting lighting embodied the absence of a stabile intellectual or emotional frame of reference with which these works could be viewed. From this point on, the lighting was more uniform, cooler, as if to indicate that the sexual content in Roee Rosen's 1995 *To Live and Die as Eva Braun*, Mat Collishaw's colored transparencies of dead, semi-dressed Nazi couples, and Elke Krystufek's 1998 juxtapositions of her nude body with photographs of Nazis should be looked at directly.

The lighting in the last room of the exhibition containing catalogues, comment books, computers, and a video was also neutral. Here, the clear light acted as a transition to the outside world, the lobby of the museum, seen through the glass doors. In many art exhibitions, there is space at the end of an exhibition where viewers can record their responses to what they have seen. The inclusion of a video with responses to the exhibition itself in *Mirroring Evil* was atypical and more closely related to survivor videos found in the last rooms of Holocaust museums. The reference to the living present is intended to provide some relief to what is called "secondary witnessing" for viewers who have walked through the harrowing history of the Holocaust.[11]

Holocaust museums are particularly attentive to viewer sensibilities, especially those of survivors. In Holocaust museums, exhibition designers place warnings about potentially upsetting images and build walls to shield viewers from unwittingly encountering disturbing images. Sometimes, exits are provided to allow viewers the possibility of leaving the exhibition without looking at the potentially provocative material. These devices have been used by art museums when displaying disturbing images such as those by Cindy Sherman in the retrospective exhibition at the Art Gallery of Ontario (October 1, 1999 – January 2, 2000). In *Mirroring Evil*, strong warnings were placed in the introductory room and before the gallery containing works by Libera, Sachs, Alan Schechner, and Arad. The Jewish Museum's use of a black background and white lettering rather than the usual black on white format made their warnings stand out. Putting these emphatic warnings on a large, free-standing panel in the middle of the entrance to the gallery with the artworks suggested a sentry blocking the route. Viewers could turn back rather than enter the darkness. Once in the gallery, viewers could leave if they wished through an "escape route," a specially constructed exit that led into the response room and to the lobby.[12]

The designers of *Mirroring Evil* also protected viewers by shielding the images in Schechner's two computer works behind walls. The Jewish Museum prepared viewers even before they entered the exhibition by reversing the usual entrance and exit pattern for the temporary exhibition galleries, thereby upending any preconceived ideas habitual visitors to the museum might have had about the art being the same as what they had previously encountered in these galleries. Once inside the exhibition, viewers found explanatory text panels throughout. Their large size called attention to the importance of reading and made the act of reading while standing, sometimes in a group, easier.[13]

One reason for safety devices was to provide relief from a sense of claustrophobia created by the oblique, sequential, and peripheral views of the carefully constructed sight lines in the dense display. *Mirroring Evil*'s presentation strategy was a theatrical *mise-en-scène* structured in three parts: a context room, the art galleries, and the viewer response video room. At times, because of the tight spaces in the galleries and the controlled choreography, viewers were confronted with images they would rather not see. Viewers felt surrounded by the images, as if there was no escape from the tight narrative path through the exhibition they were made to follow. Usually, every bit of exhibition space in Holocaust museums is filled with displays, text, or film. In *Mirroring Evil*, the small exhibition space was filled to a degree not usually encountered in group art exhibitions. As in other Holocaust museums, the density of displays diminished towards the end of the exhibition.

Within modernism, artists and curators have used the language of display to challenge conventional readings of art, sometimes in ways we approve and sometimes not. The Nazi-organized *Degenerate Art* exhibition of 1937, with its chaotic arrangement of tilted, tightly spaced paintings and disrespectful captions, is the standard example of an installation practice that denigrates the objects on display and constructs a narrative of devaluation. By contrast, Duchamp's intervention in the *First Papers of Surrealism* exhibition held in New York in 1942, where he strung string from wall to wall, making the space practically impenetrable and reorienting viewers' relationships with art, is seen as a positive example of transgressive display aesthetics. Duchamp's use of innovative display techniques to create meaning through a frustration of habitual desires is a different inflection of the Duchampian geneology usually invoked for

Mirroring Evil. Recently, especially in New York, artists such as Group Material and Joseph Kosuth have created exhibitions using the art of others for installations that departed from current norms in order to further a political agenda, and viewers literally were positioned differently so they could experience alternatives in their bodies.[14]

The syntax of *Mirroring Evil,* like the Duchamp installation, signaled that *Mirroring Evil* is not a "disinterested" exhibition. By mirroring the theatricality, the narrative impulses, the extensive use of text and pedagogic videos used in Holocaust museums, *Mirroring Evil* called these devices into question, suggesting that the genre has failed as a deterrent to evil, prejudice, and mass murder. By mirroring the pristine, orderly arrangements of exhibitions of contemporary art, *Mirroring Evil* undermined *their* latent, utopic vision of societal transformation. In a time of terror, imploding the exhibition rhetorics of two genres that once promised transcendence reopened a series of questions many would prefer to believe closed: How can a museum offer hope? How can a museum be a moral force? How can a museum contribute effectively to societal change? The lack of definitive answers may be another reason for the anger that *Mirroring Evil* attracted.

Notes

Versions of this essay were presented at *Museums After Modernism: Strategies of Engagement,* Toronto, April 2002; The Association of Jewish Studies, Los Angeles, December 15, 2002 and the Institute for Jewish Studies, Concordia University, Montreal, February 5, 2003.

1   Joan Rosenbaum, Director's Preface, in Norman L. Kleeblatt, ed., *Mirroring Evil: Nazi Imagery/Recent Art* (New Brunswick, NJ: Rutgers University Press, 2001), p. vii.
2   Ron Rosenblum, "Mirroring Evil? No, Mirroring Art Theory," *New York Observer,* April 16, 2002: <http://observer.com/pages/.asp?ID=5590>.
3   Wiesel and Rosensaft quoted in Richard Goldstein, "Managing the Unmanageable," *The Village Voice,* March 6–12, 2002: www.villagevoice.com/issues/0210/goldstein.php>. Stefan Kanfer, "How to Trivilize the Holocaust," *City Journal,* April 3, 2002: <www.city-journal.org/html/eon_4_3_02sk.html>.
4   Quoted in a press release, "YAF Calls for Jewish Museum to Cancel 'Mirroring Evil'," issued by the New York branch of Young Americans for Freedom. See <www.nyyaf.com/mirroringevil.htm>.

5   "Evil, The Nazis and Shock Value," *New York Times*, March 15, 2002, p. 35.

6   The cartoon was republished in *Die Zeit*, Nr. 17, April 18, 2002, p. 34. For Jörg Lau's earlier response to the exhibition in *Die Zeit*, see <www.zeit.de/2002/12/Kultur/200212_lego-kz.html>.

7   Norman Kleeblatt, "Impossible Bedfellows: Adolf Hitler and Marcel Duchamp," in Kleeblatt, ed., *Mirroring Evil*, p. 115. Based on a conversation with Peter Friese and Friederieke Wappler, October 20, 1999 referred to in Kleeblatt's text.

8   "Peering Under the Skin of Monsters," *New York Times*, March 17, 2002, AR, p. 36.

9   "Who's Afraid of the big, bad Adolf?," *Guardian*, March 21, 2002. <www.heretical.com/holofun/shoah7.html>.

10   The Animating Democracy Lab is a component of the Animating Democracy Initiative, a program of the Americans for the Arts, funded by the Ford Foundation. *Without Sanctuary*, 2000, an exhibition of photographs of lynchings of blacks in the United States was also funded by Animating Democracy. With *Too Jewish: Challenging Jewish Identities*, 1996, another controversial exhibition curated by Kleeblatt, both the book and catalogue appeared at the same time.

11   I have borrowed the term from Dora Appel, *Memory Effects: The Holocaust and the Art of Secondary Witnessing* (New Brunswick, NJ: Rutgers University Press, 2002). See her book for a discussion of art made from the position of secondary witnessing.

12   The emergency exit was added just days before the opening in response to survivor critique about the exhibition.

13   The Director of the Jewish Museum, Joan Rosenbaum, insisted on increasing the size of the text panels found throughout the exhibition so that viewers, especially older ones, would not have to strain to read. Norman Kleeblatt in conversation with the author.

14   Group Material created the time line structure for displaying art and Kosuth in *The Play of the Unmentionable*, 1990, expected his viewers to stand back and survey an entire wall, salon style.

6

A Place for Uncertainty: Towards a New Kind of Museum

Vera Frenkel

There is a sense in which all art can be said to represent the unrepresentable, just as it is generally understood, though insufficiently emphasized, that anyone alive, each one of us, is living on borrowed time, by which truism is meant... *what*, exactly? Time borrowed from the voids that precede and succeed our breathing and our struggle? Time as a constant, accelerating present; no looking back – until, *oops*, it's all over? Time as a braided memory path of world events, private choices, and the consolations of art; a path, for purposes of our discussions here today, shadowed and lit by the museums and art galleries where these threads meet and where, in their conjunction, meaning, perhaps, is made?

So here I am, on borrowed time, to think about what cannot be said and to consider how best to show what cannot be depicted. Yet visual artists, composers, writers, and choreographers have managed quite well over the centuries to provide reflections on love and war, birth and every kind of death. A rich range of conventions from the most literal to the most abstract shapes our perceptions of such events. (I remember once spending the better part of a day in the University of Toronto's music library listening only to operatic screams. At the close of Alban Berg's *Lulu* I found the one I needed for my then current production, but the search provided en route a tour of the dreadful things done to women in opera, and a renewed sense of how routinely their screams and the conduct that prompts them are seen as axiomatic, simply as the legitimate stuff of spectacle.)[1]

Despite the frequent assumption that key aspects of human experience cannot be represented, representations abound and are received as variously good and appropriate renderings of what is impossible to render. So why attend in particular to the notion of the unrepresentable?

Painful as they may be, birth, love, and death are generally untraumatic, and we respect the time-honored conventions (and almost equally time-honored transgressions) within art practices which describe a longing to penetrate these mysteries, taking such efforts not only as representations, but at times as even capturing the mystery itself. (While it is true that not everyone wants the statue of the Madonna to cry real tears, there is a substantial constituency of those who do, and indeed from time to time a Madonna-statue obliges, fulfilling a need on someone's part to touch the mystery, whatever it may be, that the tears signify.)

Regarding trauma, however, whether the mass, collective trauma of genocide or the cumulative private trauma of HIV/AIDS, attempts at representation carry a charged ethical and moral freight, and despite many moving attempts to find forms with which to convey the suffering and the dread, there are no equivalent conventions. Attempted modes of representation seem forced or insufficient. Quilt. Song cycle. Film. Poem. Plaque. Monument: survivors' tales named for the dead, meant for the living.

Caught between the anguish of grief, the anesthetization of shock, and the denials of the larger society, art that attempts to address horror confronts the difficulty that building a set of conventions with which to convey trauma may not only be impossible: it may also be obscene in that the result so easily becomes the opposite of what was intended, as happens when grief is fashioned into spectacle. This brings us again to the museum and its options.

As a child of European refugees for whom the formative trauma in their lives was loss in the Holocaust of family, personal history, and hope, I found compelling the thoughtful post-World War II calls to silence of such as Claude Lanzmann, George Steiner, and Elie Wiesel. Yet compelling as they are, these cautions seem not to have hampered the imperative to distill through art what most defines, integrates, or threatens our humanness. Ambivalent attempts to approach the unspeakable persist, as does the vexed issue of what can or should be represented.

When shock and upheaval are so searing that the experience is considered unrepresentable, the uncomprehending soul seems nevertheless to need to revisit the experience, seeking meaning. Doing so in the museum, however, more often than not brings one instead nose-to-nose with formulaic closure. Though a desired state following life's normal betrayals and losses, closure is nevertheless unwelcome and perhaps unachievable when survival itself has been turned toxic by events. How then is it possible, on either the individual or the institutional level, to make or display art about horror, to connect with the next generation in ways that go beyond victim narratives or the placing of blame?

Drawing on a longstanding interest in so-called cargo-cult practices, my work of the last decade or so has centered on a range of irresolvable dilemmas as they inform human longings from messianism to migration (Figure 6.1), from the madness of art-collecting fever to the calcifying amorality of bureaucracy, moving further and deeper into that place where uncertainty resides, and cherishing that uncertainty as a shield against closure, as protection against control and against forgetting. This forfeiting of closure may suggest a state of ongoing bereavement, but I don't think that's the case; more likely, it's a way of engaging with loss in ways

Figure 6.1 Vera Frenkel...*from the Transit Bar*, installation, Toronto. Courtesy of the artist.

that elude packaging. My respect for the uncertain, however, and my insistence that a work remain dilemmatic, rubs up against museum culture in strange ways.

I suspect I owe my sanity to a handful of curators and art historians, most of whom work outside the museum world or on its periphery, who have welcomed this approach and its implications, among them the late Alvin Balkind at the Vancouver Art Gallery; Denys Zacharopoulos, at *documenta* IX, now living and working in Athens; art historian and curator Sigrid Schade, teaching and practicing in Linz (Figure 6.2), Kassel, Bremen, and Zurich; Tom Sandqvist and Ulla Arnell from *Riksutställningar* (Swedish Traveling Exhibitions: see chapter 8); in Canada: the Goethe-Institut's intrepid cultural director Doina Popescu; historian, cultural theorist, independent curator Dot Tuer; and Elizabeth Legge, writing art history with a particular insight into contemporaneity. In their own practices, here or abroad, these colleagues have had a special relation to the unrepresentable and have shaped their working lives in unorthodox

Figure 6.2 Vera Frenkel, "The Apparatus of Marking Absence," photo-mural for Station 4 of *Body Missing* (<www.yorku.ca/BodyMissing>), six-station video-photo-web installation (1994 and ongoing), first realized in the exhibition *Andere Körper*, Offenes Kultuthaus, Linz. Curator: Sigrid Schade. This detail: 48 × 72 inches, Goethe-Institut, Toronto, 2000.

ways to suit. As is evident from the project of Roger Simon, discussed later on, to make a place in the public arena for work arising from what has been called "difficult knowledge" – studies of slavery or the Middle Passage, the HIV/AIDS epidemic, the Holocaust, the fates of indigenous peoples, the Montréal École Polytechnique murders, the travails of the South African Truth and Reconciliation Commission, for example – requires a tenderness and sensitivity on the one hand and a fierce passion and compassion on the other in order to make space and time for this knowledge in the lives of museums and their minders, and, by implication, in the lives of those who look to museums to shape and dignify experience; to be exemplary.

Consideration of how to transfer "difficult knowledge" between generations is nowhere more sensitively addressed, in my view, than in the context of the Testimony and Historical Memory Project at the Ontario Institute for Studies in Education at the University of Toronto. Founded by social scientist Roger Simon on a closely reasoned armature of critical pedagogy, the very existence of this program attests to the ability of Simon and his co-workers to sidestep misdirected power and build a cadre of cultural workers able to deal directly and empathetically, as well as intellectually, with personal and collective histories of unbearable pain. Considering the work of the late educator, curator, and editor Judith Mastai, whose thinking informs the chapters in this book, it remains a profound regret that she and Roger Simon were not able to fulfill their intention to work together. They recognized in each other a mutual interest in controversial questions and a shared impatience with systemic institutional nonsense. With her particular gift for entering and leading others into arenas of the irresolvable, Judith Mastai, like Roger Simon, was utterly committed to a mission to expand both consciousness and audiences, organizing events that drew into the light many instances of difficult or contested or marginalized knowledge, in that way making a place for uncertainty in the museum, and therefore for its corollary: trust.

On hearing my accounts of some of the deceits and compromises with which I was confronted at another institution, the man I was once married to said: "It's clearly a problem of double-disenfranchisement: academics are not respected in this culture, and art historians and artists are undervalued in academia. It's no wonder they're at each others' throats all the time. Having no sense of entitlement makes people crazy." Unsurprisingly, issues of entitlement underlie questions of courage, in turn the essential requirement for a transformative curatorial vision.

In her unpublished text, "Performing the Museum: Education, Negoti-ation, Art Galleries and their Publics," Judith Mastai wrote on just these issues from her position within the museum:

> In 1997 I took a post as Head of Education at the Art Gallery of Ontario and entered a world in which diverse philosophies prevailed about educational practice in a public art gallery. In short, I found myself in an environment in which the educators espoused a practice related to actual and potential visitors but the principles underlying their messages seemed to be framed by formalist principles.... While I had once described my working environ-ment at the Vancouver Art Gallery as a laboratory, I now describe it as a performance in the sense that, every day in many ways, my colleagues and I are engaged in performing a continually emerging institutional subjectivity. Change is not an interlude, but a condition of our work.... [S]etting the stage for the negotiation of transformative possibilities rather than rehears-ing old certainties is the mark of a contemporary museological practice.[2]

Whether or not contemporary museological practice can give voice and shape to the unrepresentable, the attempt requires active and brave cur-atorship and doubtless more negotiation, struggle, debate, writing, broad-casting, and moderating than would be the case with the simple commodification of art, artist, and issue which characterizes so many museum programs. This brings us back to the obliquely related issues of spectacle and entitlement, since avoiding the reductive seductions of the first means having the confidence of the second to navigate through institutional fog and its internal and external resistances.

In light of all that, there are four sources which I would like to introduce here. In alphabetical order by author, these are:

1   "Performing the Museum" (title shared with Judith Mastai's text cited above), in *Performing Pedagogy: Toward an Art of Politics*: an anthology of the writings of the performance artist and critical pedagogue Charles Garoian.[3]
2   "Dweller on the Threshold," by Bill Horrigan, Media Arts Curator at the Wexner Center for the Arts: an eloquent critique of the denial that characterizes our communication media, written in memory of his cherished colleague Gregory Patten.[4]
3   "Problems in Learning from Traumatic Pasts: A Psychoanalytic In-quiry," a paper on learning through and from trauma by cultural theorist and educator Sarah Matthews.[5]

4   Roger Simon's "The Memorial Museum in an Age of Spectacle:
    Re-thinking Practices of Remembering Mass Violence and Social Suf-
    fering," given first as a working paper at a University of Toronto
    Department of Museology Colloquium.[6]

Charles Garoian, Director of the School of Visual Arts at Penn State
University, has instituted a program that takes as its mandate the task of
addressing difficult knowledge through performance. In his own work as
an artist he considers formative the accounts he inhaled at the breakfast
table of the atrocities his parents experienced during the 1915 Armenian
genocide. He writes:

> Historically and theoretically, the political challenge of performance art has
> enabled artists to question the assumptions of traditional art and culture
> with respect to contemporary issues that are often considered "subversive,"
> "controversial," or "difficult"...
>   ...the horrifying images of events born of cultural injustice continue to
> exist and, in doing so, influence the cultural identity issues in my work.
> Through performance art I expose, examine, and critique the oppressive
> assumptions of the body politic that have inscribed my body and shaped my
> identity. In doing so, the politics of culture is at the heart of my perform-
> ance work.[7]

Arguing for "a performative museum pedagogy that repositions viewers as
critical participants and enables their creative and political agency within
museum culture," Garoian continues:

> Performing the museum is a radical pedagogical strategy that critiques the
> exclusivity of the Enlightenment mindset in order to create and open
> discourse between museum culture and viewers....Thus, by performing
> the museum, viewers challenge the museum's monologic practices through
> the discourse of their memories and cultural histories, thereby introducing
> narrative content that would otherwise remain ignored.[8]

So in working towards a museological practice that supports "difficult
knowledge," we begin to see the playing out of Mastai's assertion that change
is not an interlude, but a condition of our work and, as Garoian writes, a way
of introducing "narratives that would otherwise remain ignored."
   In her paper "Learning from Traumatic Pasts," Sarah Matthews brings
a psychoanalytic framework to the issue of how, in education, we engage

narratives of historical trauma. She explores the conditions necessary to tolerate traumatic loss as mourning, rather than repetition. "Something other than the shocking facts are at stake in the making of knowledge from traumatic loss," she writes, and proposes pedagogical conditions that can hold wish and fulfillment in abeyance long enough for thinking to take place.[9] Matthews quotes Deborah Britzman in *Between Hope and Despair*, on bonding the capacity for learning with an appeal to thought that refuses both the facile rationale or the demand to make closure.[10]

Connecting some of the above threads in his paper "The Memorial Museum in an Age of Spectacle," Roger Simon introduces a conceptual framework for thinking through practices of representation of events of genocidal violence and state-initiated social suffering, and considers the relation between the semiotic character of museum practices and the pervasive, discursive forms that regulate the way we attend to contemporary global circulation of stories of mass violence.

He discusses what he calls a new kind of museum, the memorial museum, and names several in different parts of the world. In these he perceives three functions: historicization, memorialization, and social transformation. "The centrality of questions of pedagogy to notions of remembrance is often missed, eviscerating discussions of how and why public memory matters." In a footnote he adds, "It might be argued that all museums, to the extent that they instantiate loss while attempting to enact the presence of that which was lost, serve a memorializing function."[11] He continues: "Remembrance enacts the unsettling of the present. Hope enters through a tearing of continuity. Through the recognition that institutionalized practices, past narratives, are unable to fully provide the terms for remembrance."[12]

Simon and his colleagues in the Testimony and Historical Memory Project share a concern with what they call the "spectacle of presence":

> How then is it that we see the relationship we hold of the body in ruins, the suffering body, the body subjected to state-violence and public crimes, as one of spectacle? . . . The projections and identifications made within spectacle, and the consequent defenses it elicits, both require and enact leaving ourselves intact at a distance, protected from being called into question, or altered through our engagement with stories of others.[13]

The latter, I think, describes much of what museums do and do not do. He continues:

> Before the spectatorial scene, we fall in awe – feeling deeply, but with nothing to say. . . . Assembled in terms of spectacle, we must behave as good museum visitors – leaving unthought the question of how this regulates our obligation to a testamentary legacy that demands a reckoning in the present. . . . Thus the stories of past lives and the violence they have encountered enter the commodity form.[14]

It is sometimes helpful to bring into a discussion instances from a corner of the forest sufficiently different from the matter at hand to provide perspective, while sufficiently similar as to create a kind of recognition. In that regard, what Bill Horrigan has to say allows me to draw a not altogether exaggerated parallel between the issue of representing the unrepresentable in museum culture and the treatment of HIV/AIDS by mainstream television.

In "Dweller on the Threshold," Horrigan writes of Paula Treichler's AIDS narratives on television:[15]

> She has the forbearance to trace in microscopic detail, how and why television relates to a profoundly traumatic social and sexual crisis such as the AIDS pandemic. AIDS didn't make television the way it is; television has always been the way it is. AIDS just came along as one more thing for television to miscomprehend or deny.[16]

Or, as Roger Simon might say, "In the spectacular return of the dead, what is lost is loss itself."[17]

In thinking about this, I am suggesting that in our minds we substitute the museum for television. Horrigan discusses "television's self-loathing submission to western dicta of pictorial perspective. . . . Its exhaustive replication of photographic legibility orthodoxies, its terrified adherence to theatrical and novelistic notions of dramaturgy, its profiteering enchantment with a one-way system of communication."[18] While this eloquent set of criticisms may not apply to your favorite neighborhood museum, there is an echo there, in my view, and an implicit warning. As Horrigan says of television:

> [The museum also] needs to be taken light years beyond its present fallen state, and light years beyond its presently emerging paradigm of interactivity as exercised on television most rivetingly in home shopping expeditions. . . . [I have] never witnessed television as an expressive vehicle for representation of mourning practices except on daytime soap operas which

are exempted from those rules of television . . . as described by Treichler in her essay . . . *because soap operas famously act to actively forestall closure.* No other dramatic form is able to simulate grieving and loss in the wake of a loved one's death with the emotional accuracy it's given on soap operas. Loss produces a situation in which nothing can ever be forgotten.[19]

Not that I, or Horrigan, would recommend soap opera in itself as a paradigm to follow. Rather, it offers an instance of a certain use of time and of the forestalling of closure that may permit in museum programming the transformative transfer of the difficult knowledge of which Roger Simon writes and which characterizes what he sees as a new kind of museum.

Although each of these writers approaches differently the question of the unrepresentable, their understandings converge in a shared perception of the norms that hinder growth and the prices paid for allowing this to happen. Their respective insights suggest the beginnings of another way to acknowledge and work with pain without trivializing or spectacularizing. In the case of HIV/AIDS and of genocides and traumas of all kinds, there is always the question of how much to say, how much to show, before, as was mentioned earlier, falling into the trap of perpetuating the pain, of transmitting the trauma. It seems, however, that in the course of a flow of information accepted as incomplete, relative, and subject to revision, even the unbearable can be understood and absorbed.

In another register, offered here as a descant of sorts, psychiatrist and cultural theorist Jeanne Randolph calls attention in her essay, "Technology and the Preconscious," to the idea that:

> the preconscious is in some way a medium, perhaps in some way censorship, in some way (as Freud also said) binding rather than discharging whatever reaches it from the unconscious. . . . [This] model that I am making of the preconscious, and its effect on desire, implies power relations *regarding what we can represent to ourselves, never mind what we can then carry on to represent to others.*
>
> What aspects of mental functioning have the power to designate what is and what is not unthinkable? Just on what basis is this so-called preconscious lens constructed; according to whose judgement does it have its effects as "a new medium" through which unconscious desiring must pass? . . . [What] I am trying to alert you to is the possibility that this is the site of interaction of the technological ethos with either the embodied self, the body politic, or both.[20]

In discussing her concept of the technological ethos, Randolph writes: "Technology is surely both external and intra-psychic. There is no boundary between the two.... Technology is a process or an ethos rather than a set of objects," and, quoting from an earlier essay, her argument dovetails with our discussion as follows:

> The elimination of ambiguity is exactly what the ideology of technology demands. For without ambiguity, there is no opportunity to contribute multiple and alternative interpretations. The citizenry who cannot contribute subjectively to the interpretations or perceptions of a phenomenon cannot be in a position of responsibility but must either submit to the authority of an object or attempt to dominate the object by exercising their power to explain it.[21]

This suggests that factors in the representation of the unrepresentable include the role of the preconscious as filter as well as the internalization of a technological ethos which eschews ambiguity, in that way controlling what representations we are able to make to ourselves and to others. The new museum as a place where ambiguity is cherished and closure is discouraged will require the scrutinizing and abandonment of a number of ideologies and the power relations they institute. How that is to be achieved deserves our attention.

Tragedy, which inhabits the core of the unrepresentable, shares with the unending, unfolding of soap opera – a vehicle for other kinds of "difficult knowledge" from those being discussed here – a path through an ongoing sequence of moral dilemmas. "Difficult knowledge" cannot be packaged as if it's a display of finite historic events or objects, if historic events or objects are indeed ever finite. It requires art practices and museum structures that allow space and time for difficult knowledge to remain dilemmatic, unresolvable, evoked rather than stated and made present to the imagination through a mix of absence, indirection, and incompleteness that brings the viewer out of passivity, and makes the world, the world of art, scholarship, and social engagement, a place where the difficult is understood to be at home. Regarding whether or how the unrepresentable might be addressed and the unspeakable spoken in a museum context, the issue is how we might support each other in making the museum, as Judith Mastai did, a place for uncertainty.

Notes

1 Notes from a talk given in the session, *Representing the Unrepresentable*, Museums after Modernism Conference, Toronto, April 2002.

2 Judith Mastai, "Performing the Museum: Education, Negotiation, Art Galleries and their Publics." Unpublished and undated text.

3 Charles Garoian, "Performing the Museum," in *Performing Pedagogy: Toward an Art of Politics* (Albany: The State University of New York Press, 1999). Also in *Studies in Art Education* 42/3 (Spring 2001): 235–48.

4 Bill Horrigan, "Dweller on the Threshold," in Michael Renov and Erika Suderburg, eds., *Resolutions: Contemporary Video Practices* (Minneapolis, London: University of Minnesota Press, 1996), pp. 165–72.

5 Sarah Matthews, "Problems in Learning from Traumatic Pasts: A Psychoanalytical Inquiry." Paper delivered at Testimony and Historical Memory Speaker Series, OISE/University of Toronto, January 18, 2001. Later published *in Safundi: Journal of South African and American Comparative Studies* 3/2 (April 2001).

6 Roger I. Simon, "The Memorial Museum in an Age of Spectacle: Re-thinking Practices of Remembering Mass Violence and Social Suffering." Unpublished paper presented at the University of Toronto, Department of Museology Colloquium, March 19, 2002, unpaginated.

7 Garoian, "Performing the Museum," p. 2.

8 Ibid.

9 Matthews, "Problems in Learning from Traumatic Pasts," p. 4.

10 Deborah Britzman, "If the Story Cannot End: Deferred Action, Ambivalence and Difficult Knowledge," in Roger I. Simon, Sharon Rosenberg, and Claudia Eppert, eds., *Between Hope and Despair: Pedagogy and the Remembrance of Historical Trauma* (Lanham, MD: Rowman & Littlefield, 2001), pp. 27–56.

11 Simon, "The Memorial Museum in an Age of Spectacle," p. 5.

12 Ibid.

13 Ibid.

14 Ibid.

15 See Paula A. Treichler, "Seduced and Terrorized: AIDS and Network Television," in Allan Klusacek and Ken Morrison, eds., *A Leap in the Dark* (Montreal, Quebec: Véhicule, 1992).

16 Horrigan, "Dweller on the Threshold," p. 167.

17 Simon, "The Memorial Museum in an Age of Spectacle," p. 5.

18 Horrigan, "Dweller on the Threshold," p. 169.

19 Ibid.; emphasis added.

20 Jeanne Randolph, "Technology and the Preconscious," in Randolph, ed., *The City Within* (Banff: Banff Centre, 1992), pp. 35–46; emphasis added.

21 Jeanne Randolph, "Influencing Machines: The Relation Between Art and Technology," in *Psychoanalysis and Synchronized Swimming* (Toronto: YYZ Books, 1991), p. 51.

7

The Ballad of Kastriot Rexhepi: Notes on Gesture, Medium, and Mediation

Mary Kelly

In memory of Judith Mastai – inspired curator, intellectual, activist and dear friend.

In the program dedication for the symposium, "Museums After Modernism" (2002), Judith Mastai was described, evocatively, as someone "swimming upstream," finding ways to go beyond received ideas. As I read this, another image flashed before me. It was summer 1989. Judith and I were literally swimming, in a secluded lake near Mount Whistler: icy water electrifying our pliant bodies, sunlight diffusing the charge. We were doing the backstroke, laughing and plotting nothing less than total feminist revolution for the Vancouver Art Gallery. The pleasure of that moment, so poignant now in her absence, slips beyond the grasp of my words. In another way, though, my retrospection produces a bifurcation of the image that is tightly bound to the cultural legacy of modernism. As Giorgio Agamben defines this, there are images that obliterate gesture and those that preserve it.[1] One refers to "the recollection seized by voluntary memory"; for instance, the memorializing image of a woman's courage drawn in poetic rhetoric – swimming upstream. The other invokes "the image flashing in the epiphany of involuntary memory." There is no picture, simply arms in motion, icy water, sunlight, laughter – reminiscence infused with the unpredictable fragments of being that animate loss. What distinguishes Agamben's concept of gesture from more conventional linguistic definitions is that in it, nothing is produced or performed; rather, something is supported or endured and this stance without purpose, so to speak, allows the ethical dimension of human experience to unfold. In my view, it also provides a way to consider the question of spectatorship in the museum beyond modernism.

Gesture

Often, I have thought about what this ethical stance would mean in relation to making art, but have come up against the stumbling block of passion. Whatever drives an artist's truth procedure verges on a certain kind of terror, I mean, the passionate fidelity to an idea that is necessary to enact it in some form. Yet, this seems to be precisely what must be relinquished in order to be a veracious observer of art. Passion in this sense might imply a suspension of aims. Nothing is being assumed. I am just looking (trying not to read the wall text), making myself vulnerable or open to "the situation." Unlike a critical engagement with the work, the ethical dimension of museum-going experience resides neither in judgment, nor decipherment, but in anticipation.

The importance of interpretation is not in question; rather, it is a matter of calling attention to something else, more aleatory, that pertains to the exhibition in its phenomenal form. Considered as a complex enunciative field, the exhibition constitutes a group of statements in which fragments of imaged discourse, or individual works, are anchored by signage and codes of display, yet, at the same time, dispersed in the process of their articulation as events. For Foucault, the possibilities of reinscription and transcription that define the statement are generated by an institutional order rather than a spatio-temporal localization.[2] However, the "perishable individualities" that fall outside the institutional frame are exactly what interest me here. Perhaps, a different mode of inscription is facilitated by the non-repeatable materiality of gesture. In relation to the exhibition as lived event, there are instances that suggest this possibility: performances staged as an integral part of the work exhibited, yet, bearing the trace of local contingency; receptions, conferences, guided tours – institutionally sanctioned intrusions, shaped by an uncertain public and, above all, interactions among viewers in the gallery space. In unpredictable ways, a sense of community is forged out of human ephemera – looks, sighs, shuffles, poses, and disposed to the situation, which, as I understand it, is not a constructed play of events, nor a psychological relay, but an intersection between art and life; a point from which the ethical possibility emerges as an inscription prior to the copy, anticipatory and meditative.[3]

With regard to the spectator, what significance can be accorded to this apparently indeterminate effort? A profound one, I think. It is nothing less than the recognition that the audience-as-support *is* the artwork in the process of becoming visible. That is to say, in addition to the work's concrete signifying materiality, its decipherability, there is another process of becoming legible that depends on the viewer's "good will." This gesture is linguistic, not in regard to an underlying structure, but as an existential support. Agamben refers to it as "the communication of communicability." My interest in his thesis has been provoked by the growing realization that any attempt to visualize the traumatic experiences of war-related atrocities would require more intricate forms of displacement than those I have used in earlier projects; a shift not only from iconicity to indexicality and from looking to listening, but also from the art object itself as means to the viewer as witness or *being* a means.[4]

As the critical discourse of trauma unfolded, first as a psychological and historical inquiry, then as a biopolitical and ethical concern, it also informed the visual arguments in my recent work. But, this has evolved in the process of making it, that is, making narrative installations from the residue of thousands of pounds of washing – my own clothes washed over and over again, the lint harvested according to certain rules. Although I can say it has art-historical precedents in the assisted ready-made, in another sense, this conversion of the everyday into an esoteric medium is beyond my explanation. Nevertheless, I would like to consider some of the implications of these "arguments" in relation to *The Ballad of Kastriot Rexhepi* (2001), in a way that will not, I hope, discourage other readings.

Medium

What attracts me to lint, as a medium in the physical sense, is the directness and immediacy of the process (Figure 7.1). The text is formed in intaglio as the lint blows through the filter screen of a domestic dryer.

Figure 7.1   Mary Kelly, *The Ballad of Kastriot Rexhepi* (detail Stanza III), 2001, compressed lint, 49 framed panels 17 × 48 × 2 inches each; overall length: 206 feet. Courtesy of the artist.

Although conditions, such as the temperature of circulating air, the weave of fabrics, the abrasiveness of detergents, and so on, must be controlled to produce a "clean" print every time, nothing is added. The lint is compressed and extracted from the screen in units, approximately 8 × 11 inches, and these are combined to form a continuous narrative in low relief. Technically, however, the rules are generated not only from within the medium, but also from the inquiry, informed by psychoanalysis and carried out according to a method of free association, in which material indexicality has been the privileged means of translating affect into form. In the origination phase of a project, I usually begin with an image from the news media, then close my eyes, so to speak, filter out the figurative elements, and work with the emotional residue of the event.

The Ballad is based on an incident reported in the *Los Angeles Times* on July 31, 1999. The headline reads: "War Orphan Regains Name and Family." For the photo-op, Kastriot Rexhepi appears in close-up, his startled face framed by his mother and father who, obligingly, kiss both cheeks for the camera (Figure 7.2). The photograph illustrates a story in which "patronym" – reclaiming his family name – also implies "patria" – claiming

child
S

image
a

a'

AMI VITALE / For The Times
Afrim Rexhepi, wife Bukurie and Kastriot, the son they thought had died.

A

ideal

Name of the Father

Figure 7.2   Untitled photograph from the *Los Angeles Times*, July 31, 1999 with notes by Mary Kelly. Artist's archive.

his survival as a symbol of Kosovo's national independence. Before the discovery of his "true" identity, for example, Kastriot is known among the refugees as Lirim, or "freedom." From a psychoanalytic point of view, the recurring theme of survival, as a missed encounter with death, defines the psychic structure of trauma and the way it is frequently expressed as a desire to make good the loss, to fill the gap temporarily, through denial or repetition.

Looking at the story more closely, the circumstances of his recovery reveal a coincidence that overdetermines the unconscious impact of the "accident." Kastriot, mistakenly left for dead when his family flees from the village of Kolic during "the expulsions," is only 18 months old. During the five months that follow, he is found and named by Serbs, abandoned again, then rescued and renamed by Albanians, before being reunited with his parents. This occurs, literally, at the moment he is learning to speak, and figuratively, at the point of entry into the order of language when he is assuming an identity in which sexual difference and ethnicity converge and resonate with sociopolitical as well as psychic conflict. When the reunion with his Kosovar Albanian parents takes place, Kastriot is 22 months old. At this age, linguists claim that a child shows the propensity to speak grammatically by combining words that form an elementary syntax. Symbolically, he is projecting an image of himself as "I" and, at the same time, internalizing the parental imago that, in turn, prompts the formation of an ego ideal. Significantly, the first word Kastriot utters, according to the reporter, is "Bab," Albanian for Dad.

Kastriot's legendary journey has the structure of myth; that is, it can be told many ways without altering the underlying themes, and I have tried to reflect this in writing *The Ballad*. Of course, there is a long tradition of Kosovo battle balladry, including contemporary versions by popular song-writers, but heroism, martyrdom, and retribution are *not* valorized in my account – just the opposite. In fact, it could be called an anti-ballad. What I take from the literary form is the structure of four stanzas, but the number of lines in each does not adhere to the convention (three eight-line stanzas, a four-line envoy) and a refrain is only suggested in the repetition of "downy crop, coral mien." The first stanza gives the historical precedents for the violence; the second tells the mother's story, her personal tragedy; the third describes the politics of Kastriot's recovery; the fourth parodies the media spin. My subjective investment is evident in the second stanza.

Like most mothers, I have experienced the temporary loss of a child, a close call, resolved when he is found again, alive and well. It is profoundly moving, even traumatic, but there is something more ambiguous with respect to surviving the encounter, when the child is irrecoverable, the loss final and therefore infinite. For a woman, especially, since the narcissistic relation to her love object is so deeply cathected, it mimes her own death and, in this sense, she does not survive, simply remains. An excerpt:

> Minutes pass, perhaps more, Bukurie is not sure,
> Not sure when his breathing stops,
> How to start it – shaking, calling, caressing him –
> Nothing;
> Pleading,
> Still nothing.
> She lays his body on the disbelieving ground;
> Does not scream, does not look back, but vows,
> "Always, always, always, I will think of him."
> His downy crop, his coral mien,
> Oblivious.

In the installation, the text is presented as a continuous line and read as metered prose rather than verse. But is this still relevant to the discussion of medium? Yes, I would say, in the technical sense, because narrative is generated by the limits of an aniconic practice, or put another way, by the possibilities of an invocatory image. For me, words are also things. Transposed into compressed lint, they are specific objects that invoke the voice.

Mediation

From the beginning, I wanted *The Ballad* to be sung. When Michael Nyman and I discussed the possibility of working together on this project, I had in mind his adaptation of Paul Celan's poetry – *Six Celan Songs for Low Female Voice*, in the collection called *Songbook* and his scores for Peter Greenaway's films, in particular, *Prospero's Books* which features Sarah Leonard, the soprano who, eventually, performed *The Ballad* at the premiere and subsequent venues.[5] With reference to reception, the self-directed observation of the gallery space seemed more appropriate than the focused attention of the concert hall. Disregarding both the spectacle of musical theater and the improvisational mode of performance art, the objective of my collaboration with Nyman on *The Ballad* was similar to that of a filmmaker: to produce a score for an exhibition. Although I provided compositional notes for the text, Nyman's reading diverged provocatively from my own as a method of interpretation. The addition of a musical score involved mediation in conventional terms. It had to be performed. But in this instance, the performance also mediated the installation's material representation of duration by allowing it to pass into real time. In this respect, *The Ballad* also resolved some of the formal concerns that I had referred to in previous work as the *narrativization* of space.

In *Mea Culpa* (1999), I had placed more emphasis on the phenomenological aspects of reading in the context of an exhibition – movement, surface, and peripheral vision. By using the lint units to compose a linear narrative, I found that a rhythm of viewing as well as an illusion of fading, similar to anamorphosis, could be established. Following from this, I thought it would be possible to make something comparable to a 360-degree pan in film. As an installation, *The Ballad* is more than 200 feet; 49 panels divided into 4 stanzas which wrap around the gallery in a continuous band at eye level. The composition of the lint panels is based

Figure 7.3 Mary Kelly, *The Ballad of Kastriot Rexhepi*, 2001, compressed lint, 49 framed panels 17 × 48 × 2 inches each; overall length: 206 feet. Installation view, Santa Monica Museum of Art, California. Artist's archive.

on the a-b-a structure of a transverse sound wave, with the text running through the middle as a rest line (Figures 7.3 and 7.4). When the viewer walks around the gallery, either reading sequentially or simply taking it in at glance, space functions as a temporal metaphor. By that, I mean that there is the simultaneous time of the narrative, cast in lint, immobilized, and the time of reading, animated in the present; but there is also a probable reversal – physical movement as internal reality, static image as time-based process.

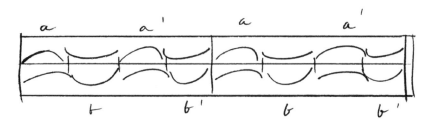

Figure 7.4 Study for *The Ballad*. Artist's archive.

During the performance, if the viewer follows from stanza to stanza, the lint-form-as-sound-wave takes on a different meaning, perhaps a different appearance, one that belongs to the singularity of the situation. *The Ballad* is performed in the round, audience enclosing the musicians in an intimate circle, "libretto" surrounding them, in turn, as the outermost boundary of the installation (Figure 7.5). The visual medium is residual; the instruments, acoustic; the voice, elusive. When Leonard sings, she resembles a boy treble; the sound is elegiac and contrasts with the intensity of the string quartet. Similarly, when the vernacular account of Kastriot's plight is filtered through the conventions of a "high art" form, a distance from the memorialized event is acknowledged.

After the performance, the musical trace remains in the visual suggestion of measures and phrases, and in memory where it is replayed in the peculiar tempo of unconscious desire. (For instance, my reverie of the opening night is infused with the sentiments of 1968.) But is there something else, neither distanciation nor subjectivism, that constitutes the audience-as-support? Perhaps, in the registration of a dissonance

Figure 7.5   Mary Kelly, *The Ballad of Kastriot Rexhepi*, 2001, compressed lint, 49 framed panels 17 × 48 × 2 inches each; overall length: 206 feet. Opening performance with soprano Sarah Leonard and the Nyman Quartet, Santa Monica Museum of Art, California. Artist's archive.

between the performance as a constructed event and the ephemeral incident as conduit of communal sensation, the disinterested and medial space of gesture emerges. To work at the liminal point of vision can conjure the voice and to force the materiality of an image through repetition can mark experiential time, but the spectatorial gesture is impossible to predict. Neither artist nor curator can devise it. But this is no reason to retreat. If, as Jacques Rancière has claimed, a moment of disidentification or declassification precedes the espousal of the cause of the other, then it would suggest that the viewer's perception of disparity, rather than the experience of a shared community, permits the formation of collective aspirations.[6] Some situations, it could be argued, are more susceptible to this than others.

Notes

1 Giorgio Agamben, "Means without End: Notes on Politics," trans. Vincenzo Binetti and Cesare Casarino, in *Theory Out of Bounds*, vol. 20 (Minneapolis and London: University of Minnesota Press, 2000), pp. 48–59.
2 Michel Foucault, *The Archeology of Knowledge*, trans. A. M. Sheridan Smith (London: Tavistock Publications, 1972), pp. 106–17.
3 See also Maurice Berger, ed., *Museums of Tomorrow: An Internet Discussion* (New York: Issues in Cultural Theory 8, 2004), pp. 172–3.
4 See Griselda Pollock, "Mary Kelly's *Ballad of Kastriot Rexhepi*: Virtual Trauma and Indexical Witness in the Age of Mediatic Spectacle," *parallax* 10/1 (2004): 100–12.
5 See *Mary Kelly: The Ballad of Kastriot Rexhepi with an original score by Michael Nyman*, exhibition catalogue including a conversation with Elsa Longhauser and essay by Maurice Berger (Santa Monica, CA: Santa Monica Museum of Art, 2001). See also *Mary Kelly: La Balada de Kastriot Rexhepi, Musica original de Michael Nyman*, exhibition catalogue including an interview by Trisha Ziff and essay by Jorge Reynoso (Mexico: Museo Universitario de Ciencias y Arte, Ciudad Universitaria, 2004).
6 Jacques Rancière, "The Cause of the Other," trans. David Macey, *parallax* 7 (1998): 25–34.

8

Riksutställningar: Swedish Traveling Exhibitions

Ulla Arnell

A Temporary Experimental Study on Traveling Exhibitions

During the 1960s there was in Sweden, as in other countries, lively debate about culture. Books and articles were published dealing with how to promote a democratic and just cultural policy. Sociological studies showed that visitors to museums and exhibitions were a pretty homogeneous group. Major consumers of culture were mostly young, well-educated people from the major cities, which was where the big national museums were situated. In 1965, the Swedish government accordingly set up a commission to look into how objects from central museum collections could be shown safely and in an educative manner beyond the limits of Stockholm. What was unusual about the brief given to the commission was that it included practical work in producing traveling exhibitions as well as a theoretical study. It was this initiative which gave rise to what is now *Riksutställningar* which started as a temporary experiment commissioned by the Swedish government. The key concept was that of geographical and social justice. The idea was that cultural justice could be achieved in a distributive fashion from the center to the periphery.

A Century of Sweden's Museum of National Antiquities – The First Exhibition

One image that illustrates well the ideas that lay behind Riksutställningar is that of the very first exhibition, entitled *A Century of the National Museum*, that is of the Museum of National Antiquities. This exhibition was organized as a celebration of the centenary of the national art collections. It contained a succession of masterpieces by famous artists. During the previous summer, visitors to the museum had been asked which works of art they liked best. These were now gathered into an exhibition that became a sort of hit list, with works by Rembrandt, Gauguin, Degas, Toulouse-Lautrec, and Picasso, as well as eighteenth-century tapestries and ancient Chinese sculpture. The exhibition was shown in more than 20 venues – galleries, museums, schools, and tourist centers throughout the country from north to south – and received massive publicity. Newspapers wrote about the hugely valuable treasures and how they were protected at night by armed guards with fierce dogs. A news photograph shows the director of Riksutställningar kneeling in front of Rembrandt's painting of *Simeon and the Infant Jesus* together with the only woman member of the museum's governing board and the men in charge of packing the exhibition watched over by policemen (Figure 8.1).

I had just finished my degree in sociology and art history and was engaged to travel with the exhibition to find out from visitors who they were, where they came from, and how they responded to the exhibition. These were important questions for the commission with regard to the practical experiment.[1]

What Do You Think of the Exhibition? Exhibition? What Exhibition?

In the course of the next ten years the operation grew and a succession of exhibitions was organized with the intention of trying to reach a new public which was not familiar with museums. We experimented with the form of the exhibition as well as the contents. We collaborated with museums, libraries, schools, and the extramural adult educational organizations that are a feature of Swedish life. We tried to find new venues

Figure 8.1   *A Century of Sweden's Museum of National Antiquities.* Photo: Olof Wallgren.

for exhibitions, even outdoors in public parks. Sociological studies showed that a stream of visitors cannot be guaranteed just by holding an exhibition at a place that is much frequented, such as a shopping center. New visitors could be attracted to some extent by an interesting subject, but the challenge lay in getting them to come back again.

Great importance was attached to conditions for different forms of activity during exhibitions which were to be pedagogical instruments while stimulating mutual exchange. One main focus was the function of the exhibition as a medium of communication, the museum or the exhibition venue becoming an environment for communication. Traveling exhibitions were not something new to the world of museums. What was new lay, rather, in the growing insight that there was a need for a specialized institution that could develop the concept of traveling exhibitions that was not bogged down in its own collections. It was seen as important for the institution to build up its own production resources in order to meet the special needs of traveling exhibitions: durability, flexibility, and mobility.

There were people in the museum world who were not entirely happy about Riksutställningar; some senior staff were very suspicious of us, precisely because we were not a "real" museum, had no collections, no conservation staff, and no scholarly expertise. There was also jealousy about the exhibition studio that we built up in these early years. We were frequently told just how many exhibitions could have been mounted with the money that went to us. What many people did not understand was that Riksutställningar was, in point of fact, a joint resource for the entire museum sector and that we also provided assistance and consultancies of which other museums could make use.

Beautiful Moments: A Most Provocative Art Exhibition

The exhibition that certainly aroused the most interest during the experimental years was a manifestation called *Beautiful Moments*, which was produced during the politically turbulent year of 1968 (Figure 8.2).[2] The idea for the exhibition came from an artist who was passionately involved in the problems of the Third World. He wanted to shed light on the relations between the industrial and the underdeveloped countries. The main aim of the exhibition was to stimulate debate. Riksutställningar

Figure 8.2 *Beautiful Moments.* Photo: Olof Wallgren.

supported the theme of the exhibition but also stressed the importance of finding out about the possibilities of creating opinion through art. A group of nine artists, several of whom were central figures in Swedish art in the 1960s, produced the exhibition within the framework of the original concept.

The exhibition was designed as a fairground, with colored lights between the sideshows and taped noise from a real fair. The catalogue looked like an evening newspaper. It was highly critical of Sweden's policy towards the Third World as well as raising questions for politicians concerning trade unions, Swedish democracy, business, world trade, global starvation, the US bombing of Vietnam, the Swedish armed forces, and so on. The exhibition received considerable publicity in the media; probably no other exhibition has been written about to such an extent. People questioned whether museums were really the right place for a political exhibition, which they considered would be more appropriate in the sort of premises used for political meetings. There were articles about the exhibition almost daily in the national press. Most of the debate dealt not with the art but with the message that it conveyed. Was it right for a government-funded operation to use its grant for what was termed "violently extreme communist propaganda"? The exhibition was attacked on the grounds of one-sidedness and an excessively subjective perspective. The debate even reached Parliament. The Minister of Education, who at the time was Olof Palme, defended the exhibition. His view was that it was unavoidable and, indeed, desirable that political values found expression in different forms of art and that, merely because the operation was financed from the public purse, this did not mean that the government supported the ideas that were being represented. The Director of Riksutställningar gave his opinion that exhibitions were becoming a medium, an opportunity for debate, and a forum for gatherings; it was important that the institution should provide opportunities for presenting different opinions.

A Permanent Institution

A decision in Parliament in 1976 turned Riksutställningar into a permanent institution. By then, the institution had established itself and had gained a great deal of publicity for several other controversial exhibitions as well as for its method of working. This consisted of engaging artists in producing exhibitions, whether these were cultural or scientific. This was not common at that time; it stimulated people in the museums to emulate the practice in their own exhibitions. Becoming a permanent institution did not change things very much but was, rather, confirmation of the fact that Riksutställningar was now a vital institution in Swedish cultural policy.

The Museum Commission 1993–1996

In 1993, a Commission was set up to consider the aims and structure of the nationally owned or government financed museums of Sweden. The background to the Commission was the decline in the public finances during the 1990s, which caused reductions in the funds available to the cultural sector. The museums were fiercely criticized as being too inward-looking. Exhibitions, it was argued, were not sufficiently interdisciplinary and were seen by too few people. The Commission's brief also included consideration of the role of Riksutställningar in society. As regards operations, the Commission's proposals maintained that the need for centrally produced exhibitions was not as great as it had once been. There had been a great expansion of the county museums in Sweden over the last 20 years; many museums had sprung up. This meant there were now far more producers of exhibitions. It was proposed that a large part of Riksutställningar's production grant should be distributed among these other producers and that Riksutställningar should offer to organize exhibitions produced by other institutions.

This was the most serious threat the organization had hitherto encountered. We protested forcefully against the proposal, claiming that it is precisely in the practical work of producing exhibitions that expertise in the field can best be conveyed to others. We managed to produce a convincing argument for not only retaining our studio resources but for increasing them with further investment in new technology in order to live up to the expectations that people actually had of our projects. In our counterproposal, we suggested that our resources should be gathered together and used for productions that no other institution could undertake. We also proposed developing and strengthening our work with Swedish and international contemporary art. It was thus that Riksutställningar had the pleasure of inviting Vera Frenkel to make a tour around Sweden, and then to Norway and Poland, with her multimedia installations on

Figure 8.3   ... *from the Transit Bar.* Photo: Olof Wallgren.

migration:... *from the Transit Bar* (Figure 8.3; see also Figure 6.1 above) and on cultural looting, *Body Missing.*[3]

Riksutställningar: Today a Government Department

In 2000, Riksutställningar became a government department financially depending on an annual grant from the Ministry of Cultural Affairs of almost 40 million Swedish krona. The institution earns a further 10 million krona from joint ventures and from exhibition rentals. After salaries and fixed costs, some 44 percent of the grant is free for disposal. Riksutställningar is accountable to the Ministry, which also lays down certain guidelines. These require the institution to contribute to the preservation of cultural heritage by developing and disseminating knowledge and experiences and, in this way, affording people a perspective on the development of their society. The fundamental mandate is that of contributing to the protection of free speech, of promoting cultural diversity, cultural exchange with other countries, and meetings between different cultures in the home country. At the same time, Riksutställningar has great freedom to interpret the way in which this brief is carried out.

It is to produce traveling exhibitions and to distribute both its own productions and productions from elsewhere in a number of different fields. It is also to contribute experience and expertise pertaining to the science of exhibitions and to work with the artistic, educational, and technological development of the exhibition medium.

Every year Riksutställningar receives between 100 and 150 proposals for new exhibitions, approximately 10 of which are realized. Exhibitions are produced in our own workshops. Riksutställningar also has resources for producing photographs, films, and audio-visual productions. The production group almost always includes artists and designers as well as various consultants and specialists on a freelance basis. Technicians are involved at an early stage in order to find suitable technical solutions for the particular exhibition and to fulfill the demands for environment-friendly but durable materials that will withstand transportation and the wear and tear involved in repeated packing and unpacking. Large exhibitions are installed by a team of Riksutställningar technicians working together with the local organizer. Exhibitions are normally transported in the institution's own vehicles to the local organizations, which are mainly museums and public galleries. Venues can, however, include libraries, schools, and adult education organizations. The tour coordinator is responsible for the tour as such, which often involves producing an educational program for the exhibition.

The director of the Exhibition Department, who is also the artistic director, makes the final decision about what exhibitions to produce. Fundamental criteria are that exhibitions should shed light on and problematize actual phenomena in society as well as cultural identity. We aim to strengthen our role in contemporary art both as a producer of exhibitions and a builder of networks. We tour with exhibitions throughout the country and reach a broad public, with the emphasis on children and school-aged youngsters, especially in places with a very limited cultural infrastructure. Riksutställningar also continues to develop the exhibition medium by boundary-crossing collaboration, experimental forms of exhibitions, concern for the environment, and the use of IT.

The Expotek is a department within Riksutställningar which offers information and expertise on the exhibition medium based on experience of producing exhibitions as well as the extensive archives which can be accessed on the institution's website.[4] The Expotek hosts visits, organizes specialized seminars, produces informative brochures, and provides expert advice to both professionals and the general public.

The Exhibition Train, 1987–2000

One project in Riksutställningar's history that generated a very great deal of interest and that fitted in very well with the policy aims was the exhibition train (Figure 8.4). In the mid-1980s Riksutställningar's then director, Bengt Skoog, returned from a trip to Australia, where he had seen an exhibition train, and he launched the idea of a Swedish train very persuasively and with vast enthusiasm. By 1987, there was an exhibition train with four coaches: three for the exhibition and one for the staff. The first exhibition to be made for the train, entitled *The Landscape in a New Light*, was produced by Lars Nittve, who was then a curator at Moderna Museet in Stockholm. The next exhibition, *Good Heavens – Such Beauty*, sought to promote discussion of beauty. *Good Heavens* consisted of more than 100 objects loaned from some 20 museums around the country. An unusual and much debated feature of the exhibition was the fact that there were no texts accompanying the objects. My task was to fit out the so-called media coach with a library: a collection of illustrated catalogue covers, pictures, and posters so that visitors could learn more about the

Figure 8.4   The exhibition train. Photo: Olof Wallgren.

objects in the exhibition. Yet a further dimension feature was our plan to expand the role of the museum guide by working together with mime artists, dancers, and actors.

The train toured all over the country from north to south, summer and winter alike. It stopped for about a week at stations in many small and distant places that often had no other exhibition premises. "How amazing that you take the trouble to come to us!" was a frequently heard comment. It soon became evident that we had succeeded in meeting a public that was not used to exhibitions. It was equally obvious that we were working with new categories of venues. For each place we visited, there were several months of preparation to do with activating and preparing local schools and societies. In order for the exhibition *The Dream Train* to visit a place, the local authority had to guarantee to arrange a youth-culture week in the town. *The Dream Train* was only open to youngsters in the eighth grade. *Track down the City* was, sadly, the last train exhibition (Figure 8.5).

The exhibition train was made possible with support from Sweden's government-owned Railway Corporation, which made the train available, serviced it, and provided the necessary drivers and maintenance staff.

Figure 8.5   *Track down the City.* Train interior. Photo: Olof Wallgren.

Riksutställningar was responsible for the contents and for running the exhibitions. In fact, the train acted as a complete museum with an exhibition and staff, a media coach, and a small museum shop. Details differed depending on the exhibition being shown. From 1987 to 2000, six exhibitions were produced, two of them aimed specifically at children and young people, and more than 350 places were visited.

From the point of view of Riksutställningar, the exhibition train demanded very large resources. As the exhibitions became more complex, they required a longer period of planning and production, as well as the dedicated time of a significant number of staff and related technology. Building the exhibitions was an exciting challenge. Since we controlled the space ourselves and were building fixed installations, we could try out advanced techniques and stretch the limits. Ambitions increased with each production, as did experiments with new materials and solutions, which simultaneously meant greater uncertainty and vulnerability. In the last exhibition, for example, concrete was used and this necessitated exchanging one of the coaches for another that could support the greater weight.

Real commitment was required to keep the tour going. Special staff had to be engaged and trained at Riksutställningar to learn about the operations and act on our behalf. There were many problems to be solved, from determining the working hours of the guides to finding financial support for the running costs of each exhibition. Finally, the whole enterprise became too demanding and when the Railtrack Authority pulled up old rails that were no longer in use, we lost many possible stopping places and, at the same time, the possibility to visit many smaller localities.

Difficult Matters in the Exhibition Trailer, 1999–2000

Difficult Matters: Objects and Narratives that Disturb and Affect was cited as the reason for awarding Riksutställningar the title of Museum of the Year 2001. *Difficult Matters*, a mobile exhibition, but also a field station, was installed in Riksutställningar's trailer (Figure 8.6). A number of museums were invited to participate by choosing objects from their collections. The objects were to be of a controversial or explosive nature. In the end 54 objects were picked up along the route and placed in showcases together with their narratives. The general public was also invited to submit items.

Figure 8.6   *Difficult Matters.* Exhibition trailer. Photo: Olof Wallgren.

Two field ethnologists registered and photographed the objects, which were then placed in the exhibition. In this way, the exhibition became a process in which visitors were very much co-creators. Almost 300 objects were registered. Contemporary catastrophes, like the sinking of the ferry *Estonia* and the terrible fire at a discotheque in Gothenburg, when many young people lost their lives in the autumn of 1998, were included in the material (Figure 8.7). At the end of the tour, the objects were placed in the archives of Nordiska Museet.

The project involved collaboration with Samdok, the Swedish museums' network for researching contemporary society. The background to the project was a discussion of the museums' collecting policies and what it is that museums collect and keep for posterity. Have museums become monuments to success and progress, successful and well organized? What has happened to the objects that are associated with disappointments, with sorrow and distress, with intolerance and vulnerability?

The discussion continued because the exhibition was, at the same time, a case study that formed the basis for the conference *Museum 2000 – Confirmation or Challenge*, arranged jointly by the Swedish branch of ICOM, Riksutställningar, and the Swedish Museum Association. In the

Figure 8.7 *Difficult Matters.* Trailer interior. Photo: Olof Wallgren.

Congress publication, Barbara Kirschenblatt-Gimblet writes: "*Difficult Matters* is not only *in* the medium of the exhibition and *in* the medium of the museum. It is also *about* the medium of the exhibition, it is also *about* the museum. It is at once museological and metamuseological. That is to say it reflects on the museum."[5]

Developing New Mobile Exhibitions Spaces

The Museum of the Year title awarded in 2001 by the Swedish Museum Association came as a surprise. It served, however, as confirmation of the fact that, after almost 40 years of operations, Riksutställningar, now accepted in the museum sector, was seen as an important cultural institution. The institution's most important mandate continues to be that of showing exhibitions in non-traditional venues, thereby reaching out to a new and larger public. One strategy is to develop ideas of new mobile exhibition spaces for all possible and impossible spaces or in public spaces as arenas for many acitivites.

In 2001 a new mobile space – the exhibition towers – was conceived. Three of these exhibitions towers have been constructed for outdoor use in public places. They can be positioned anywhere that can be accessed by a lorry with a lifting arm or a forklift truck and where electricity is available.

Figure 8.8   Summit meeting, Gävle, April 2003. Photo: Olof Wallgren.

The towers are burglar-proof, climate-controlled, and fully equipped. The first exhibition in the towers dealt with the questions of democracy and power, taking as its starting point the events which accompanied the EU Summit meeting in Gothenburg in June 2001 (Figure 8.8). People passing the exhibition could respond day and night by sending text messages; or they could drop commentaries in the letterbox in one of the towers. The exhibition showed symbol-laden objects linked to events. Each object was accompanied by a personal narrative. With the help of local organizers, an arena was created for debate as well as activities such as films and cultural events.

At the time of writing, a new expandable trailer has been under consideration, offering an exhibition space of 100 square meters (Figures 8.9 and 8.10). This has presented many technical and aesthetic challenges. Ideas for the first exhibition in this magical vehicle have been numerous. The aim was to create a project for children with a focus on children's own stories.

It is still relevant and important to ask whether, at this moment, Riksutställningar would still be able to produce an exhibition that was as controversial as *Beautiful Moments*. Such a powerful, political exhibition was so much in the spirit of the day while Riksutställningar was still just a young and experimental institution. There is an enormous difference now that Riksutställningar is an established institution. Yet any institution

Figure 8.9 The expandable trailer. Model. Photo: Olof Wallgren.

must remain open to contemporary questions, to maintain creativity, and to have the courage and flexibility to engage with and participate in processes, discussions, and interactions, while avoiding the fate of becoming rigid in undesirable fixity.

Figure 8.10 Interior and plan. Expandable trailer. Photo: Love Arbén.

Notes

1 Ulla Arnell, Inger Hammer, and Göran Nylöf, *Going to Exhibitions* (Stockholm: Riksutställningar, 1976).
2 Ulla Keding Olofsson, "Beautiful Moments: An Art Exhibition With a Shock Effect," *Museum* 1 (Unesco, 1970/71).
3 Vera Frenkel, ... *from the Transit Bar, Body Missing* (Stockholm: Riksutställningar, 1977): <www.yorku.ca/BodyMissing>.
4 <www.riksutstallningar.se>.
5 Barbara Kirschenblatt-Gimblett, "The Museum as Catalyst," in Per-Uno Ågren, ed., *Museum 2000: Confirmation or Challenge?* (Stockholm: Riksutställningar, 2002).

9

Reframing Participation in the Museum: A Syncopated Discussion

Janna Graham and Shadya Yasin

From the late 1990s, the Director of Public Programming at the Art Gallery of Ontario (AGO), Judith Mastai, with colleagues in the Education Department she headed, developed strategies of engagement that marked a decisive move away from current understandings of the audience as other, seeking instead collaborative community experimentation and participation. In this text, we offer a framing discussion and, integrating poetic texts and reflections from participants in some of the projects realized under Judith's initiative, a dialogue about the ways in which these strategies became practices, unfolding to suggest what the public and civic role of this museum might be.

Performing Away the Insider/Outsider Divide

In 1999, the Art Gallery of Ontario wanted to start a youth program. Crafted by then Head of Education, Judith Mastai, this program, *Teens Behind the Scenes*, sought to move beyond the youth docent or young curator model of programming for teens (in which young people are trained into the profession by museum staff and curators, often for credit, or money) and into a more open programmatic, community, and critically based project. *Teens Behind the Scenes* invited young people to make and implement programming decisions at the Gallery and to develop exhibitions, interpretive strategies, and actions that related to the way in which they saw the museum and its functions. I, Janna Graham, was the program's first coordinator; Shadya Yasin was a member of the first group of youth who entered the program.

Where some models of arts education and museum practice at the time seemed to center on the museum (I remember diagrams of concentric circles around an inner circle called "museum" inserted into a departmental planning session), offering its histories, knowledge, and authority up as gems, as services to a large public (usually for a fee), a group led by Judith Mastai in the Education and Curatorial Departments looked at other ways communities might be engaged to take ownership of the museum, to read and to write upon its history and its future.

Much like the AGO's educational founder, Group of Seven member Arthur Lismer, we saw the museum as a space of use, of participation, and as part of a much broader and more complicated configuration of subjectivities operating within the civic sphere.

Judith Mastai once told me that she was always acting. Although it is true that late at night before a deadline or after a large public event, one might have found her performing show tune routines outside her office, this is not what she meant. Her theater located itself at the juncture of the perceived insider/outsider framing of the museum's relationship with the public. As a critical agent within the museum, Judith Mastai saw this institutionalized and ideological barrier as a construction that secured power, dedicating much of her time to disrupting and disabling this dichotomizing and often fiercely protected division. Mastai argued that staging performances that pulled at this division of and within the museum had deep social and political consequences. She believed that the relationships formed in the space of the gallery had the potential to mirror, or even to connect with, change occurring in the world outside its walls. She often quoted the German Frankfurt School philosopher Jürgen Habermas: "The paradigm of the knowledge of objects has to be replaced by the paradigm of mutual understanding between subjects capable of speech and action." This was an agenda that went well beyond bringing audiences into the museum, or simply making the museum accessible. It was a belief that the museum might, as Habermas continued, "make possible a different relationship of the subject to itself than the kind of objectifying attitude that an observer assumes toward entities of the external world."[1]

Rather than enforcing the line that separates those who provide, those who receive, and those who create from those who learn, and seeking not to confirm traditional hierarchies about the relationship between the private connoisseur and public agent of the museum, the lines of interaction which interested us were more akin to those described by urban theorists in the 1930s as "desire lines."[2] Desire lines, or, as we referred to them, "lines of desire," are the routes that people insert into the landscape that amend, oppose, and reconfigure paths designed by planners, bureaucrats, and other city officials. They are the shortcuts, the marks made in the dirt across a corner, the ways in which people insert themselves and their movements into the highly regulated zones of urban life. "Desire lines" produce what Henri Lefebvre called "representational space," the lived space of inhabitants and users.[3] In the museum, these are seen in the ways in which people, when enabled, by accident or subversion, use spaces, collections, exhibitions, and processes idiosyncratically, politically, and creatively to activate the museum's public role.

Building on the work of other educators at the AGO and elsewhere, Mastai institutionalized these ideas in her many "special projects." These were initiatives that developed collaborative practices and relationships, engaging groups and individuals in participatory, self-determined initiatives in the museum. As practices, "special projects" were strategic, political, intellectual, and, for her, sometimes lonely. For those of us who watched, collaborated, and are left to carry this work forward, she modeled a self-reflection and performativity that attempted to connect theoretical concerns, artistic practice, political work, and social reflection in the museum, a place understood as, on the one hand, deeply inscribed with division, hierarchy, elitism, objectification, and problematic relationships with its "others" (whether determined by historical circumstance or pressures resulting from current forces of privatization), and, on the other, still full of potential for overcoming these forces and realizing its full public meanings.

Between You and Me

In one of her first "special projects," Judith Mastai commissioned writers in exile living in Canada and associated with PEN Canada to create works in response to the AGO.[4] Each was given a year's family pass and free rein to explore the museum's public spaces and "behind-the-scenes" functions.

The writers' texts appeared in a booklet called *Making Meaning*, which was available to all visitors to the AGO. One of the participating writers, Martha Kumsa, an Oromo born and raised in Ethiopia from which she fled to refuge in Canada, wrote "The Space In-Between," about her encounter with a sculptured bust in the Gallery's Canadian Collections entitled *Head of a Negress*, by Elizabeth Wyn Wood:

> This rigid curve between you and me
> is just a contingent turn of a spiral
> just a spot in the expanse of continuity
> But lo and behold!
> It wears an illusive face of a border
> It takes the name of divide and conquer
> Am I the object and you the image?
> Am I the real and you the fake?
> Am I the original creature and you the copy?
>
> This border slaps me in the face with shame
> My hope melts into despair
> The hate of you consumes me
> and my head turns away with a jolt
>
> I glimpse around. To gaze at eyes gazing at you.
> To see your reflection in the lights of their eyes.
> Yes I see eyes see you. And drift away
> the moment they see you
> Oh yes, I see eyes see me through you
> and I shrink away from you lest they see me see you...[5]

Provoked by Wyn Wood's sculpture and the interplay of gazes around and beyond the work of art, Martha Kumsa, describes the complexity and unforeseen experiences of looking in the museum, which may generate responses not anticipated by those who plan its spaces. She suggests that conceiving of museum spaces as locations in which "visitors" are imagined to be merely visual consumers of narrative, chronology, and interpretation, rather than as agents of a public and civic process, is both dangerous and distrustful. Understanding the complex acts of looking and of being together that occur, however, might provide the opportunity for people, as Hannah Arendt suggests, to "create that public space between themselves where freedom could appear."[6] In Mastai's conception of the museum, insiders play outsiders, and outsiders play insiders, to the point where the line between the two, she hoped, would begin to disappear, opening up a much larger text of social interaction in which the museum is read from a variety of perspectives and connected to a much larger sphere of personal and collective subjectivities.

This text of social interaction might be seen in the ongoing legacy of such "special projects" as *Teens Behind the Scenes*, an initiative through which 100 young people participate annually in the design and delivery of programs for their families, friends, and communities. The young people involved, from all social and geographic strata of the city, are not solicited through a cool hunting focus group poll or the corporate youth think-tank that has been fashionable; rather, they were invited to perform the fluctuation of their desires, using the museum's spaces, collections, and profile. Since its inception in 1999, there have been skateboard ballets, anti-racism advocacy initiatives, performance art projects, protests, family workshops, film festivals, trips, breakdancing lessons, and critical investigations of the museum's holdings.

The following text, initially performed by us, Shadya Yasin and Janna Graham, as a spoken dialogue in 2002, is an attempt to present the positions of, and collaborations between, participant and museum worker at play within these strategies. Each text is prefaced by the author's initials – SY or JG; Janna Graham's text appears in italics.

SY: In 1999, I joined *Teens Behind the Scenes* at the AGO, a program originally inspired by Judith Mastai. Coming from the outside culture/community and being involved in the inside of the AGO for me was a series of firsts. Being a newcomer to Canada, downtown Toronto was a place to explore. After an application form and interview, the AGO enabled me to enter and participate in creating a welcoming space for youth.

JG: *Much of the strategizing around audience happens behind closed doors in the museum. In an effort to hear a wider selection of voices and to better respond to the slippery and elusive audience, in recent years there have been more and more opportunities for feedback in museums. Focus groups, evaluation forms, public soundings have been set up to "hear" the audience. Here, insides and outsides are constituted by the relationship established between the questioned and the questioner. As Irit Rogoff points out:*

> *We [as a society] uphold and approve the rhetorics of participation as they circulate in political culture. What we rarely question is*

*what constitutes the listening, hearing or seeing in and of itself –
the good intentions of recognition become a substitute for the kind
of detailed analysis which might serve to expand the notions of
what constitutes a mode of speaking in public, of being heard by a
public.*[7]

*The problem with merely asking questions, she points out "is that the
question – whatever the question might be – is inevitably articulated at
the centers of power and it is only the response to which is paid attention." How do institutions learn to listen differently?*

SY: Like the majority of our group, I came from communities that were
not attached to the institution. We were invited by this program to say
that the AGO is for everyone. We were given the chance to create a
new community of our communities and to collaborate in showcasing
what art looks like in the eyes of our generation.

JG: *At museum meetings and conferences, it is common to hear museum
administrators discussing the audience: they talk about attracting the
audience, captivating the audience, engaging the audience, holding
the audience. They talk about maneuvering the audience, targeting the
audience, educating the audience, helping the audience to better understand. At one conference recently, an educator asked: Now that we have
this audience, should we attract them again or work with another? Each
time, "audience" is uttered with a rhetorical tone of certainty. Heads
nod. "Ah yes . . . the audience!" Conceived and spoken of in such ways,
this audience is positioned as the museum's "other." It is relegated to a
geographical and conceptual outside.*

SY: I was an insider as soon as I was chosen to participate on the Teen
Council. It was all about us and our ideas. In our first project, we
created an exhibition attended by thousands. It challenged traditional
art and exhibition concepts at the gallery. Our productions and arts
were coming from people of different communities. Where the institution often creates static perceptions of art, glorifying and isolating
the object, we allowed interaction, dialogue, and communication
between the public and the institution, the youth and the institution.

This event was called *Shocking Vibes: A New Beginning* and was our
statement of change at the AGO. It included work by 200 young artists
in a variety of media. *Shocking Vibes* happened over six months. We
invited youth to exhibit whatever they wanted. They came back again
and again. We showcased fashion designers, music performers, visual
artists. We wanted to remove boundaries between art forms. We
were interested in youth and their expression through art. This was
important, as it occurred during the time of the Columbine shooting.

There was tremendous fear about youth culture and events in the city, and the mayor, following the example of a number of American cities, declared a war on graffiti in Toronto.

But being an insider still did not make everything easier. We communicated with the AGO staff and we learned how things were done in the institution. The institution needed to allow room for change, and a space for conversation. We challenged the organizational culture from its traditional rigid forms to become fluid and to open its doors to other forms of culture. We were supported, but did not win all of the battles.

JG: *This audience can be rewarding. "Last night we had a great audience," a huge audience, but more often than not, it is difficult. Where was the audience? There is no audience for art in this town; that audience, "they say one thing and do another"; "they do not understand our workload, the audience. The audience doesn't read, they never follow directions, they just don't get it." The audience is slippery, unpredictable, off the charts, unattainable, uncivilized, untrainable, wild.*

The museum searches for its audience, frantically attempting to contend with it, meet its demands. Sometimes conversations with museum heads of security indicate that we must control the audience, tame the audience, and monitor their actions through gallery and non-gallery spaces.

SY: Next, we created a ballet on skateboards (Figure 9.1). We invited youth from both the suburbs and the inner city to work with composer Terence Dick and dance choreographer Zoja Smutney. We selected two spaces that skaters used, two places in which they consistently made their mark and from which they were often banned, to showcase skateboarding as an art form. Skaters (and their graffiti artist friends) at this time were targeted as part of a "clean up the streets" campaign in Toronto. With the Teen Council, they worked for weeks to develop an improvised "ballet on wheels." This was performed at two one-day events advertised as *Decked*, held at a mall in the suburbs and at the AGO. Inscriptions by skaters were like marks on paper, traces of youth in the city. We wanted to challenge the commodification of what skateboarding had become. There were no ramps, no boarding competitions, and no multinational sponsors. Each skater was endorsed by a local skate shop. Old school skaters came to talk about the early days of freestyle skateboarding and using construction sites to develop their style.

JG: *In the museum, the audience is also constructed as a series of demographic categories. There is a general audience, a family audience, an art audience, a local audience, audiences divided by ethnicity, gender, and interests. These categories of audience are sampled. Information is*

Figure 9.1   From *Decked*, a ballet on skateboards at the Art Gallery of Ontario and Oakville Place suburban mall, 2000. © Art Gallery of Ontario.

collected, offering often crude simplifications, abstractions of the people who come to, or could potentially come to, a museum. These audiences are presented as homogeneous categories, relying on stereotypical character-istics for the purposes of analyzing and predicting audience behavior.

In a paper entitled "Stalking the Wild Viewer," Ien Ang calls these attempts "civilizing techniques" that are "aimed at the codification, routinization, and synchronization of the audience's viewing practices, so as to make them less capricious and more predictable." [8] *The stereotype in this case functions, as Sander Gilman points out, as "a momentary coping mechanism" to overcome the anxiety of the strange and unknow-able entity of "audience."* [9]

Attempts at knowing the audience in this way are an extension of the colonial model operating in museums in its functions of collection, object-ordering, and narration. With the pressures of defunding and privatiza-tion, manifestations of globalization in the museum, old paradigms of the object/observer reinscribe themselves onto late capitalist techniques of intensified market research.

SY: Our largest event was an exhibition of hip-hop culture-in-the-making. We wanted to change stereotypes about hip-hop culture. We worked with many other youth organizations with the same goals. We wanted to take it back and showcase what was happening in the scene and show youth that spoken word could be used as a powerful tool for public voicing. We invited leaders from the grassroots hip-hop community to give workshops on how to build community, how to think critically about representations of women and violence in hip-hop. We did this for three years in a row. More than 2,000 people came in its second year. We used our affiliation with the AGO to get press at HYPE (Helping Young People Excel) and create counter-representations to what was circulating out there about youth and gangs and street culture.

HYPE (Figure 9.2) invited youth organizations from across the city to become involved. What appeared as one day was six months of negotiating: would security staff allow bandanas – indicators to them of gang activity? Could we use the walls for the graffiti artists? Would union staff stay late? Who were the partners? Where were the partners? The amorphous nature of hip-hop culture met with its very opposite in the museum. Some of us worried about whether the art we showed was appropriate in the eyes of the institution, since it was known for its high art collection and the Teen Council was working with "amateur" artists instead of professionals. Some of us didn't care. We learned quickly to work against and around these limits, practicing our motto to the

Figure 9.2 From HYPE, an advocacy project celebrating urban youth culture during Toronto's crackdown on graffiti, 2000. © Art Gallery of Ontario.

fullest with the belief of bringing our generation to the gallery with our concept of "art."

JG: *A conversation amongst "us" about "them" is a conversation in which "they" are silenced, says Trinh Minh-ha.[10] How then does the museum hear the many and multiple voices of people, rather than "the people" or "the audience"? How does the museum hear these voices without reinforcing the mechanics of historical silence? How does it relate outside of the framings of objectification?*

SY: Since my time on the council, I have mentored other youth at the Gallery. In 2001, I was invited to be one of 15 respondents to the museum's first home in a project created by the Teen Council and associated with the exhibition *House Guests: Contemporary Artists at the Grange.* The Grange is a nineteenth-century home that was donated to the City of Toronto and later became the Art Gallery of Ontario. *House Guests* was a series of interventions by seven artists into the historical home. I worked with the artist Luis Jacob to create a 30-second audio piece. This audio intervention was placed, along with the others, in a kiosk in the basement of the house. I found this statement written in a very small font, in the Grange library beside the fireplace: "Great is the power of truth that can easily defend itself by its own force."

I asked, "Was the statement in the library there to start a debate, or was it just a philosophical quotation?" The Grange was built in the 1800s. Marcus Cicero, who made this statement, was born in Rome in 106 BC. When I first read the quotation, I did not know what it meant. I started asking people what they thought it meant. I was puzzled, as were they. I wanted people to think about it and find their own interpretation. The audio piece was my own way of interpreting it.

> Great is the power of truth that can easily defend
>   itself by its own force.
> Force own its by itself defend easily can that truth
>   of power the is great.
> Great is the power of truth that can easily defend
>   itself by its own force.

I read each word backwards. It is not often that you hear people speaking backwards, so you have to figure out what the person is trying to say. It is like hearing a new language from the perspective of a different culture. You have to question what you hear. Reading it backwards makes it questionable.

Even though Cicero's is a definitive statement, it fills us with questions. Whose truth is powerful in the Grange or in the Library? To whom does this truth belong? Who wrote it? Who believes in it? Then I read the quote forwards to indicate my point of realization. I have achieved an understanding of what the words mean when they are put together. Coming from outside a language or a culture, this is how you make sense of words, sentences, and ideas. You make your own interpretation. The museum is a language that is foreign to many of us.

Future Questions

The Art Gallery of Ontario reminds me of a ship. You enter it the way people walk off a gangplank and then find your place in the ship either above or below deck. Aesthetically, what you see above deck is only part of the story. The more interesting parts might be below deck, hidden from view but providing the assumptions and expectations on which everything in the gallery, or galley, is based. Below deck lies not only the foundation but the superstructure, the established order that dictates how every artifact is interpreted, how the world beyond the AGO must fit into a perfect order within the AGO.[11]

In disrupting the authority of the question by inviting conversation based on collaboratively negotiated terms, we use the museum as a site for exploring the complex subjective relationship between individuals, communities, objects, and power within the broader project of social transformation. Rather than solely disseminating object-based knowledge, we unpack the difficult knowledge that exists in all aspects of the museum, from the positioning of objects to the conceptual framing of audience, bringing disparate things into relationship – in communal celebration, uneasy juxtaposition, intimate conversation, and ferocious debate.

Since these earlier projects, we have continued to work on strategies that invite intervention into the regular and regulatory narratives and functions of the museum. Projects such as *Private Thoughts/Public Moments* (initiated by Judith Mastai), a collaboration between artist/curator Sutapa Biswas and Toronto's South Asian Visual Art Collective, generated a series of interventions into interpretive material narrating the AGO's Canadian art installations in 2001. Bringing to light everything from little-known histories of Canadian Immigration Law to the relationship between key members of the Group of Seven, Canada's nationalist painting movement, and their South Asian contemporaries, the project unsettled the museum's interpretive voice (Figure 9.3).

Figure 9.3   From *Private Thoughts/Public Moments*: image of *Tagore and Mrs E*, fictionalized diaries of Mrs E, the subject of a painting by Group of Seven member Fred H. Varley, inserted by Rachel Kalpana James into sketch drawers in the AGO's Canadian Wing. *Tagore & Mrs E*, 2000, artist's books. © 2000 Rachel Kalpana James.

In 2003, the AGO's blockbuster exhibition space was turned over to Debajehmujig Theatre Group, an Anishnaabeg storytelling collective, which replicated the home of its Artistic Director, Audrey Debassige Wemigwans (Audge) from the Wikwemikong Unceded Reserve as a set for public performances (Figure 9.4). For many days, members of the Debajehmujig Theatre Group intervened into existing Gallery interpretations, took over staff training sessions, and invited Gallery visitors to eat corn soup, perform improvised vignettes of life on a northern reserve, and discuss what these performances revealed about stereotypes of Aboriginal people. *Audge's Place* was a parallel location that inserted another spatiality into the museum, a space of encounters that generated often challenging interpersonal experiences for visitors at the threshold (symbolized by an open screen door) of cultural difference. Their performative and deterritorializing approach (which included a special issue of the local newspaper created for the space) enabled museum staff to contemplate what practices of relationality, hospitality, and improvisation might lend to the museum-going experience.

Figure 9.4 On the set of *Audge's Place*, Debajehmujig work with AGO visitors and members of the local Aboriginal community to develop improvised performances over corn soup, 2003. © Art Gallery of Ontario.

In 2004, this exploration continued with Tauqsiijiit, a temporary media lab and drop-in space that brought First Nations, Inuit, and non-Aboriginal artists and youth into residence as part of the *Ilitarivingaa? (Do You Recognize Me?)* exhibition of Inuit art (Figure 9.5). Through these encounters, artists and members of the public began to unravel their simplified perspectives of one another, incorporating these explorations into media productions that were developed in the Gallery and broadcast from the group's blog. Using the Gallery as a laboratory for the exploration of relationships between cultures and art forms, the group struggled to develop a framework through which the extension of hospitality across a range of cultural differences, including summer tourists, could be politically and creatively generative. A residency on Manitoulin Island built upon these relationships in the summer of 2005.

This is how "special projects" were positioned – as a stage for collaborations, experimentation, and negotiations of difference on the museum's contradictory terrain. Many years later, these projects and methodologies have proven to be important test sites for this reorientation of the museum's understanding of its public role. They have shown us what

Figure 9.5   Artists and youth in the Tauqsiijiit residency interact with AGO visitors in the *Ilitarivingaa?* Inuit exhibition, and generate media projects for broadcast, 2004. © Debajehmujig Theatre Group.

might happen if we resist the models of consumption currently at play in conceptions of the audience and actively move toward a notion, described by Danielle Allen, of a "citizenship of political friendship."[12] "Special projects" have begun to change perceptions within the museum and, more importantly, they have begun to create expectations, among some, but by no means all, people, that this form of participation is their right. Most recently, a former Teen Council member relayed to me her unsuccessful attempt at starting a youth group at a museum in another city. Her response to the museum's lack of interest was to start a collective of young people who would come up with projects and lobby all of the museums in the city, and start their own museum if necessary.

No longer "special," these programs have now been institutionalized. They have shifted some perceptions at all levels of staff at the AGO toward a form of access that is not the delivery of services and programs to those "in need," but rather toward a series of explorative collaborations that initiate social process and see the interpretive act beyond didactic labels, as generating discussion and relationship. As contemporary artists and community groups continue to push this agenda of participation, one can only hope that this will continue.

The barriers to this kind of movement, however, must be recognized. While these projects have begun to take hold conceptually and program-matically at the AGO and in other galleries and museums, they have not managed to alter the habitual and hierarchical way in which knowledge is delivered and read by most people who enter their doors. As museums, and the AGO in particular, continue to struggle with the forced move toward privatization that has been dictated by public defunding, evi-denced in such pervasive forms as the blockbuster exhibition, the product launch, the for-profit education department, and the build-a-better tourist-mecca scheme, the divide between the connoisseur (now less an issue of curatorial authority and more a conflation of the desires of private donors, collectors, and a consumer public) and the participant becomes more acute.

Creating programs that attempt to alter social relations in this conflict-ual location and within an intensified version of the contradictory logic that has always been at the heart of the museum can bring about exciting and unexpected fusions, but one is never sure of how long commitments will stick. Capable of foregrounding multitude, while, in the same stroke, reinscribing familiar structures of power, one is never sure whether the tension of our efforts is generative or futile. In the face of such shifting terrain and predictable uncertainty, rather than succumbing to the market researcher's command to "answer this!" we continue to ask, as Judith Mastai always did: "So – what do you want to do?"

Notes

1   Jürgen Habermas, *The Philosophical Discourse of Modernity: Twelve Lectures*, trans. Frederick G. Lawrence (Cambridge, MA: MIT Press, 1990), pp. 295–6.
2   Janna Graham encountered this concept in her undergraduate studies in geography. The term was used by traffic statisticians in urban planning in the United States during the 1930s to identify routes or pathways through open space used by people in opposition to or in the absence of planned pathways and marked traffic routes. Graham encountered the term in artistic use in the performance of Tim Brennan at the Henry Moore Institute in Leeds in 1998.
3   Henri Lefebvre, *The Production of Space* (London: Basil Blackwell, 1991).

4   PEN is an international organization of writers instituted to defend freedom of expression and to counter censorship.

5   Martha Kumsa, "The Space In-Between," in Judith Mastai, ed., *Making Meaning* (Toronto: Art Gallery of Ontario, 2000).

6   Hannah Arendt, *Truth and Politics: Between Past and Future* (New York: Penguin Books, 1977).

7   Irit Rogoff, "Looking Away: Participations in Visual Culture." Paper presented at *Museums After Modernism*, Toronto: Centre CATH, York University, 2002, in Gavin Butt, ed., *After Criticism: New Responses to Art and Performance* (Boston and Oxford: Blackwell Publishing, 2005), pp. 117–36.

8   Ien Ang, "Stalking the Wild Viewer," *Continuum: The Australian Journal of Media & Culture* 4/2 (1991).

9   Sander L. Gilman, *Difference and Pathology* (Ithaca and London: Cornell University Press, 1985). According to Gilman, only pathological personalities hold on to too rigid stereotypes about a group they fear on a consistently permanent basis.

10 Trinh T. Minh-ha, *Woman-Native-Other: Writing, Postcoloniality and Feminism* (Bloomington: Indiana University Press, 1989).

11 Cecil Foster, "A Ship and Its Cargo," in Mastai, ed., *Making Meaning*.

12 Danielle S. Allen, "Talking to Strangers." Excerpt from Key Note Address. Carolina: Foundation for the Carolinas, 2003.

10

"There Is No Such Thing as a Visitor"

Judith Mastai

I have chosen to call my short paper: "There is no such thing as a visitor."[1] To be more accurate, perhaps I should have said, "There is no such thing as *a* visitor." This inflection puts the emphasis where it belongs. My intention here is to address the relatively recent rise of the arena of museological research known as "visitor studies," which attempts to refocus the interpretive concerns of museums, away from authoritative curatorial and art-historical narratives and toward responding to the various questions which are raised by the presence of visitors in the museum and by the need to attract visitors to the museum.

For the sake of clarity and efficiency, here is my argument, in a nutshell. As government support for museums has been reduced, the strategies for maintaining the financial health of these institutions have shifted to serving the customer (or, in the jargon of Museum Studies, the visitor). Along with all the other services of museums – and I speak primarily from my experience of art museums – the contemporary focus of museological practice has incorporated strategies from commercial marketing in order to create and sell products. The major product, from which most other products are generated, is the exhibition. In striving to create appealing exhibitions, museum staff have become interested in what city planners call "paths of desire" – the ways in which visitors choose their paths through the environment as well as the ways that they like their information packaged and how much information they like to have.[2] With the zeal-to-appeal has come a blurring of two concepts: the visitor-friendly museum and the museum as an educational environment. While critical analysis is preoccupied with the museum and the exhibition as meta- phorical texts, the visitors' paths of desire might be more appropriately examined as hypertext – bobbing, weaving, and webbing from sensation to question, from perception to discovery, among various nodes of information and experience.

Having given it all away, here at the start, let me now go back and flesh out the various points in my argument.

At the present time, and for the past 15–20 years, ever-increasing attention has been paid to the accountability of the museum to its publics. For the most part, this concern has arisen as a result of reduced govern- ment support for museums (and here I include art galleries, or art museums, which have permanent collections, rather than Kunsthallen or art galleries that only show temporary exhibitions and do not have collections that must be maintained and developed). The changing fund- ing environment for museums, in North America and Europe particularly, has usually been characterized by a reduction in public funding from government sources and a turn to the "development" of sources of fund- ing directly from the public, through corporate sponsorships, foundation grants, admission fees at the door, and a variety of "cost centers," ranging from cafés and shops to the rental of the museum for functions such as weddings, bar mitzvahs, and events hosted by corporations for their clients. So the need better to understand the experience of the visitor has risen, in my opinion, from the need better to serve the customer; indeed, to attract the customer and gain their allegiance through mem- bership, while ensuring that they spend as much money as possible each time they visit the museum. This is not a cynical view. It is the reality faced by these institutions since the early 1980s and the era of fiscal restraint by governments. The caution, however, is in capitulating to the attendant, extreme, and reductive view that the visitor (read "the customer") is always right.

While academic and critical analysis often focuses on the exhibition as a text, the real struggle faced by museum staff is between the paradigms of marketing and education. At one time, this struggle was enacted by conflict between members of the various departments of the museum, between curators and the new cadre of museum educators, who claimed the visitors' view as their own point of view. Then these forces (curators and educators) joined in battle with the new marketeers who began to appear on the staff of large museums by the end of the 1980s. The new corporate reality is a practice that recognizes and incorporates the marketing paradigm in all facets of operation. The ideological differences that once divided staff in different departments of the museum have morphed into shared strategies for success – financial success – where working together for financial solvency on large, popular projects has provided the funds to do less populist, even more esoteric, research-based projects.

As a gallery educator myself, I have a fundamental disagreement with treating visitors as merely sources of information based in perceived needs and desires, so that the museum can appear to be publicly accountable by meeting them. My disagreement arises in the difference between what have been called "felt" and "unfelt" needs, for instance for further knowledge. If, for example, we characterize the museum as an institution with an educational mandate, then, in the same way as schools and universities have curricula which must be mastered in order to achieve the appropriate credentials, there is a body of information inherent in understanding the knowledge that is housed within the collections of the museum. Like any other educational institution, the mandate of the museum is not to pander to "felt" needs, but to use them as a starting point from which to build bridges between what is known and what must be known. Therefore, if the educator's practice incorporates the marketing paradigm, the educational approach begins and ends with following the paths of the visitor's desire, finding so-called "sexy" content, using current, popular, or "accessible" themes to sell the museum experience. If the educator's philosophical orientation, however, is that the museum is an educational resource for lifelong learning, the task changes in order to identify multiple points of entry for visitors of many sorts and kinds, based on differences in age, gender, race, ethnicity, levels of knowledge about history, about art history, and so on. To wit, this recent email that I received: "Browsed around the Gallery a bit. Came across... etc."

At the Art Gallery of Ontario, we define stratified audiences. Various program staff specialize in programming for particular interest groups. These include children in school, children out of school, pre-school children, children with their families, adults with their families, adults on their own, adults visiting during the day, adults who work during the day, young, unmarried adults, teens, senior citizens, those who have a great deal of knowledge about art, those who have very little knowledge about art, and so on. Our assumption is that individual visitors bring their own narratives to the museum and, using the hypertext metaphor, their paths of interest and desire lead them to land on various points of entry into relationships with our institution. Their first experience could as likely be meeting a friend for coffee in the café as buying a ticket for a temporary exhibition, or spending a few hours in the studio finger-painting with their child on a Sunday afternoon. Some of our visitors only have their first experience of the galleries because they are looking for something else – the restaurant, the bathroom, or a puppet show. Obviously, I am overstating the case. Our hope is still that the art is the main attraction. . . .

In conclusion, I reiterate my main point. There is no such thing as *a* visitor. The people who visit museums bear differences of many sorts. Our task is to talk to them in person, through comment cards, and over the world wide web, and to design multiple possible entry points for their interests. Of course, within our own experimentation, some projects do this more successfully than others. In that sense, the museum is a laboratory for constant experimentation. The points of inquiry, the learning tasks, the personal narratives, and the insecurities that people bring to the environment of the Art Gallery of Ontario are all of interest to us, and we seek to provide as many opportunities as possible to hear from and respond to our various publics. Unlike the curator's task of creating an exhibition – a task much beleaguered by exhibition critique – the task of the educator is to bridge the gaps between inquiry and authority, between desire and satisfaction, between length of attention span and volumes of potential information. In relation to the ways that people seek knowledge, as George P. Landow pointed out in his book *Hyper/Text/Theory*, the "merging of creative and discursive modes simply *happens* in hypertext." It is a medium that tolerates the "blending and blurring of genres" and offers "a powerful means of understanding by comparison."[3] I look forward to the development of critical inquiries appropriate to these sorts of practices.

Notes

1   This is an unpublished lecture that was given during Judith Mastai's tenure as Director of Public Programs at the Art Gallery of Ontario.
2   Editors' note: Janna Graham introduced Judith Mastai to the urban planning concept of "desire lines" developed by traffic statisticians during the 1930s in the United States to describe the routes people took through open space, as opposed to or in the absence of those marked by planned pathways or traffic

routes. Janna Graham has informed me that she not only encountered the term in her geography studies, but in a performance by Tim Brennan at the Henry Moore Institute, Leeds, in 1998, since when it has been explored by a number of artists and poets. Judith Mastai renamed the concept in her writing as "paths of desire," while in chapter 9 Graham uses "lines of desire" as her modification of this expanding concept.

3 George P. Landow, "What's a Critic to Do? Critical Theory in the Age of Hypertext," in Landow, ed., *Hyper/Text/Theory* (Baltimore: Johns Hopkins University Press, 1994), pp. 39–40.

11

"Anxious Dust": History and Repression in the Archives of Mary Kelly

Judith Mastai

Rustling the Dust[1]

In 1996, the MIT Press published the collected writings of American contemporary artist, Mary Kelly, under the title *Imaging Desire*. The articles, interviews, and essays assembled in the book represent Kelly's history, tellingly and very deliberately, from 1976 to the present. The year 1976 – defined by Kelly herself as the official beginning of her oeuvre - was the one in which she first exhibited *Post-Partum Document*, her celebrated study of the first six years in the relationship between a mother and her child. Shown at the Institute of Contemporary Art in London, England, the exhibition became immediately notorious because Part I of the Document included the laundered liners of the baby's diapers, containing traces of stains from the baby's feces, which were the sign, for the mother, of the baby's health, as she introduced his first solid foods. In the opening paragraph of the *Imaging Desire* Kelly wrote:

> Until recently, I could not even open, much less examine, the contents of a certain folder. It contains reviews that appeared in the tabloid press during the exhibition of *Post-Partum Document* at the Institute of Contemporary Art (ICA) in London, in 1976. Just a glimpse of the insalubrious prose descrying "dirty nappies" was enough to prompt a swift return to the

archive where they remained gathering anxious dust for almost twenty years.[2]

My task in this paper is to rustle the "anxious dust" and discover for you much that lay buried in the archive. Needless to say, Kelly's oeuvre did not begin in 1976, but rather in 1966, although some of the early work would correctly be labeled "juvenilia."

My own association with Mary Kelly goes back to 1988, when I was Head of Public Programs at the Vancouver Art Gallery. Two topics were of particular interest to the artists in that community at the time: postmodernism and feminism, or, more correctly, feminism's many forms, and the figure of particular interest was Mary Kelly. By coincidence, Kelly was in residence at the Banff Center that winter. We conspired to meet and began a collaborative process that has lasted more than ten years. In 1993, I had occasion to ask her about the founding of the Artists' Union in Britain. Kelly had been the first Chair and kindly arranged to share with me her files on the Union during my next visit to England. That was when I became aware that, although she had moved back to the US after 20 years in the UK, the material relating to her early history was still stored in Britain. Unfortunately, the conditions under which the material was being stored were less than ideal and, in December, we agitated to remove it to a better situation.

In addition to my questions, Mary Kelly was now being contacted on a regular basis by students and curators engaged in many forms of research about her work. It seemed an appropriate time to consider organizing her papers and moving them to the United States. We imagined an exhibition project and, with the help of Greg Bellerby, Director of the Charles H. Scott Gallery at the Emily Carr Institute of Art and Design in Vancouver, I applied for a research grant from the Canada Council, which covered the costs of assembling the material and shipping it to North America. During the summer of 1995, I spent six weeks in a dusty, hot storeroom in Kingston-upon-Thames, sorting through papers and boxing them up for shipping. At the same time, Mary Kelly was spending her summer in California, writing the introduction to her collected essays, *Imaging Desire*, from which I have just quoted. Our almost daily telephone conversations were difficult for her at times. In my excitement over each new find, it took me a while to realize that some of this material had been buried, both actually and metaphorically. I had to learn a suitable sensitivity to various aspects of her history, which may be inherent in organizing archival papers, but is probably more pronounced in the case of a living artist. In answering my questions, there were often moments when she would have to get back to me, to allow time to deal with feelings associated with some of her history which may have been preventing remembrance. In return, Mary often made requests for me to find material in England which she needed for the book and which was not available in the US, such as excerpts from *Control* magazine, one of the many ephemeral visual arts publications, and in which she had published some of her first writing about *Post-Partum Document*. The exhibition that resulted from the reassembling of her archival papers is called *Social Process, Collaborative Action: Mary Kelly 1970–75*.[3] My hope in mounting the exhibition was that, by recontextualizing her oeuvre to include the early work, much of which was collectively produced, Kelly's audiences would gain a wider understanding of the conditions for the production of the *Post-Partum Document* and, particularly, of the strong socio-political underpinnings of a work that has largely been interpreted in light of its intellectual roots in psychoanalytic theory.

The Early Work of Mary Kelly

In hindsight, I can see now that there were many reasons why Kelly was not anxious to draw attention to her early work. For one thing, because some of the work was collaborative, there would inevitably be issues related to authorship. A second factor was that in the period in the 1980s, prior to the fall of the Berlin Wall, if one had Leftist political affiliations during the 1960s and '70s, they were rarely discussed. But after 1989, and certainly by 1995, when art historians had begun anew to unpack and interpret the art of the late 1960s and early '70s, there seemed to be a strong rationale for blowing the dust off some of Kelly's early work and seeing how it stood up in the harsh light of the end of the century.

The earliest record of Kelly's work is an exhibition invitation for a show at the Jafet Memorial Library in Beirut in June 1968, where she took up a post as an instructor at the American University after completing postgraduate training in painting in Florence, Italy. While in Lebanon, Kelly produced and exhibited a series of relief paintings which pushed the envelope of Greenberg's formalist definitions of the difference between painting and sculpture. Kelly wrote:

The works on exhibit began with a series of minimal line drawings based on variations of the human figure. Although I was attracted to their intimacy, they seemed too private, too introverted and generally limited in terms of making a definite visual impact. In an attempt to "materialize" the image while conserving at least the illusion of linear progression, I decided to work with wood; cutting the general shape mechanically, carving the final details manually, and then giving the surface a calm, mat [sic] finish with vinyl-latex. I wanted to explore the psychological effects of the figure variations as well as the physical possibilities of relief and finally let the form break the boundaries of a "literal" picture frame.[4]

In 1968, she moved to London and began further postgraduate training at St Martin's School of Art. Here Kelly extended her studies of abstraction and the female form, moving entirely into three-dimensional works as well as creating *An Earthwork Performed* with Stephen Rothenberg at the London New Arts Lab. In an exhibition of work by Senior Overseas painting students at St Martin's in 1970, an art critic known only as J.G. had this to say of Kelly's work: "Her multi-layer 'prints' on perspex, based on a mosque plan, show an integrity of style and disciplined colour which is outstandingly mature."[5]

At this time, Kelly's engagement with Leftist politics in the Middle East brought her into contact with members of the New Left in London and particularly the Women's Liberation Movement. One of her early pieces of writing, on "National Liberation and Women's Liberation," which appeared in *Shrew*, charts these interests.[6] In order to better understand the time, I interviewed a number of Kelly's friends and associates, including feminist historian Sally Alexander, who had this to say:

Mary was a very interesting person in the Women's Movement in London at that moment because, not only was she North American and from the mid-West, she'd studied in Lebanon and married a French Lebanese man and had traveled and studied in Italy, as well as the Lebanon. She brought an active politics of the aesthetics into the concerns of the Women's Liberation Movement in London. She was one of several. The Women's Liberation Movement was by no means a homogenous group, but Mary was interested in having a deliberate and self-consciously more internationalist approach to political questions of the women's movement. And she was very important for that reason. The article, making an analogy between women's liberation and national liberation, I think, was a kind of mistaken attempt but it was a very interesting one and a fruitful and creative one.

Fundamental to the development of the Women's Liberation Movement in Britain at the time was the formation of Gramscian-style, community-based study and support groups which aimed to provide a place for women's voices to be heard through local discussion of shared experiences and study of important texts which formed the basis for analysis and debate about class, society, and women's roles. Sally Alexander described the way she and Kelly met through this network of study groups.

> I believe I met Mary first of all in 1970 in a history study group. We had a meeting in Notting Hill Gate, in Laura Mulvey's flat. Mary came... to speak about the Palestinian Liberation struggle. She was writing an article which we were going to include in our issue [of *Shrew*]. Our study group was the History Study Group, which was part of the Women's Liberation Workshop in London, which was a network of consciousness-raising groups, local groups, study groups, and action groups.
>
>   Mary was very Marxist and very socialist and very correct. Another friend lived here named Maxine Mollineaux. Mary and Maxine were in a group called Theoretical Practice, which used to read Marx and Lenin, and Mao and Althusser, and so on. She was very, very theoretical and very much into the politics of art practice.[7]

I would like to stress the importance of reading at this time and of the model of the working-class intellectual. Reading, study, and discussion had great importance for the post-war generation, interested in the revolutionary possibilities of social change at a time of relative economic plenty. Through reading and study groups on Women's Liberation, women's health, history, unionization, and the arts, Kelly met other women equally committed to social change. A familiar expression at the time was "the personal is political" and, like others, Kelly was motivated by this ideology to experiment in many facets of her life: as a student during the turbulent days of the actions at Hornsey and Guildford Colleges of Art, as a founding member and first Chair of the Artists' Union, and a founding member of the Women's Workshop of the Artists' Union, in her home life, in her teaching, and in her work as an artist. For women, reproductive rights were at the top of the liberationist agenda, and the roles of women and men in relation to childcare and the family was of particular interest to Kelly as, in the midst of her other activities, she contemplated parenthood. In every way, her interests and her work reflected her ideological commitment and political engagement.

For women, and particularly for feminists like Mary Kelly, this period was unquestionably a radical break from former times. Medical science had found a practically perfect method by which women could take charge of their reproductive functions for the first time in the history of humankind. While birth control had been publicly debated in Britain for over a century, it had never been widely accepted as a method of family planning. Provision of birth control information to unmarried women was still considered taboo. In countries like Canada, the provision of information about birth control, even to married women, was illegal under the Criminal Code until the late 1960s. With the legalization and wide availability of the birth control pill, the attention of women turned to redefining feminine subjectivity in light of these new conditions for self-determination in relation to reproduction and the family. Kelly's *Post-Partum Document*, based on her reading and application of psychoanalytic theory, was a contemporary study of motherhood after choice.

In attempting to define her own practice at that time, in hindsight, Kelly has argued that *Post-Partum Document* followed the meta-discursiveness of the 1960s. But what she had assumed to be inevitable – that the prevailing interrogations would necessarily include the question of the subject and the construction of sexual difference – was not the case. "Although there was a move to extend the analytical method beyond the exclusive parameter of aesthetics, it stopped dramatically short of synthesizing the subjective moment into that inquiry."[8]

Most people in the visual arts who are aware of Kelly's work know about *Post-Partum Document*, but two other works by Kelly overlapped with the research period for *Post-Partum Document* and greatly influenced it. One was *Women and Work: A Document on the Division of Labour in Industry* (1975), a Collaborative project with Kay Hunt and Margaret Harrison.[9] The other was *Nightcleaners* (1975), a film produced with the Berwick Street Film Collective (Richard Mordaunt, Marc Karlin, James Scott, and Humphrey Trevelyan). An experimental, feature-length documentary, much influenced by Brechtian aesthetics, *Nightcleaners* followed the campaign in 1972 by May Hobbs of the TGWU (Transport and General Workers' Union) to unionize working-class women employed by janitorial companies to clean office buildings during the night in the City of London. Members of the Women's Liberation Movement had become actively involved in this campaign, and exploring the collaboration between the various women was part of the film's project.

Women and Work was an analysis of the division of labor in a Metal Box factory at the time of the introduction of Equal Pay legislation in Britain in 1970–5.[10] First installed at the South London Gallery, near the location of the factory, *Women and Work* clarified differences in the relationships of men and women to the workplace as well as the fact that "women's unpaid work in the home not only maintains the labour force in the physical sense, but also mediates the relations of production through the ideology of the family."[11] Kelly has ascribed this work fundamental importance as the stimulus for questions addressed by the *Post-Partum Document*. She described *Women and Work* as:

> a document on the division of labor in a specific industry, showing the changes in the labor process and the constitution of the labor force during the implementation of the Equal Pay Act. At the same time we were discovering how the division of labor in industry was underpinned by the division of labor in the home and that the central issue for women was in fact reproduction.

Sally Alexander said:

> I was very close friends with a woman called Sheila Rowbotham, as was Mary, and we were very involved in socialist politics and trade union politics. I suppose, in our very naive way, we wanted to work with women who were wage earners and not noticed by the trade union movement and working in domestic labor, in the market place. I suppose the preoccupations were with women's confinement to the domestic role and the way in which waged work echoed and repeated women's domestic labor. We wanted to be involved in trying to organize, collectively, women who were engaged in that kind of women's work.

I asked her: "Were issues around abortion and birth control coming up in your work with the night cleaners, domestic workers, and other women?" She responded: "As you know, this is what women talk about all the time. One of the points of contact between us, as feminists, and the women workers was children and our reproductive histories because that's always what women talk about."

Central to women, central to Women's Liberation, central to women's place in society and in the workplace, and central to Kelly herself, as an artist, a teacher, and a mother, reproductive rights took precedence over other forms of institutional, structural, and social critique for women.

At the moment when the birth control pill provided women with a stronger case for equality and choice than had previously existed, it also meant that they became engaged in redefining the terms of femininity and the gendered construction of women's roles in the family and society. Kelly's attention, like that of many other women, was focused on sexuality and gender as well as class and institutional critique. As Sally Alexander put it:

> What Marxist women were interested in at that time was the relationship between sex and class. We were not socialists; we were Marxist feminists. And we were studying the texts. Now and again, we went off on a conference of socialist economists. We were the Political Economy of Women Group. Mary was not involved in that, but we met at our home, and Mary would ask, "What did you all talk about today?" I'd tell her what the Political Economy Group was doing and she'd tell me what the Theoretical Practice Group was doing. There'd be all this exchange of ideas. We went off to the big conference with our paper on women and work in the First World War which is all about trade union exclusion and structural inequality and sexual division of labur. The sexual division of labor now is a commonplace, isn't it? but it was a concept that was very revolutionary at the time. It came out of all that empirical work. For Mary and Kay to go off and do the work they did on *Women and Work* – interviewing, systematically breaking down the structure of an industry, and re-presenting its structure and form and the experience of working in that industry in different aesthetics – it was an extraordinary piece of work to do.

In particular, Kelly's reading and study turned to the psychoanalytical construction of "woman," participating in a wide variety of contemporary and subsequent investigations of subjectivity, gender, and sexuality. Kelly's practice, while feminist, was not aesthetically or politically distinct from other conceptualist art practices at the time. Its distinction lay in its content, providing a contemporary investigation of mother and child, invested with a utopian impulse toward equality for women within the structures of the family and society, and equality for men too, for that matter, within the context of the family, by acknowledging their active role in childcare. Kelly's concerns were realized at both the level of material practice and the meta-discourse about art and society, constructing a set of propositions, working these out conceptually within the frame of reference of a visual arts practice, and presenting them as exhibitions which challenged the conventions of aesthetic and institutional practice.

I asked Sally Alexander what distinguished *Women and Work* as an art show. She said: "Well, it didn't just feed you information and facts, while there was lots of information and history and analysis. We wouldn't have used the term 'deconstruction' then. It laid it out for you." I asked: "When you entered the room and looked at it, did you have the sense that something beautiful was there?" She answered: "Not beautiful, but – being Mary and Kay – it was aesthetically very pleasing and stylish and very easy to find your way around. It was clear and very aesthetically pleasing." I wondered if it had an aesthetics based on the use of the mind, laying out information in a way that made complex ideas clear. She countered:

> But [it] also [revealed the] complexity of an economic structure. I'm not a very visual person, so what I recall is the clarity. That distinguishes all Mary's work. It's all very beautiful and clear. I remember when she first showed me the nappy and she told me what she was doing. It was hilarious, so exciting and wicked. She told me as a sort of confession – that I'd think she was mad – what she was doing. You know that sort of thing of women shrieking with laughter. It was utterly wicked and mad and crazy, but brilliant as well, just brilliant. And she wasn't sure that this was going to work. And then seeing that exhibit, *Post-Partum Document*, it was just stunning. There is a clarity.
>
> When it caused this kind of mayhem and furor, I couldn't believe that they were describing the same thing, because it was so beautiful and so clear and so perfectly saying what she wanted it to say, and ironical and witty and moving, terribly moving.

Such an obvious moment of *jouissance* seems to bring us full circle, back to the opening statement of Kelly's introduction to her recent volume of published writings: "I could not bring my self to open the folder containing the reviews," she said. "Just a glimpse . . . prompted a swift return to the archive where they remained gathering anxious dust." Such thrilling fear and transgression, the hysterical public reaction, and the burial in the archive. No wonder, 20 years later, it called for caution and courage to open those boxes and folders again.

Twenty Years On

In producing this exhibition, Mary and I had to clarify our relationships to it. We decided to approach it as an exhibition of an archive, not as a display of works of art. In this way, we could distinguish my work of uncovering, interpreting, and displaying from her artistic production, and this body of historical material, viewed with hindsight, from current exhibitions of her work, which relate to contemporary life. She is an artist and her work is making art; mine, as a curator, was to make a place for the work in relation to its history.

Epilogue: February 26, 2000[12]

Three years after its first opening, the exhibition *Social Process/Collaborative Action* traveled to three Canadian and one English venue.[13] In the meantime, a number of events have taken place in reaction to the rustling of the "anxious dust" of Kelly's archive which have led me to a better understanding of the anxiety surrounding the archive. While the exhibition toured in Canada, it was of historical interest, but it remained relatively benign. Once I began to speak of it at conferences in England, however, and once it opened in its first English venue at the Leeds City Art Gallery in October 1999, the works in the exhibition re-entered their discursive arena and their meanings became open for renegotiation, through the gauze of memory and history.

Women and Work had been virtually forgotten when I went looking for it in 1995.[14] As far as Mary Kelly knew, the work had been donated to the Museum of Labour History in London. Through friends and a few phone calls, I was able to determine that this Museum had been moved to Manchester, but when I called the curators to inquire after the work, they had never heard of it and were distressed to imagine that something that was thought by the artists to be in their collection was not. To all intents and purposes, the work had vanished.

Persevering further, I tried to locate Mary's collaborators on the project, and when I managed to contact Kay Hunt, it turned out that when the Museum's curator had come to pick up the work, she had decided not to give it to him. Unfortunately, she had never communicated this to the other artists who had worked with her on the project and who, to that day, thought that it was safely located in the public domain of the Museum. While Mary had the original audio-tapes and film loops in her archives, Kay had packed up the photographic material and stored it in her attic. Luckily, she was amenable to allowing it to be exhibited, and together we spent some weeks unpacking it and examining it together, preparing it for its journey to Canada. During this time, Kay told me many stories about the work, what it meant to her, and how it had come into being over two years of weekly research and documentation at the Metal Box factory.

For Kay, the production of this work had been a personal journey of exploration to better understand the life of her mother, who had also been a factory worker in South London, but in the leather trade. This memory was entwined with her decision not to part with the work.

Kay Hunt also outlined the breakdown in relations between the third member of their group, Margaret Harrison, and herself, and, finally, the estrangement between herself and Mary, over the years. While all of this remained part of the past, when the exhibition opened at the Leeds City Art Gallery in 1999, it became clear that, now that *Women and Work* had come "home" again to England, the hostilities and estrangements that had lain buried in the archives for more than 20 years also had their dust rustled. Without going into great detail, suffice it to say that the three collaborators are now in contact with each other again. As a result of this, portions of *Women and Work* were collectively lent to the exhibition *Live in Your Head* at the Whitechapel Gallery in London and the Chiado Gallery, Lisbon, in 2000.

A few days ago, I was speaking to someone who had been at the opening of that exhibition earlier this month. In particular, they mentioned the fact that a work by the original members of Art and Language – their final work together, the *Index* – was also being shown in the Whitechapel exhibition. The large cabinet, with many drawers containing the index of their works during 10 years of practice, which is the centerpiece of the *Index*, much to everyone's surprise, was locked, presumably for reasons related to conservation. In direct opposition to the intentions of the work, visitors could not actively participate in using it. This was particularly ironic since, after more than 20 years of antipathy amongst the various members of that collective, they had finally had something of a reunion in Barcelona in 1999, burying the hatchet after a particularly acrimonious parting that had been the subject of much hostile rhetoric in the various art press in England during the 1990s. Perhaps it was just as well, I thought. Better, perhaps, I thought, to leave the hatchet buried and locked, in the archive.

Notes

1   First presented as a plenary session for the Third Biennial Conference of the Feminist Arts and Histories Network ("Virtue and Vulgarity: a feminist conference on art, science and the body"), University of Reading, September 18–21, 1997, which I co-convened with Sue Malvern.

2 Mary Kelly, "Introduction: Remembering, Repeating, and Working-Through," in *Imaging Desire* (Cambridge, MA/London: The MIT Press, 1996), p. xv.

3 Judith Mastai, ed., *Social Process/Collaborative Action: Mary Kelly 1970–1975*, (Vancouver: Charles H. Scott Gallery, Emily Carr Institute of Art and Design, 1997) included papers by Kelly, Sue Malvern, Peter Wollen, Margaret Harrison, Kay Hunt, and Griselda Pollock. The exhibition ran from February 1 to March 16, 1997.

4 Mary Kelly Trabulsi, *Painted Reliefs*, exhibition invitation, Jafet Memorial Library, American University of Beirut, June 21–July 5, 1968.

5 J.G., *Arts Review*, London (April 25, 1970).

6 *Shrew*, special double issue (December 1970), pp. 2–5.

7 Some of the women were in more than one study group; for instance, Kelly was also engaged with the Family Study Group.

8 Mary Kelly, *Imaging Desire*, p. xx.

9 Kay Hunt was actively involved (as an instructor) in advocating equal pay for women and better conditions for part-time instructors.

10 See Rozsika Parker and Griselda Pollock, *Framing Feminism: Art and the Women's Movement in Britain 1970–85* (London: Pandora Books, 1987 and 1992), pp. 11, 19, 32, 99, 201. Includes reprint of Rosalind Delmar's review from *Spare Rib* 40 (1975): 32–3.

11 Women's Workshop/Artists Union," *Spare Rib* 29 (1974): 40.

12 This epilogue was added, three years later, in response to an invitation by the organizers (Alphabet City) of the one-day symposium "Lost in the Archives," which took place at the Art Gallery of Ontario in Toronto on February 26, 2000. Mastai, "Anxious Dust" for "Lost in the Archives," February 26, 2000, p. 14.

13 In addition to the Charles H. Scott Gallery, the exhibition was shown at the Edmonton Art Gallery, the Agnes Etherington Art Centre, Kingston, Ontario, Leeds City Art Gallery, Norwich Gallery. As a result of this display, some of the core work of *Women and Work*, by Harrison, Hunt, and Kelly, was shown in *Live in Your Head: Concept and Experiment in Britain 1965–75*, Whitechapel Art Gallery, 2000.

14 It had been 'archived' or documented in Parker and Pollock's *Framing Feminism*.

12

On Discourse as Monument: Institutional Spaces and Feminist Problematics

Juli Carson

Prequel: The Discursive Site

> *The building site is the site for a story, a story that acts as if the site preceded it. But there is no site without project. The project actually produces the site it appears to be aimed at. . . . In a sense, the project is never more than an image, an image that, like all images, can be occupied. . . . The project is the story that produces the image of the site's reality.*
>
> Mark Wigley, *On Site*

Here is a story about an emblematic building that many feminists are discussing today. In 1971 Judy Chicago and Miriam Schapiro initiated the Feminist Art Program at the California Institute of the Arts (CalArts). Their curriculum, as former graduate student Faith Wilding recalls, addressed:

> the myths of (male) genius and mastery deemed as necessary to the making of art; the lack of social expectation of achievement and ambition for women; and the traditional hierarchies of materials and methods taught in art schools which devalued many of the skills and experiences women have been trained in.[1]

From this program came *Womanhouse*, a group of collaborative installations mounted in a condemned Hollywood house for just one month in 1972. As Arlene Raven recalls, the house was "eventually destroyed by the city as planned, but not before *Womanhouse* made a widespread difference in art-making and in all subsequent art."[2]

Twenty-three years after *Womanhouse* was torn down, the Bronx Museum of Art recreated parts as a museum installation for a show entitled *Division of Labor: "Women's Work" in Contemporary Art* (Figure 12.1).[3] This was a chance for the original participants of *Womanhouse* to defend the project, which they believed had been wrongfully maligned by feminists in the 1980s for its empirical emphasis on women's

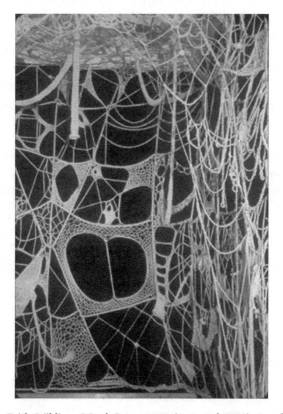

Figure 12.1   Faith Wilding, *Womb Room*, 1972 (recreated 1995). Installation in the exhibition *Division of Labor: "Women's Work" in Contemporary Art* at the Bronx Museum of Arts, 1995. Courtesy of the Bronx Museum of the Arts. Photo: Tony Velez.

known experience. The exhibition's curator restaged this debate by including *Womanhouse*'s psychoanalytic Other, Mary Kelly's *Post-Partum Document*, which had been made in Britain at roughly the same time. Unlike Chicago's model, Kelly's work interrogated models of intentionality by taking up the unconscious drives that made men *and* women complicit with patriarchal structures of representation. The only problem with evoking this debate in a show historicizing the 1970s was that the debate never actually took place at the time either project was made. Rather, it is one that retroactively came to define both that moment's spirit as well as each project's original intention.

Although it is not only interesting but also fruitful to restage feminist debates implicit within feminism's nascent moments (I plan to do just that in this chapter), to naturalize them as explicit positions is problematic because doing so concretizes a modernist notion of a site – that is, a one-to-one relation between a given idea and the physical work representing it. This historical dilemma is not just one of *Womanhouse*'s reception, for this notion of site characterized Chicago's project from the start. In their original press release, participants of *Womanhouse* asserted that their installations represented a pre-existing condition of women's experience, without acknowledging that the project itself came to form and define an image of such "experience," an image with which women could later identify or debate. In this way, as Mark Wigley argues, such sites are always already discursive. To ignore that sites are at once physical and discursive leaves unacknowledged the fact that such projects as *Womanhouse* and *Post-Partum Document*, for instance, only came to debate each other explicitly through discourse at a much later date.

To think of *Womanhouse* this way, as a work constituting a "discursive" site, rather than reflecting a physical one, is useful beyond problematics concerning "site-specific" feminist art.[4] It tells us something about historical context, which is traditionally viewed as the stable "ground" upon which an analysis of a given event or object is situated. But it is imperative that critics and historians listen to what *Womanhouse* (against its will) teaches us about history – that meaning is not only discursive but, in fact, metaleptic. Jonathan Culler has theorized just that: "Context is not given but produced; what belongs to a context is determined by interpretive strategies; contexts are just as much in need of elucidation as events; and the meaning of context is determined by events."[5] Thus, Culler concludes, context is just more text, and the manner in which it is produced in the present needs to be understood from the beginning of any analysis.

The inability to locate an "authentic" context for a given project is not to say that we throw our hands up in the air out of frustration. It acknowledges the futility of such context-driven hermeneutic strategies, for they will only lead one into a fruitless infinite regress. As Norman Bryson argues:

> The context-idea invites us to step back from uncertainties of text to "context" posited as platform or foundation. But once this step is taken it is by no means clear why it may not be taken again; that is, "context" entails from its first moment a regression without breaks.[6]

Better, then, to make the very framing of one's analysis actively a part of said analysis. This involves accounting for how debates surrounding contemporary feminist polemics, through which we study various 1970s art projects, come retroactively to define them. This is precisely the manner in which a return to the subject of 1970s and 1980s feminist theory and art practice should be made, and the means by which we can assess the formative role played specifically by such institutions as The New Museum of Contemporary Art, New York in sustaining that discursive site. At this moment, however, many artists and intellectuals are returning to the topic of 1970s and 1980s feminist art production without acknowledging the text/context dilemma and thus teleologically restaging current feminist polemics as part and parcel of a revisionist historicism.

Most notable on this account are recent writings by Mira Schor, an artist who attended CalArts' Feminist Program under Chicago's direction. Schor's writings are led by a "sadness" that people today resist "reconciliation and synthesis [of the] split between theoretical positions of the essentialism/social construction debate."[7] What gets lost in this sadness, however, is the recognition that a debate over representations of gender that engages theories of essentialism (Chicago's model) versus constructionism (Kelly's model) is a second generation of feminists working in the 1980s who were heirs to these models, devised (separately) by such artists and theoreticians in the 1970s. Moreover, while it is true that debates over constructionism versus essentialism are being waged again today as they were in the 1980s, their discursive formation – which is to say, the terms of their debate, their very pulse – are radically different now. What really drives such historicist models (as Schor's in particular) is the dissatisfaction that one type of feminist art practice (psychoanalytically informed semiotic work) seemingly trumped another (an expressive, oppositional model) in New York City during the 1980s. It is exactly this moment – or rather, discursive site – to which I will now return. Or perhaps, better put, this is the site that has recently returned to us.

Two Theoretical Trajectories

In the early 1980s, within a year of each other, two feminist exhibitions were mounted by The New Museum in New York. One was *Events: En Foco/Heresies* (June 1983), the other was *Difference: On Representation and Sexuality* (December 1984). The first exhibition, as the name implies, was associated with *Heresies,* a New York-based feminist collective/magazine, founded in 1976, which was founded as a consciousness-raising platform for women artists primarily concerned with cultural issues surrounding gender. The second exhibition was associated with *Screen,* founded in 1969 as "the British journal of the Society for Education in Film and Television." Initially, *Screen* had a pedagogical function: to provide filmmakers with lists of books-in-print, available 16-millimeter films, relevant courses, exhibitions, and so forth. During the 1970s, however, *Screen* underwent several theoretical evolutions, whereby Marxist and feminist considerations of ideology, semiotics, and psychoanalysis were discussed through the lens of film practice and later art practice.[8]

Within these two exhibitions, *Difference* and *En Foco/Heresies,* lies what appears to be the hypostatization of a regional divide in feminist theory and art practice in the 1980s. When looked at more closely, however, it is actually the culmination of a discursive divide characteristic of feminist theory during the previous decade. In the 1970s, American feminists (largely New York-based artists) associated with magazines such as *Heresies,* took as their theoretical model the combined writings of feminists Simone de Beauvoir (*The Second Sex*), Kate Millett (*Sexual Politics*), and Shulamith Firestone (*The Dialectic of Sex: The Case for Feminist Revolution*) in a fight for gender parity on the job and at home.[9] At the same time, the *Screen* model (attracting artists and film-makers in Britain) took up psychoanalytic writings by feminists Juliet Mitchell (*Psychoanalysis and Feminism*), Laura Mulvey ("Visual Pleasure and Narrative Cinema"), and Julia Kristeva ("The System and the Speaking Subject") in an analysis of women's representation in the visual field.[10]

Like many other critics and art historians subsequently, Schor misrecognizes the heterogeneity of 1970s feminist art practice when she periodizes "academic," "text-based," and "text-driven" feminism following the works of Jacques Lacan, Michel Foucault, Roland Barthes, and Jean Baudrillard (again associated with *Screen* in the 1970s) as a 1980s backlash against the American model.[11] Her confusion arises from the fact that American feminist artists and writers working in New York were introduced to the British model in the early 1980s, in large part through The New Museum's publications. I am speaking not only of the *Difference* exhibition catalogue, but also of the New Museum's 1984 anthology *Art After Modernism: Rethinking Representation*, which translated and introduced relevant historical texts by Barthes, and others, including the republication of such feminist texts as Mulvey's "Visual Pleasure" essay, first published in *Screen* in 1975.[12] We can now see how The New Museum's discursive project has retroactively come to define its "original" physical site founded in the 1970s, a metalepsis we can and must expect. However, if we do not recognize the operations of this metalepsis, we naturalize the manner in which the reception of 1970s art and theory has been conflated with its production. From there, we get Schor's dialectic: first American cultural feminism, followed by British text-driven model. But there is a more interesting story at hand, one that begs us to consider the following questions: how did two art practices associated with two theoretical models indirectly define themselves in relation to questions of sexuality and representation in the 1970s? And: what were the conditions that their legacies finally met and directly engaged during the 1980s? Moreover, what role did The New Museum play in facilitating this rendezvous?

Let's digress here, and look at the intellectual development of the American feminist position (the story) leading up to the founding of The New Museum in 1977 and later the *Difference* and *Heresies* exhibitions in 1984.

On March 19, 1970 the *Village Voice* published an article by Muriel Castanis entitled "Behind Every Artist There's a Penis," addressing the historic question Linda Nochlin would ask a year later in *Art News*: "Why are There No Great Women Artists?" Nochlin noted that women artists in the nineteenth century had no access to such pedagogical norms as nude models, outside encouragement, educational facilities, and intellectual circles. Extending the premise of Betty Friedan's *Feminine Mystique* (1963) to an analysis of art production, Nochlin concluded that women artists were trained to excel in the artifice of femininity, not professional art careers. How then did artists like Mary Cassatt or Berthe Morisot get around this in the nineteenth century? They had male mentors. In the same vein, Castanis's article considered the masculinization of women once they gained access to art education in post-war American universities. Moreover, male work, she argued became more phallic as it reacted to female presence:

> Their reaction is reaching desperate proportions, what about sculpture, where they can step away from the wall and really grab hold of a lot more space? The controlling aspect of plaster-casting life in a frieze or of massive cubes balanced effortlessly on their corner, huge steel pipes positioned like tinker toys or sewn with steel thread, the hardness of steel, the lightness of lead, the largeness of Brillo Boxes, the softness of a telephone – veritable giants in mother's kitchen. And let's not leave out the wrapping up of a whole skyscraper or even a mountain. Recently we are being led into the backyard to appreciate the mile-long hole big junior has dug in the earth.[13]

As to whether there is a female counter-voice, Castanis dialectically affirms: "When we see sexism (like racism) take over, we know there must be a female voice by negation." In an art market dominated by masculine "brutal confrontation," the solution was therefore an expressionist, humanist one: "Art must be the expression of the total human world, and only an art fed by male and female views interacting can be vital." As a revolutionary coda, she adds the following imperative: "The time is now and is overdue."[14]

This was the discursive background, against which Lynda Benglis would assert: "I don't have penis envy," an anti-Freudian utterance that paradoxically informed her infamous 1974 advertisement in *Artforum*: a nude photograph of the artist sporting sunglasses and an enormous dildo held at her crotch (Figure 12.2).[15] Yet the same year that Benglis took out her advertisement, Juliet Mitchell published *Psychoanalysis and Feminism*, a book that mounted a critique of American feminists' rejection of Freud. Mitchell's contention dealt with their overall denial of the unconscious. She argued that such a denial serves to overdetermine social realism at the expense of the subject's desire and fantasies – the latter of which is the cause for the subject's "knowable" social existence or gender identification. As Mitchell's text was absolutely central to subsequent psychoanalytic developments within British feminism (standing as a counterpoint to the American model), it is necessary to go over her approach at length.

It should be underscored that Mitchell's psychoanalytic reading of the subject was devised as a political model, though importantly it was not

Figure 12.2   Advertisement by Paula Cooper Gallery in *Artforum* 13 (November 1974): copyrighted "centerfold" of artist Lynda Benglis. © DACS, LondonVAGA, New York, 2005.

separatist, drawing as it did on her earlier socialist reading of women's oppression. In her essay, "Women: The Longest Revolution" (1966),[16] Mitchell tried to understand women's sexuality through Engels' claim that women's condition derived from the economy and Marx's symbolic equation of it to society. Without the concepts and terminology afforded by Freud's reading of the women's condition, however, Mitchell's Marxist reading hit an impasse. Just what was Marx naturalizing when talking about "women's experience"? Mitchell would subsequently ask through Freud. If we know that our conscious gender identification is not innate, but constructed, how psychoanalytically speaking does the subject come to build it, and on behalf of what hegemonic structure are such constructions built? Through Freud's analysis of the subject's unconscious motivations ("what does the woman want?"), we could thus come to understand, and possibly get to, the conscious, oppressive motivations that construct a patriarchal society.

From this standpoint, a turn to the unconscious was not a bourgeois flight of fancy into the unknown. For, as Mitchell stressed, Freud's notion of the unconscious is not a "deep, mysterious place, whose presence, in mystical fashion, accounts for all the unknown." On the contrary, the thoughts contained by the unconscious are "knowable and normal," though the (patriarchal) laws of repression transform them. The purpose of psychoanalysis (extended by Mitchell as a political, feminist imperative) is to decipher the operation of these laws, which are recognizable and readable. The importance of the unconscious for Mitchell's feminist practice, then, was the manner in which it exposed sexuality – femininity specifically – as that which is "lived in the mind."[17]

American feminist writers, such as Friedan, Millett, and Firestone, were also addressing a women's sexuality at the time, but their investigations were polemically waged against psychoanalysis in general and Freud's presumed sexism in particular. Subsequently, Freudian tropes, such as "anatomy is destiny" and "penis envy," were widely circulated and attacked in a populist context. Mitchell argued that this was a debased form of psychoanalysis, one that merely recapitulates the very hegemonic structure of patriarchal ideologies that feminism seeks to undo.

Diametrically opposed to such feminists critiques, Mitchell found just the opposite of sexism in Freud's texts. What compelled her most was his assertion that an individual's acquisition of human culture was less voluntary and more internally duplicitous. Mitchell explains this internal duplicity via the bisexuality of the drives:

> Each little baby can't repeat the whole meaning of human history, it has to be acquired very, very rapidly. That infant has to find its place within the human order. And while that place is a feminine or masculine one, it's never absolutely so. That's the psychological concept of bisexuality, which I do think is true. Bisexuality, not in the popular sense of object-choice, loving either a man or a woman, but in the sense that one has the possibility of the other sex within one's self, always. One's social orientation is always to the repression of the psychological characteristics of the sex that one, anatomically, is not.[18]

The popular American notion of bisexuality, based upon the subject's conscious dual object choice, with its concomitant counter-cultural polymorphous perversity, was of little interest to Mitchell on its own. Indeed, *Psychoanalysis and Feminism* interrogated the revolutionary potential of such nonconformity or "libertine" practices, popularized by the radical psychology of Wilhelm Reich and R. D. Laing, both of whom were popular among Americans in the 1960s and 1970s for their repudiation of Freud.[19] As they advocated a kind of separatism, Mitchell argued, such models offered little analysis of the existing ideological structures unconsciously taken up by the subject. A psychoanalytically informed feminist practice, on the other hand, looked for the material base for these internalized attitudes.

According to Mitchell, the material base for such attitudes, however, is not exclusively located within a knowable, empirically defined "masculinist" structure. A psychoanalytically informed feminist practice, therefore, would engage in a textual analysis of the site in which these attitudes are unconsciously reiterated. Also directly related to our topic at hand is Mitchell's interrogation of the conventional feminist response to Freud's passage on penis envy. She begins by citing Freud's most "offensive" statement:

> So far there has been no question of the Oedipus complex, nor has it up to this point played any part. But now the girl's libido slips into a new position along the line – there is no other way of putting it – of the equation "penis-child." She gives up her wish for a penis and puts in place of it a wish for a child: and with that purpose in view she takes her father as a love-object. Her mother becomes the object of her jealousy. The girl has turned into a little woman.[20]

Mitchell proceeds with an explication of the unconscious in this passage.

The unconscious, of course, revolves around the fact that the little girl wants a penis. Since this desire is incompatible with convention, she represses it into the unconscious. On occasion the desire will resurface, transformed in the guise of a symptom, ultimately sublimated into the desire for a child, which is perfectly compatible with convention. The woman's wish – bifurcated into unconscious (penis) and conscious (baby) – thus establishes her subjectivity as a divided one. The obstacle for most feminists in this passage, however, is the original "wish" for a penis. Yet, this reified wish can only be posited at the expense of the unconscious. That is to say, the subject's "conscious decisions and perceptions" replace the "mechanism of unconscious life." In doing so, the psychoanalytic principle of "penis envy" is transformed into the conscious wish for a penis. According to Mitchell, this move re-enacts (rather than analyzes) the subject's unconscious repression of fantasy and desire in favor of the subject's knowable experience, thus replacing the unconscious into the mysterious realm of the "unknowable." Such a move, she argues, only naturalizes conventional femininity because it leaves the original repression mechanism that defines normative sexuality un-interrogated.

Should such a social-realist model of knowledge be privileged, Mitchell argues, the subject is only re-sutured into an indivisible, discrete unit – the "woman," as it were, under patriarchal law. To substantiate this claim, Mitchell cites Millett's response in *Sexual Politics* to the same passage by Freud:

> What forces in her experience, her society and socialization have let [a woman] to see herself as an inferior being? The answer would seem to lie

in the conditions of patriarchal society and the inferior position of woman within this society. But Freud did not choose to pursue such a line of reasoning, preferring instead an etiology of childhood experience based upon the biological fact of anatomical difference...it is supremely unfortunate that Freud should prefer to bypass the more likely social hypothesis to concentrate upon the distortions of infantile sexuality.[21]

Not only was such consideration of the unconscious anathema to Millett's understanding of a woman's "real" experience, she later asserts that Freud's invention of the unconscious was meant to deny a woman's life experience outright.

If Millett thus saw Freud as a quintessential misogynist, incapable of acknowledging the real-life experience of women (rape not castration constituting such experience), Mitchell in turn points out the inability of Millett's social realism to account for the primacy of the subject's unconscious "experience." For Millett, desire exists in the conscious world alone, arguing, as she does, that a girl envies not the penis but what the penis can give her in a world dominated by "the male superior status." What is completely denied, Mitchell argues in turn, is the psychic origin of such structures as "male superiority." From Mitchell's perspective, then, Millett's child is born "directly into the reality principle," bypassing the moment of infantile sexuality, Oedipal development, and subsequent gender identification. For feminists like Millett, Mitchell would argue, Freud's starting point – the subject's "reality" – is the end point.

British feminists following Freud thus saw the development of the subject's sexuality as originating with the repression of unacceptable impulses within the Oedipus complex, while American feminists saw the "reality" of incest (a repressed fantasy for Freud) as formative of the subject's sexuality. Put simply, Millett wanted to recognize the reality principle as formative of a woman's sexuality, whereas Mitchell wanted to put such a reality principle itself under analysis as a means of finding the material, ideological basis of the structures that form such a sexuality. The effects of these two opposed theoretical positions would be far-reaching in feminist art production throughout the 1970s, coming directly together as a polemic in the mid-1980s, as I have noted. I will return to the British model via The New Museum's *Difference* exhibition shortly. First, we should look at the effects of the American model, one that in part contributed to Marcia Tucker's founding The New Museum.[22]

Gender Parity and the Institution

Although American feminists may have over-determined the subject's "reality" factor at the expense of analyzing the unconscious roots of such reality, their demand for parity of representation was, nevertheless, instrumental in challenging the administrative hierarchies of such major museums as the Museum of Modern Art (MoMA) and the Whitney Museum of American Art. In fact, one could argue that the proliferation of alternative spaces and galleries in the 1980s, centered on politics of difference (in terms of class, race, and gender), was in part a result of this early feminist demand for parity. Of note are New York spaces developed in the late 1970s and early 1980s – spaces such as the Clocktower, PS.1, Artist's Space, Fashion Moda, Longwood Arts Gallery, ABC No Rio, and the Alternative Museum – where women and artists of color were provided a forum to develop their practice at the margins of the mainstream gallery system.[23] These alternative spaces exhibited a hybrid of concerns surrounding parity and representation, reminding us that feminist challenges to the museum were initially conceived within broader coalitions centered on general socialist challenges to cultural institutions.

In 1970, the same year that Castanis sarcastically argued that "behind every artist is a penis," a collective called Women Artists in Revolution (WAR) demanded accountability for the discrepancy between the fact that while 65 percent of art students were women only 3 percent of them were represented by New York galleries.[24] WAR was founded in 1969 as an offshoot of the Art Workers' Coalition (AWC), both of which argued for the democratization of art production and exhibition.[25] In June 1969 WAR and AWC jointly made the following demands of MoMA: free admission, racial and gender parity in the exhibition schedule, decentralization of the institution to include outreach to "black, Spanish, and all other communities," a public registry of all artists, an emphasis upon supporting non-represented artists, as well as the artists' disposition over the destiny of their work, including rental and resale charges. On September 28, 1970, Brenda Miller and Poppy Johnson added to the AWC's agenda the demand that in future 50 percent of the artists in the Whitney Annuals should be women. The demand for gender parity exposed an internal contradiction within the group – the desire for open Whitney shows (regardless of gender) being more preferable to some of the men. Jon Henricks, of Guerilla Art Action Group, ultimately saved the motion from foundering.[26]

That fall, an Ad Hoc Committee was formed to wage a letter-writing campaign, spearheaded by Johnson, Miller, Lucy Lippard, and Faith Ringgold. A central issue was how to afford museum access to women artists denied by the canon:

> How many one-man exhibitions of men's work have been held at the Whitney since the new building opened, and what is the percentage of those to the four full-fledged and two one-room women's exhibitions of which you are so proud? With all respect to Louise Nevelson's achievements, the fact that two of the four large shows have been hers indicates the Whitney's narrow outlook on women's work in general...we consider this a "lousy" record. As you say, the curatorial staff is new and can't be blamed for anything but the last few years. Unfortunately, your Director has been at the Whitney for some 20 years.[27]

Recalling Castanis's complaints, initially there was an attempt to connect gender parity with a gendered aesthetics. In a previous letter to MoMA, the committee had emphasized that those women achieving access to the institution (artists such as Nevelson, Frankenthaler, or O'Keeffe, whom the Whitney touted) had been corrupted, or masculinized, by the structure in which they were assimilated:

> The central point of the WAR committee was that discrimination versus women – including women artists – is so general, profound, and long-standing that it can be reversed only by a positive and conscious reconstruction program, which will seek in frankly experimental ways to discover and establish truer feminine values, and thus a genuinely feminine aesthetic. Women artists should not be judged solely on presently available criteria (intellectual or intuitive), since these criteria are the product of the dominant male culture.[28]

The feminist art movement in New York City in the early 1970s was based on the belief that total gender parity in the museums' economy of exhibitions, coupled with a feminized aesthetic criterion, should be achieved by means of an oppositional women's practice. Its founders contended that this would revolutionize the existing "masculinist," hegemonic museum structures.

Such was the spirit in which the Ad Hoc Committee founded the Women's Art Registry in 1970, which at that time contained slides of more than 600 women artists. Developed by Lucy Lippard, the registry served as a network in which women artists – under-represented by the

gallery/museum system – could encounter each other's work and strategize alternative practices and exhibitions. Though New York-based, the
registry bridged the east/west coast divide, such that artists in New York
would have access to projects like *Womanhouse* in addition to related
projects associated with the Women's Building in Los Angeles, described
by its founders as "a new art community built from the lives, feelings, and
needs of women."[29] In this same oppositional spirit, a collective of women
artists, including Howardina Pindell, Nancy Spero, Mary Beth Edelson,
and Ana Mendieta, founded the New York Artists in Residence Gallery
(AIR) in 1972, an alternative space run by the collective in order to show
the work of its members. The collective's first press release defined its
intended (professional) demographic: women artists in their early 30s
who "have been working for a number of years, some in total isolation,
others exhibiting extensively." According to Corinne Robins, the dominant
aesthetic of AIR's opening exhibition (September 17, 1972) drew upon the
"eccentric, non-fine-art materials" of Eva Hesse and Louise Bourgeois,
with an added emphasis on "domestic materials and erotic and autobiographical content," something perceived by the group as missing in mainstream work of the time.[30]

Although a common aesthetic was indeed apparent, AIR's collective
focus rapidly shifted to the professionalization of women artists, at the
expense of promoting a particular theoretical, political, or aesthetic investigation. Barbara Zucker, one of the group's founders, makes this clear in
her account of AIR's evolution:

> The thing that differentiated AIR from other women's collectives at that
> moment is that it was never intended to be a support group. It was a
> professional organization.... Though not all of us would acknowledge
> standing behind the work of each of the twenty original members ... there
> was enough respect and commitment to enable us to work together. We
> wanted to demonstrate that there were at least twenty women artists
> producing innovative, professional work in 1971.[31]

Nevertheless, the artwork produced and exhibited by the collective had
in common the general look of "non-traditional" artwork (decorative,
autobiographic, intimate-scale), as the collective believed such an aesthetic would "change attitudes about art by women ... [showing that
women's work] is as innovative, transitory, or unsaleable as the *artists'*
conceptions demand."[32] Autonomy of the artists' aesthetic and professional intentions was thus the group's emphasis, as was the intervention

of such intentions into the mainstream art world, a sensibility that AIR shared with such groups as WAR.

Referring to the Women's Art Registry, Lippard has similarly asserted that its contribution to the movement empowered women's sense of being gendered, working artists. In 1974, defending the registry against challenges that "quality" was overlooked in the selections, Lippard sarcastically argued back: "Men have always shown bad art. Until recently, most of the bad art has been made by men. We should have less privilege?" Parity was parity, good and bad art alike. The fight here was clearly on the side of the woman-as-practitioner. At the same time, Lippard with others emphasized the aesthetic discourse of "cultural" feminism, a sensibility Lippard took to even though she had been drawn to socialist feminism during her stay in London in 1977–8. In 1993 she reflected upon this time, recalling that although British socialist feminists developed theories on women and class "far in advance of theory and praxis in the American art world," she had nevertheless become "obsessed" with cultural feminism's interest in "great prehistoric stone and earth monuments on Dartmoor, at Avebury and elsewhere" that allegorically spoke to women's roots in both nature and culture. Many cultural feminists viewed socialists feminists as "male-identified, unfeeling intellectuals bound to an impersonal and finally anti-female, economic overview," while socialist feminists saw cultural feminists as "a woozy crowd of women in sheets taking refuge in matriarchal 'herstory,'... reactionary, escapist and possibly fascist in its suggestions of biological superiority." Lippard's position amongst and between these two camps speaks to the contentious diversity of early feminist rhetoric.[33] But given their contrasting yet entangled emphasis on the aesthetic and economic factors that distinguished these two approaches, both camps sought a type of materialist parity.

While the emphasis on professional empowerment indicative of American cultural feminism was undeniably momentous (witness the subsequent alternative spaces engendered by the collaborative efforts of WAR and AWC), we would, however, be remiss to overlook the manner in which this discourse's tone has encoded other like-minded, revolutionary movements long before Lippard's own conflicted identification. Specifically, the tone of cultural feminism's rhetoric recalled some key traits of what early twentieth-century Marxist theoreticians called Zhdanovism, the theoretical backbone for socialist realist art in the Soviet Union from 1922 to 1953. Based on an economic determinist understanding of the relations of material base to cultural superstructure, Zhdanovism proposed the direct superstructural reflection of society such that the art of the bourgeoisie would only ever reflect bourgeois economic decadence. The art of a socialist society would therefore mirror revolution in the form of proletarian art. A post-Leninist position, Zhdanovism held three main principles: (1) the return to a prior glory oppressed by the dominant power structure; (2) the rejection of theoretical complexity in favor of populist narrativity and realism; and (3) a rejection of dissenting models challenging the first two principles. In 1934 Andrei Zhdanov characterized the crisis of representation under capitalism this way: "The decadence and disintegration of bourgeois literature results from the collapse and decay of the capitalist system. Now everything is degenerating – themes, talents, authors, and heroes."[34]

The tone and logic of Zhdanov's statement parallel the feminist rhetoric associated with both AIR and *Heresies* in the mid-1970s, should we substitute the word "bourgeois" with "patriarchal," "capitalist" with "masculinist," and "heroes" with "goddess." Certainly it recalls the motivation behind *Womanhouse*, in which "women took on power, metaphorically confronting the symbolic penis with the symbolic vagina."[35] The desire for a mythic, oppositional return also mirrored a dominant faction (though certainly not all) of the *Heresies* collective. In particular, issues such as "The Great Goddess" (spring 1978) were best-sellers on this account, described by Carrie Rickey as "a veritable multi-cultural textbook in its discussions of the many paths of female spirituality." Temples from Anatolia to Chartres were framed in terms of the Goddess debate, as were Navajo rug-making, ancient Anasazi structures in Chaco Canyon, not to mention earthworks by Mary Miss, Nancy Holt, and Alice Aycock.[36]

Implicitly, this attitude also recalled Georg Lukács's position on revolutionary aesthetics. Lukács believed that "modernist theories of popular art, strongly influenced by avant-garde ideas" had "pushed the sturdy realism of folk art very much into the background."[37] Lukács ultimately desired a space of production outside capitalism and its concomitant modernist theories, as a means of returning to a pure pre-capitalist moment. In much the same manner, feminists such as those in the "Great Goddess" *Heresies* collective seemed to desire a space outside patriarchy and its concomitant avant-garde strategies of minimalism and conceptualism, as well as burgeoning theories of postmodern psychoanalysis. This was seen as a means of returning to a homogeneous, utopic female space, outside 1970s masculinist practice and antecedent to a theoretical 1980s model.

It is important to note that American feminists in the 1970s were not unanimously engaged in the promotion of a utopic female space or practice. At the same moment, a different model maintaining an interventionist relation to the museum (rather than an oppositionalist one) was initiated by Mierle Laderman Ukeles' performances "Maintenance Art Activity" and "Transfer: The Maintenance of the Art Object," both from 1973 (Figure 12.3). Informed by her maintenance "manifesto" from 1969, the performances utilized the aesthetic strategies and rhetoric of the avant-garde in order to wage a feminist problematic within it. Contemporaneous with Marcel Broodthaer's mock Museum of Modern Art (which exposed the falsely "naturalized" curatorial hand of museum exhibitions) or Mel Bochner, Michael Asher, and Daniel Buren's respective projects (which exposed the falsely conceived "neutral" physical framework of the museum exhibition), Laderman Ukeles' performances exposed the purposefully hidden labor force that maintained the cleanliness of any and all museum exhibitions. Here, gendered labor (which metonymically signifies domesticity) entered the exhibition space, not as a separatist representation, but as a performative signifier of what is excised from our perception of any given space, be it at home or the public institution.[38]

Such strategies would later come to fruition in the works of Andrea Fraser, whose work in the mid- to late 1980s similarly took up gender in the space of institutional critique, though her mock docent performances, specifically *Museum Highlights* (1989), extended this critique to include psychoanalytic considerations. A central contribution of this project was Fraser's interrogation of the public's psychic identification with cultural institutions, something she came to consider through exposure to Mary Kelly's *Post-Partum Document*.[39] The issue of gender in the public space of the museum, initiated by Laderman Ukeles and continued by Fraser, may have been one that incorporated the strategies of the avant-garde in a deconstructive move. Nevertheless, the motivating politic was congruent with the initial activities of AWC and WAR.

As for the outcome of WAR's activism, the committee's demands were never met in the case of either MoMA or the Whitney (the letter campaigns eventually turned to guerilla actions). Notable, however, in the correspondence that circulated between WAR and the Whitney was the inclusion of Marcia Tucker's name – one of four curators targeted by the group. After being fired from the Whitney in 1976, Tucker founded The New Museum, an institution informed by the agendas of the women's movement, the history of civil rights, and the anti-Vietnam

Figure 12.3 Mierle Laderman Ukeles, *Hartford Wash: Washing, Tracks, Mainten-ance: Outside*, 1973; performance at Wadsworth Atheneum, Hartford, CT. Part of *Maintenance Art Performance Series*, 1973–4. Courtesy Ronald Feldman Fine Arts, New York.

War movement.[40] It was also the site in which the aforementioned feminist models – British and American – with their concomitant semiotic, oppositionist, and interventionist theories, would directly enter into debate, as was The New Museum's founding intention.

Aesthetic Models and Institutional Spaces: The New Museum

> To me, a museum of contemporary art should be a place where dialogue and controversy are synonymous. There is a posture of inquiry that certain artists have that can be shared by museums. (Marcia Tucker)[41]

Starting out in 1977 as two small rooms in the Fine Arts Building at 105 Hudson Street, The New Museum was intended to fill the gap between "challenging contemporary" and "non-commercial forums." What made it a museum and not an alternative space, such as AIR, was not only its structure – it had a 501-3C (not-for-profit status), a Director (Tucker), a staff, and a board of trustees – but its commitment to scholarship around contemporary art. On the other hand, what made it different from mainstream museums was its commitment to being an "exhibition, information, and documentation center for contemporary art made within a period of ten years prior to the present." It was also unique at the time for focusing on living, practicing artists "which until [then] could not readily be seen outside the studio."[42]

The effect of AWC's activism is obvious here. Omitted, however, was the group's imperative for gender parity in museum staff and exhibitions. Rather than the advocacy of a unified feminist art, space, or exhibition thematic, The New Museum took up the problematic waged by feminism. This is an important distinction, because it allowed for different theoretical models of social change to debate each other. Tucker had been involved in feminist activity while she was the target of WAR's campaigns. In 1968 she was already a member of Redstockings, one of the early groups associated with the Women's Liberation Movement that waged public demonstrations of the kind associated with the New Left. Nevertheless, the feminist perspective that informed her museum project was more deconstructive and theoretical, employing as it did a feminist problematic rather than a feminist model. A "feminist problematic" intervenes into hegemonic structures, be they institutions or discourses, but without propagating a stable solution. If feminism is a problematic, rather than a style or politic, then any notion of a "feminist art" is something that should be problematized. Mary Kelly, who in 1977 articulated the difference between feminism as a problematic and feminism as a style, has put it this way: "Perhaps we should not maintain this formulation 'feminist art,' because an ideology does not constitute a style. Rather I would say 'art informed by feminism.' "[43] We can extend this question of a "feminist art" to consider the notion of a "feminist space" in terms of our discussion of The New Museum's founding project and Tucker's role in structuring it differently from such separatist feminist exhibition spaces as AIR.

Although The New Museum was in fact conceived in terms of feminist demands to restructure the museum, the challenge for Tucker was to take this up as an insider practice of dismantling museological authority. Tucker recalls that this distinguished The New Museum from other alternative spaces. In the early 1970s people had focused "more on the way things [were] done on the outside," such as the number of women included in exhibitions. "In museum culture," she asserted, "feminism never penetrated the actual *structure* of the organization."[44] This would be The New Museum's project, to the extent that exhibitions were conceived both as a theoretical challenge to normative art culture as well as administratively enacted as a "team" effort among the staff. As such, administratively and theoretically, the museum attempted to exist as a "social space" rather than a private one.[45] The initial result was a series of contradicting temporary exhibitions, each of which was accompanied by a catalogue of essays on the show's topic, written by the curators and invited contributors. As an "investigative" rather than a "didactic" space (the latter of which Tucker saw as promoting an authoritative attitude of expertise), the idea was to "have enough variety in... perspectives to be able to deal with different audiences at different times in different ways."[46] At the start, then, the space was devised to formulate different discursive practices, rather than being ideologically fixed to a given aesthetic or permanently monumental as an institution itself.

It took a while, however, for this discursive gesture to meet with a rigorous intellectual project, the first shows being unremarkable in their critical vision and scholarship. For instance, the inaugural exhibition, *Memory*, was generalist and pop-psychological in tone: "memory... is common to us all and is our primary means of understanding ourselves and sharing our lives with others."[47] The second, *New Work/New York*, an exhibition with no unifying theme, featured unknown artists, "highly individualistic and resistant to interpretation in terms of prevalent aesthetic or formal issues."[48] A performative shift occurred with *Bad Painting*, which Tucker defined as "figurative works that defied the classic canons of good taste, draftsmanship, acceptable source material."[49] The exhibition's anti-Greenbergian rhetoric was not its most engaging aspect. More interesting was the manner in which statements by contributing artists resisting the term "bad" actually demonstrated – via the contingencies of artistic desire and canonical identification – the residual problematics of Greenberg's claims for the categories of kitsch and the avant-garde. Specifically, it exposed the manner in which Greenberg's dichotomy was still (unconsciously) operative: Tucker striving to herald "kitsch" against the "avant-garde," the artists' maintaining notions of "quality" in their work against such claims.[50] It was precisely this combination (a theoretical investigation, an historical aesthetic debate, and the active engagement of artists in the form of participation and/or critique) that would come to characterize The New Museum's more mature exhibitions throughout the 1980s at its new space in the Astor Building at 583 Broadway.[51] I shall concentrate here on two such shows – *Events: En Foco/Heresies Collective* and *Difference: On Representation and Sexuality* – through which the two feminist approaches I have discussed in this chapter debated feminist art practice vis-à-vis what came to be known as "essentialist" vs. "constructionist" strategies.[52]

In June 1983, the *Heresies* collective mounted an exhibition, which they described as a "visual version" of an upcoming issue of the magazine entitled "Mothers, Mags and Movie Stars: Feminism and Class."[53] Lucy Lippard wrote a portion of the group's statement of purpose:

> "Mothers, Mags and Movie Stars"... [was] a way of getting to know each other better and discussing politics and aesthetics more directly, outside of our usual business-meeting format. For several months we discussed our own relationship to our mothers in terms of feminism and class. As we unraveled our histories and those of our families, trying to name and analyze our class backgrounds and foregrounds, we found that no one's family had stayed in one class, that there were endless subtleties, that very little of sense and use has been written on the subject. Our meetings took on the double aspect of sewing circle and study group. Most of our anecdotes centered on images, clothes, objects, and spaces.[54]

At the fore of the project was not the operation of a bodily essentialism, as had come to be associated with the vaginal works of such artists as Judy Chicago. Yet, something else was nevertheless essentialized: the conscious condition of social relations between men and women, an idea that in part echoed the writings of Guy Debord, translated to consider issues of femininity. This was clear in the rhetorical tone of the subsequent magazine version of the show. Lucy Lippard's concern with a fragmented feminine subjectivity along class lines was continued by the magazine's editorial statement:

> There are bits and pieces of us all over the place. Cutting up is rebellion. We're formed by an alienated society, parts of which are severed from mothers by a class system that is largely ignored or denied. The cutting edge, the political, is cut off from the personal. Racism cuts us off from other cultures. Cut it out. This is the cut off point. Operation, penetration, incision, intersection, a cutting remark, cut the cards, Reagan's cut backs for our own good, cut a new pattern, not trimmed down to fashionable lines. Lights, action, cut.[55]

Both exhibition and magazine focused upon images of women – in various roles, as mothers, daughters, sisters, etc. – reclaimed from "false" images women encountered in mass culture. Debord's claim had been that "[t]he whole of life... in which modern conditions of production prevail presents itself as an immense accumulation of spectacles," such that "all that was directly lived has become mere representation";[56] similarly, the group claimed that a woman's experience had fallen into the commodified condition of spectacle.

Moreover, if Debord longed for a space of "real-life experience" outside the hegemony of spectacle, the latter defined "not as a collection of images; rather... a social relationship between people that is mediated by images,"[57] so too, the *Heresies* collective sought a space outside patriarchy's spectacle. In such a space, the social relation between men and women would no longer be mediated by demeaning images of women. This was conceived in the guise of an alternative visual culture – one initiating a counter social relation among women mediated by empowering images of women's "true" lived experience. Hence, the "Roomful of Mothers" installation by Sabra Moore: a group of images from 12 women, assembled by Moore, each of which provided a photo of the woman's mother and a handwritten text of their history. The result was "shared stories, describing our families' work histories, the crossings between classes through marriage, political refuge, or education."[58] Other pieces attempted to "deconstruct" the meaning of mother, especially the 1950s stereotype in which women were taken "back into modernized jail cells," that is, to the modernized domestic space in which the mother "ran" the family unit via commodities of efficiency (washing machines, refrigerators, etc.). The Situationists themselves had commented upon the parallel spaces in which personal experience was commodified – domestic and public – but stopped short at the recognition that each space was gendered as feminine or masculine, respectively.

Sally Stein's article, entitled "The Graphic Ordering of Desire" (in the subsequent *Heresies* issue continuing the show's thematic), directly took this up. Stein diagrammed and analyzed the manner in which middle-class women were modernized in women's magazines, specifically the way in which graphic techniques of color, photography, and serial cartoons "were orchestrated in a more dynamic layout to sustain the reader's interest and draw the reader closer to the marketplace." At the heart of Stein's essay was a quasi-Debordian argument, well documented and convincingly articulated, that women's magazines had lulled the reader, through the combination of lengthy literary texts and advertising, into a visual experience that constituted women homemakers as "an audience of spectators and by extension consumers."[59] Accompanying her essay was an elaborate graph system, devised by Stein, that charted the development of women's magazines (such as *Ladies' Home Journal*) to include advertisements for a wifely lifestyle that circulated around recipe catalogues, fashion design, and whatnot, literally demonstrating the graphic order of feminine desire. The theoretical support for Stein's graphic analysis included such essays on reception theory as Robert Venturi, Denise Scott Brown, and Steven Izenour's *Learning from Las Vegas*, and Raymond Williams's *Television: Technology and Cultural Form*.[60]

Stein's article was indeed the most analytic and theoretically informed text in the *Heresies* "Mothers, Mags and Movie Stars" issue. It was also decidedly Situationist in tone, referring as it did to "the sense of fragmented leisure time that characterized women's work in the home," which, of course, readily lent itself to the commodification of her personal experience. It is important to note that the *Heresies* issue, unlike contemporaneous projects associated with CalArts' Feminist Program, delineated a female subjectivity apart from an essentialist, bodily practice. Its intellectual investigation, however – best represented by Stein's article – omitted two things: (1) psychoanalytic theories concerning the role of the unconscious in the development of a woman's subjectivity, and (2) theories of interventionist art practices, characteristic of debates over postmodern aesthetics. Consistent with Kate Millett's theories, the *Heresies* collective offered no psychoanalytic model of practice to explain or strategize the problematic of the spectacularization of a woman's personal experience, nor did they advocate a given visual strategy in combination with their theories. These two elements, however, defined the model offered up by the organizers and participants of the *Difference: On Representation and Sexuality* show, and it was there that the feminist debate between Millett and Mitchell over the unconscious and subjectivity, which I described above, found itself re-enacted in the field of visual art practice.

Guest-curated by Kate Linker and Jane Weinstock, *Difference: On Representation and Sexuality*, which took place in 1984 (and in London at the Institute of Contemporary Arts) was distinguished by the role it accorded theory. Although its line-up of artists was impressive (those who would soon after be known as defining the "New York School": Judith Barry, Dara Birnhaum, Victor Burgin, Hans Haacke, Mary Kelly, Silvia Kolbowski, Barbara Kruger, Sherrie Levine, Martha Rosler, and Jeff Wall), equal focus was given to the accompanying theoretical texts. Linker's curatorial statement from the catalogue made this clear:

> As the title suggests, this exhibition pertains to recent interest in representation and, particularly, in the powers inherent in representation. However, it diverges – differs – in the role it accords theory. The essays collected here indicate the influence on this work of psychoanalytic theory and its account of the development of sexed subjectivity. Central to it are Jacques Lacan's writings on the subject's construction in language. Underlying Lacan's theory is the conviction that the human subject is never a discrete self, that it cannot be known outside the terms of the society and, specifically, of the cultural formations of patriarchy. Implicit in his speculations is awareness of how gender informs, infuses, and complicates a range of social "texts," permeating supposedly neutral fields.

Just as the show's premise was that the sexed subject could not be considered outside his/her construction within language (i.e. patriarchy), neither could the work of art be considered outside theoretizations of its own representation. Practice and theory were thus chiasmatically intertwined much the way women were constructed within patriarchy. As such, *Difference* argued not only that there was no separate space in which women could define their social relations merely amongst each other, neither was there an aesthetic particular to the woman or her experience. For the woman, like aesthetics, is bound up in a larger signifying system, one which Lacan called the "symbolic" and which post-structuralists since the 1960s were intent on deconstructing.

On this account, one of the most important essays in *Difference* was Jacqueline Rose's "Sexuality in the Field of Vision," whose title alone came to define a type of American art discourse centered on a psychoanalytic definition of sexual difference versus a materialist one. A dominant figure in British circles studying psychoanalytic theory in the mid- to late 1970s, Rose was instrumental in the introduction of Lacan's writings to British and American feminists, much the same way Mitchell had made an earlier argument for Freud.[61] For the *Difference* show, Rose extended Lacan's model to the postmodern imperative of "disrupting visual form and questioning sexual certainties and stereotypes of our culture." This connection – the relation between sexuality and the image – was substantiated by Rose's return to Freud's essay on Leonardo da Vinci.[62] Rose asserts: "There can be no work on the image, no challenge to its powers of illusion and address, which does not simultaneously challenge the fact of sexual difference."[63] For Freud, Rose argued, voyeurism, fetishism, and castration are all related to sight. In such terms, the little boy refuses to believe the anatomical difference that he sees, while the girl sees what she does not have and immediately knows she wants it. Rose continued, however, to argue that sexuality relies less on what is consciously seen than it does on the subjectivity of the viewer who sees it – that is to say, what it comes to signify later in a moment of deferred action. Thus, seeing, like subjectivity, is always caught in a state of fracture, its meaning always somewhere other, embodying the dialectics of recognition/misrecognition, pleasure/pain, identification/disgust. The manipulation of images can then be either complicit, reinforcing sexual identity, or disruptive, exposing "the fixed nature of sexual identity as a fantasy."

Rose argued that this Freudian paradigm – one that "unsettled our certainties" – was consistent with a postmodern practice that resisted the certainty in a sign. Roland Barthes's reading of Balzac's *Sarrasine* was seen as a quintessential example of a psychoanalytically informed postmodern practice, as Barthes argued that the character's undecipherable sexuality is the actual source of the pleasure/pain in Balzac's text. Modernism (of the Greenbergian paradigm), on the other hand, emphasized the purity of the visual signifier – a Gestalt akin to the "I" of Lacan's mirror stage. But this "I" is a lie – a primordial misrecognition that is masked by the belief in a pure, unified signifier. Again, the image – like the subject – is split, troubled, decentered, along the division between conscious and unconscious desire.

This connection, between visual production and the psychoanalytic means of theorizing sexuality in the field of the visual, was a major development in feminist art practice. Throughout the 1980s and 1990s, The New Museum would continue mounting exhibitions that incorporated a psychoanalytically informed feminist problematic within postmodern logic. Two shows in particular come to mind. In 1986, *Damaged Goods: Desire and Economy of the Object,* organized by Brian Wallis, afforded Andrea Fraser the opportunity to develop her performative docent tours in the context of work by Judith Barry, Gretchen Bender, Barbara Bloom, Jeff Koons, Justen Ladda, Louise Lawler, Ken Lum, Allan McCollum, and Haim Steinbach. In 1990, The New Museum hosted Mary Kelly's *Interim* exhibition, a show that addressed a number of discourses relevant to the history of feminism – fiction, fashion, medicine, family, media, and social science – at the level of women's psychic identification across generational lines.

Difference, Damaged Goods, and *Interim* accorded with an art practice in which feminist theories incorporated a psychoanalytic approach in order to question the politics of visual practice, rather than promoting a separate sociological or ideological imperative for gendered production. From this position, Rose and others advocated a deconstructive approach (akin to that of Barthes), in place of a feminist corrective, such as gender parity. Postmodern artists utilizing such deconstructive strategies, the argument went, would necessarily draw upon the same critical and artistic tendencies they sought to displace. In this way, a separatist strategy was purposefully averted, allowing "reference" itself (e.g. "woman") in its problematized form to re-enter the frame.[64]

Conclusion: The Historical Left and Second Wave Feminism: Debates on the Unconscious

The debate invoked by the emblematic comparison of the *Difference* and *Events: En Foco/Heresies* exhibitions recalls an older debate among the Left concerning the role of the unconscious in revolutionary politics, specifically the debate between André Breton and Georg Lukács.[65] Breton wrote in accordance with the avant-garde feeling that unbridled imaginative freedom was the ultimate resistance against bourgeois conventionality and rationality – hence the most "liberated." This move toward internalization, of course, was decidedly anti-realist, which he claimed was "inspired by positivism...hostile to any intellectual or moral advancement."[66] Obviously, then, Breton opposed any art group with state affiliation, such as Russia's Proletkult, with the effect that the Communists deemed the Surrealists elitist. Influenced by Freud's dream-work theories, Breton argued for the revolutionary potential not of consciousness-raising, but of consciousness-lowering. This line of thinking would culminate in his book *Communicating Vessels* of 1932, which defended the revolutionary power of a Freudian approach against Marxist claims that it was reactionary and bourgeois. Breton argued that there was a link between conscious and unconscious states, a link that held disruptive, revolutionary potential in terms of challenging deadened bourgeois and communist sensibilities alike. Put simply, Breton's model posited a psychoanalytic concern with dialectics against a materialist one.

Breton's "Second Manifesto" took this up directly, whereupon he responds to two Marxist questions that were asked of him in 1928:

> Do you believe that literary and artistic output is a purely individual phenomenon? Don't you think that it can or must be the reflection of the main currents which determine the economic and social evolution of humanity?
>
> Do you believe in a literature and an art which express the aspirations of the working class? Who in your opinion are the principal representatives of this literature and this art?[67]

Breton answered that the first question, being too positivist, presumes a "sovereignty of thought." The question that should instead be taken up is the relation between the nature of human thought (which is unconscious) and the reality of human thought (which is conscious). Citing Engels, Breton argued, "in this sense human thought is [both] sovereign and is not; and its capacity to know is both limitless and limited." It is the space in between these two states, or rather their inextricable, chiasmatic relation, that art should underscore. To the second question, he answers "no" to a working-class art, as the pre-revolutionary bourgeois cannot accurately translate working-class aspirations.[68] Although Breton argued that Marx was right regarding the social phenomenon, the utopic proletariat as yet had no real kinship and hence no real aesthetic. Instead, the point of entry for a revolutionary art was the space provided by the divided subject – divided between conscious identification (in society) and unconscious drives (internalized, conflicting identifications).

Herein lies the reference for a Lacanian approach, continued by the British School, that was skeptical of a realist, materialist practice – specifically in the form of a separatist, feminist aesthetic. If an emphasis is placed upon establishing an innate aesthetic for a given social group, be it the proletariat historically or feminists recently, class then takes precedence over subjectivity, a move to which Breton, Lacan, and later certain British feminists were all opposed. In fact, the founding editorial statement of *m/f*, a British feminist journal on art and culture, explicitly denied such a privileging of a working-class aesthetic as it applies to feminism:

> A tendency in the application of classic Marxist ideas of class to women can be seen in any political project which claims that it is working-class women alone who will form the vanguard of any feminist politics. Doubly exploited, at work and at home, it is these women who will become conscious of their exploitation and form the vanguard of a transition to socialism. While no one would want to dispute the double pressure on working-class women, it cannot be said either that they are necessarily politically progressive, or that they are the only women who are exploited. The operations of the law, education, and employment discriminate against women of all classes. To ignore these areas is to miscalculate the current situation.

The editors instead advocated a psychoanalytic evaluation of the social structures that place women in positions where they are exploited.[69]

We can consider the feminist debate further in these terms. For it would not reduce the complexity of the feminist debate (as it was played out at The New Museum) to argue that two practices or aesthetic concerns were in part defined by their respective relation to the unconscious, in general, and to theories of penis envy, in specific. For as I have argued, in Freudian terms penis envy is not a conscious desire for an organ, but an unconscious desire for a symbolic (masculine) position of authority. While one model – 1970s American – consciously focused on women's access to institutions of power via the strategy of gender parity, another model – 1970s British – sought to theorize how those institutions constituted a symbolic to which men consciously had access but from which women were psychologically barred because they were sexually marked within it. The *Difference* model thus begged a deconstructive approach, positing as it did that women could not disentangle themselves from the structures of patriarchy, much the way Breton argued that one could not disentangle one's "sovereignty of thought" from those registers of the unconscious that mark it. The *Heresies* model, on the other hand, focused on the establishment of a feminist practice as a counter-institution, initiated by consciousness-raising, and was thus Lukácsian in tone. Ironically, the American model established a precedent for institutions such as The New Museum, which would then consider such "opposing" feminist theorizations of the subject in art, such as those which were defined, in part, by the British model. If we were to search for a point of reconciliation between these two models, as Mira Schor begs us to do, perhaps one can be found in the ironic contingency of their collaboration.

Today, after many shows and articles have continued to argue the theories and practices initiated by the *Difference* and *Heresies* exhibitions, the two models have come to be hybridized. For instance, artists such as Barbara Kruger, whose work takes up Situationist tactics of direct address and public consciousness-raising, have also been theorized around psychoanalytic considerations of feminine sexuality, most prominently the role of the "male gaze" in fetishizing the woman's body as commodity. Similarly, artists such as Mary Kelly have more recently been rehistoricized in light of 1970s practices that addressed the subject of domesticity.[70] While the development of these hybrids are entirely the subject for another paper, I have sought here to underscore the manner in which institutions such as The New Museum were both product and producer of feminist discourses as they evolved over the mid-1970s and '80s. Moreover, it is important to note how earlier Marxist debates over social relations implicitly return to us, modified as they are in the guise of contemporary feminist debates over identity and sexuality. The manner in which The New Museum was designed to facilitate such debates distinguished it from other cultural institutions – promoting as it did discussions about theory and aesthetics rather than the promotion of any given position or practice. As such, in its earliest formation, The New Museum openly showcased the manner in which all institutions constitute a discursive site, though some (i.e. The New Museum) were defined by contentious debate, while others (from MoMA to AIR) constituted a specific discursive position within such debate. Thus, should we wish to return to the theorization of feminist practice in the arts over the course of the 1970s and '80s, one cannot eclipse the importance of museums, alternative spaces, and collectives as discursive monuments through which related historical debates are recalled.

Notes

1 Faith Wilding, "The Feminist Art Programs at Fresno and CalArts, 1970–75," collected in Norma Broude and Mary D. Garrard, eds., *The Power of Feminist Art: The American Movement of the 1970s, History and Impact* (New York: Harry N. Abrams, 1994), p. 39.

2 Arlene Raven, "Womanhouse," in Broude and Garrard, eds., *The Power of Feminist Art*, p. 48.

3 See Lydia Yee et al., *Division of Labor: "Women's Work" in Contemporary Art* (Bronx: The Bronx Museum of the Arts, 1995).

4 I have chosen to discuss *Womanhouse* as a discursive site because the topic of this chapter is feminist art. However, it is important to note that the same argument could be readily made about any work or building. Richard Serra's *Tilted Arc* is a perfect example of this phenomenon, as is Rachel Whiteread's *House*.

5 Jonathan Culler, *Framing the Sign: Criticism and Its Institutions* (Norman: University of Oklahoma Press, 1988).

6 Norman Bryson, "Art in Context," in *Studies in Historical Change* (Charlottesville: University Press of Virginia, 1992), p. 21.

7 Mira Schor, in response to my piece "Why This Return Now," in which I take issue with Schor's account of my participation in "The F-Word: Contemporary Feminisms and the Legacy of the Los Angeles Feminist Art Movement," at CalArts (October 1998). Both pieces are collected in *Documents*, no. 17 (Winter/Spring 2000). For other returns to Chicago's project in the context of this debate, see Amelia Jones, *Sexual Politics* (Los Angeles: Armand Hammer Museum, 1996); and Laura Cottingham, "Interview with Laura Cottingham," collected in *Environ 27 ans, Les Cahiers de la Classe Des Beaux-Arts*, Genève (no. 113, February 1997). For a more critical engagement with the subject, see Emily Apter, "Essentialism's Period," *October 71* (Winter 1995); and Helen Molesworth, "Cleaning up in the 1970s: The work of Judy Chicago, Mary Kelly, and Mierle Laderman Ukeles," in Michael Newman and John Bird, eds., *Re-writing Conceptual Art* (London: Reaktion Books, 1999).

8 Anthony Easthope, "The Trajectory of *Screen* 1971–79," in Francis Barker et al., eds., *The Politics of Theory* (Colchester: University of Essex, 1983), pp. 121–33. The inclusion of art practice/theory debates included papers by T. J. Clark on Manet (*Screen* 21/1 (1980)), Griselda Pollock on Van Gogh and Concepts of Genius (*Screen* 21/3 (1980)), Mary Kelly on Modernist Criticism (*Screen* 22/3 (1981)).

9 Simone de Beauvoir, *The Second Sex* (London: Jonathan Cape, 1960); Kate Millett, *Sexual Politics* (New York: Doubleday, 1970); Shulamith Firestone, *The Dialectic of Sex: The Case for Feminist Revolution* (New York: Morrow, 1970).

10 Juliet Mitchell, *Psychoanalysis and Feminism* (London: Penguin Books, 1974; New York: Vintage Books, 1974); Laura Mulvey, "Visual Pleasure and Narrative Cinema," *Screen* 16/3 (Autumn 1975); Julia Kristeva, "The System and the Speaking Subject," *Times Literary Supplement* (October 12, 1973).

11 Mira Schor, "Backlash and Appropriation," in Broude and Garrard, eds., *The Power of Feminist Art*, p. 255.

12 Brian Wallis, ed., *Art After Modernism: Rethinking Representation* (New York: The New Museum of Contemporary Art, 1984).

13 Muriel Castanis, "Behind Every Artist There's a Penis," *The Village Voice* (March 19, 1970).

14 This would be the referent for more recent discourse by the American writers such as Anna Chave who also focus upon the masculine, industrial connotations of minimalist forms. See in particular Chave's "Minimalism and the Rhetoric of Power," *Arts Magazine* (January 1990). See Rosalind Krauss's "Sense and Sensibility," *Artforum* (November 1973) for the original post-structuralist account of minimalism. For more recent arguments counter to the Chave position, see Hal Foster's "Crux of Minimalism," in *The Return of the Real* (Cambridge, MA: MIT Press, 1995).

15 *Artforum* (November 1974). Ironically, although Benglis's intention was "to mock the idea of having to take sexual sides – to be either a male artist or a female," the literalization of gender roles around the possession of a penis created a controversy among the editors of *Artforum* (who wrote letters of complaint to the magazine) as well as among feminists (who accused Benglis of having penis envy after all). See Susan Krane, *Lynda Benglis: Dual Natures* (Atlanta: High Museum of Art, 1990), p. 42.

16 Juliet Mitchell, "Women: The Longest Revolution," originally published in *New Left Review* 40 (1966), expanded and reprinted in *Women's Estate* (New York: Pantheon, 1971) and collected in *Feminism in Our Times* (New York: Vantage Books, 1994).

17 Carol Morrell, "Interview with Juliet Mitchell," *Spare Rib* 22 (April 1974).

18 Ibid.

19 Laing's theories, in particular, were important to feminist writers such as Eunice Lipton, who cited his work in a liberationist attack on patriarchal ideology and violence. See Lipton's "The Violence of Ideological Distortion: The Imagery of Laundresses in the 19th Century French Culture," *Heresies* 6 (1978). The editors ran this story side by side with Suzanne Lacy's "Evolution of Feminist Art," a survey of feminist artwork based upon the "expanding self" – a "metaphor for the process of moving boundaries of one's identity outward to encompass other women, groups of women and eventually all people." At the base of these arguments was the belief that a return of the repressed – the radical feminine voice – would have liberationist effects. Indeed, in the issue's editorial statement is a diagram of the registers of the

conscious, unconscious, and preconscious, with a screaming woman in the unconscious register, repressed by the "Eye" of (patriarchal) consciousness. This is fundamentally different from Freud's reading of gender and repression, as that which is repressed differs among individuals as a result of their individual formative traumas and subsequent neuroses. Moreover, according to Mitchell's reading of Freud, it is more likely that the other "masculine" drive would unconsciously be repressed by the conscious position of "woman." In a liberationist, separatist community, Mitchell's reading of the unconscious has critical resonance.

20   Juliet Mitchell, *Psychoanalysis and Feminism* (New York: Vintage, 1974), p. 7.
21   Ibid., pp. 352–3.
22   For a more inclusive account of these events, presented anecdotally by someone central to their making, see Lucy Lippard, *The Pink Glass Swan* (New York: The New Press, 1995).
23   A decade later, many of these spaces would be subsumed into the very system they initially interrogated – PS.1's current affiliation with MoMA is most notable on this account.
24   WAR solicitation flyer, February 1970. The year before, the Whitney Annual exhibited 8 women artists among 143 men. They included Sara Saporta, Dolores Homes, Jacqueline Skiles, Juliette Gordon, Silvia Goldsmith, and Jan McDevitt.
25   Similar activist organizations were being formed at the time in Britain. The Artists' Union (aligned with the Trades Union Congress) made similar demands. The Women's Workshop was also formed within it.
26   Anon.,"50% No Joke," *New York Element* (November–December 1970).
27   Letter to Stephen E. Weil, Whitney Administrator from the Ad Hoc Committee of Women (November 9, 1970).
28   Letter to Petsy Jones and John Szarkowski, MoMA staff, from the Ad Hoc Committee of Women (December 1969).
29   Founding statement by Judy Chicago, Sheila de Bretteville, and Arlene Raven, quoted in Faith Wilding, *By Our Own Hands: The Women's Artists' Movement, Southern California, 1970–1976* (Santa Monica: Double X, 1977), p. 83.
30   For a history of AIR's beginnings, see Corinne Robins, "The AIR Gallery: 1972–1978," *Womanart* (Winter 1977–8). Again, mainstream work at this time would be characterized by the minimalist industrial aesthetic of Donald Judd and Robert Morris, or the conceptualist analytic aesthetic of Lawrence Weiner, Sol LeWitt, Mel Bochner, or Joseph Kosuth. AIR's aesthetic, on the other hand, was most likely drawn from Lucy Lippard's *Eccentric Abstraction* (New York: Fischbach Gallery): see *Art International* 10/9 (1966).
31   Barbara Zucker, "Making AIR," *Heresies* 7, 2/3 (Spring 1979).
32   Robins, "The AIR Gallery"; my emphasis.

33 Lippard, *The Pink Glass Swan*, pp. 9-10.

34 Cited in Maynard Solomon, ed., *Marxism and Art: Essays Classic and Contemporary* (New York: Knopf, 1973), p. 237.

35 Norma Broude and Mary D. Garrard, "Conversations with Judy Chicago and Miriam Schapiro," in Broude and Garrard, eds., *The Power of Feminist Art*, p. 78.

36 Carrie Rickey, "Writing (and Righting) Wrongs: Feminist Art Publications," in Broude and Garrard, eds., *The Power of Feminist Art*, p. 128.

37 Georg Lukács, "Realism in the Balance," in *Aesthetics and Politics* (New York: Verso, 1977), p. 55.

38 For more on Mierle Laderman Ukeles' work in this context, see Miwon Kwon, "In Appreciation of Invisible Work," and Helen Molesworth "Work Stoppages," both in *Documents* 10 (Fall 1997).

39 For a script of the performance, see Andrea Fraser, "Museum Highlights: A Gallery Talk," *October 57* (Summer 1991).

40 Unpublished interview by Julie Ault with Marcia Tucker (July 11, 1995).

41 "A Museum in the Village: An Idea Whose Time has Come," *The Villager* (October 20, 1977).

42 Mission statement, ibid.

43 Mary Kelly et al., "A Conversation on Recent Feminist Art Practices," *October 71* (Winter 1995), p. 50.

44 Tucker, unpublished interview; my emphasis.

45 While the approach was intended to be democratic and "self-critical," it is important to note that the ultimate veto power still rested in the hands of the Director. Nevertheless, the tone of the museum – from the beginning and throughout the 1980s – was one of continual internal debate. See statement by Alice Yang, curator from 1988 to 1993 in *Temporarily Possessed: The Semi-Permanent Collection* (New York: The New Museum of Contemporary Art, 1995), p. 152. This administrative model was one that more greatly valued the theorizations of institutional critique by artists (such as Buren, Haacke, Asher, Smithson, and Laderman-Ukeles, etc.) than that of nineteenth-century museum practice (continued by museums such as MoMA, the Whitney, or the Metropolitan).

46 Ault/Tucker interview.

47 Marcia Tucker, *Memory*, May 10–May 21, 1977 (New York: The New Museum of Contemporary Art, 1977).

48 Marcia Tucker, *New Work/New York*, June 25–July 13, 1977 (New York: The New Museum of Contemporary Art, 1977).

49 Marcia Tucker, *Bad Painting*, January 14–February 28, 1978 (New York: The New Museum of Contemporary Art, 1977).

50 See "Avant-Garde and Kitsch," collected in Clement Greenberg, *The Collected Essays and Criticism*, ed. John O'Brian, vol. 1 (Chicago: University of Chicago Press, 1988).

51   I am thinking here of the series of exhibitions that were formative in defining a theoretical/aesthetic model of practice, known loosely as a New York school of critical postmodernism: *Art & Ideology* (February 4–March 18, 1984), curated by Benjamin Buchloh, Donald Kuspit, Lucy Lippard, Nilda Peraza, and Lowery Sims; *Difference: On Representation and Sexuality* (December 8, 1984–February 10, 1985), curated by Kate Linker and Jane Weinstock, with essays by Craig Owens, Lisa Tickner, Jacqueline Rose, and Peter Weinstock; and *Damaged Goods* (June 21–August 10, 1986), curated by Brian Wallis, with essays by Hal Foster and Brian Wallis. *The Art of Memory: The Loss of History* (November 23, 1985–January 1986), curated by William Olander, significantly marked the Museum's passage from a gestural engagement with discourse indicative of its first exhibition on memory, to more analytical use of discourse engaged in contemporary debates on aesthetics, history, and art practice.

52   The *Heresies* Collective exhibition was one of the last shows to be mounted at the New Museum's 65 Fifth Avenue space, while *Difference* was amongst the first at 583 Broadway. We should also note that the *Heresies* show was part of a series called *Events*, dedicated to showcasing projects by local alternative galleries and collectives.

53   *Heresies* 18, 5/2 (1985).

54   Lucy Lippard, "Classified: Big Pages from the Heresies Collective," in *Events: En Foco/Heresies Collective*, June 11–July 20 (New York: The New Museum of Contemporary Art, 1983), p. 27.

55   *Heresies* Collective, "Editorial Statement," *Heresies* 18, 5/2 (1985): 3.

56   Guy Debord, *Society of the Spectacle*, trans. Donald Nicholson-Smith (New York: Zone, 1994), p. 11.

57   Ibid.

58   Sabra Moore, "A Roomful of Mothers," in *Events*, p. 30.

59   Sally Stein, "The Graphic Ordering of Desire: Modernization of a Middle-Class Women's Magazine, 1914–1939," *Heresies* 18, 5/2 (1985): 7–8.

60   Robert Venturi, Denise Scott Brown, and Steven Izenour, *Learning from Las Vegas: The Forgotten Symbolism of Architectural Form* (Cambridge, MA: MIT Press, 1977); and Raymond Williams, *Television: Technology and Cultural Form* (New York: Schocken, 1975).

61   In 1982, two years prior to the *Difference* exhibition, Rose and Mitchell co-edited *Feminine Sexuality: Jacques Lacan and the École Freudienne*, trans. Jacqueline Rose (New York: Norton & Company, 1982), an anthology of articles by Lacan and his school.

62   Sigmund Freud, "Leonardo da Vinci and a Memory of his Childhood" (1910), *The Standard Edition of the Complete Psychological Works*, vol. 11 (London: Hogarth Press, 1953).

63   Rose, "Sexuality in the Field of Vision," in *Difference*, p. 31.

64 In 1985, such arguments on deconstruction were familiar among New York intellectuals and artists, initiated in part by the work of Craig Owens and Douglas Crimp. In particular, see Craig Owens, "The Allegorical Impulse: Towards a Theory of Postmodernism," Parts 1 and 2, *October 12 & 13* (Spring and Summer 1980); and Douglas Crimp, "On the Museum's Ruins," *October 13* (Summer 1980). This was the moment that Hal Foster canonized the modern/postmodern debate within the field of art criticism in his *Recodings: Art Spectacle, Cultural Politics* (Port Townsend: Bay Press, 1985). Rose was among the first critics to advance these debates on art production to more rigorously consider and include psychoanalytic theories of gender.

65 Again, the ties between feminism and other historical discourses of change are important to note such that we can value feminism's larger contribution to the history of critical thought.

66 André Breton, "Manifesto of Surrealism," in *Manifestos of Surrealism*, trans. Richard Seaver and Helen R. Lane (Ann Arbor: University of Michigan Press, 1977), p. 6.

67 André Breton, "Second Manifesto of Surrealism," in *Manifestoes of Surrealism*, p. 154.

68 It should be noted here that this formulation is consistent with Marx's belief that (1) revolution is initiated, in part, within the intellectual circles of bourgeois society, and (2) that there is no one aesthetic for revolutionary advancement. The argument for a Marxist, revolutionary aesthetic would be left to Marx's followers, of which Lukács was one.

69 Parveen Adams, Rosalind Coward, Elizabeth Cowie, eds., *m/f* 1 (1978): 4.

70 In the 1980s, Laura Mulvey's essay "Visual Pleasure in Narrative Cinema," *Screen* (Autumn 1975) came to define or canonize an American feminist practice concerned with the "male gaze." In the 1990s, I am again referring to the Bronx Museum's *Division of Labor* exhibition, which conflated Kelly and Chicago's work around the subject of maternity and domesticity.

Bibliography

Adams, P., Coward, R., and Cowie, E. (eds.) (1978). *m/f* 1.

Adorno, T. (1962). "Commitment." In A. Arato and E. Gebhardt, eds., *The Essential Frankfurt School Reader* (Oxford: Basil Blackwell, 1978).

Agamben, G. (2000). *Means Without End: Notes on Politics*, trans. V. Binetti and C. Casarino (Minneapolis and London: University of Minnesota Press; *Theory Out of Bounds*, vol. 20).

Allen, D. S. (2003). "Talking to Strangers." Excerpt from keynote address (Carolina: Foundation for the Carolinas).

Alpers, S. (1983). *The Art of Describing: Dutch Art in the Seventeenth Century* (Chicago: University of Chicago Press).

Alpers, S. (1991). "The Museum as a Way of Seeing." In I. Karp and S. D. Lavine, eds., *Exhibiting Cultures: The Poetics and Politics of Museum Display* (Washington, DC: Smithsonian Institution Press).

Ames, M. (1992). *Cannibal Tours and Glass Boxes: The Anthropology of Museums* (Vancouver: University of British Columbia Press).

Anderson, B. (1991). *Imagined Communities: Reflections on the Origin and Spread of Nationalism*, rev. and extended edn. (London: Verso).

Ang, I. (1991). "Stalking the Wild Viewer." In J. Hartley, ed., *Continuum: The Australian Journal of Media and Culture* 4/2 (Perth: Murdoch University).

Anon. (1977). "A museum in the village: an idea whose time has come," *The Villager* 20 (October).

Anon. (2002). "Evil, The Nazis and Shock Value," *New York Times*, March 15.

Anon. (2002). "Peering Under the Skin of Monsters," *New York Times*, March 17.

Anon. (2002). "Who's afraid of the big, bad Adolf?" *Guardian*, March 21.

Appadurai, A. (1996). *Modernity at Large: Cultural Dimensions of Globalization* (Minneapolis: University of Minnesota Press).

Appel, D. (2002). *Memory Effects: The Holocaust and the Art of Secondary Witnessing* (New York: Rutgers University Press).

Arendt, H. (1977). *Truth and Politics: Between Past and Future* (New York: Penguin Books).

Arinze, E. N. (2000). "Glimpses of Africa: Museums, Scholarship and Popular Culture," *Journal of Museum Ethnography* 12: 1–14.

Arnaut, K. (ed.) (2000). *Re-visions: New Perspectives on the African Collections of the Horniman Museum* (London: The Horniman Museums and Gardens).

Arnell, U., Hammer, I., and Nylöf, G. (1976). *Going to Exhibitions* (Stockholm: Riksutställningar).

Arnoldi, M. J., Kreamer, C., and Mason, M. A. (2001). "Reflections on 'African Voices' at the Smithsonian's National Museum of Natural History," *African Arts* 34/2: 16–35.

Bal, M. (1991). *Reading "Rembrandt": Beyond the Word–Image Opposition* (New York and Cambridge: Cambridge University Press).

Bal, M. (1991). *On Story-Telling: Essays on Narratology* (Sonoma: Polebridge Press).

Bal, M. (1994). "The Rape of Lucrece and the Story of W." In A. J. Hoenselaars, ed., *Reclamations of Shakespeare* (Amsterdam: Rodopi), pp. 75–104.

Bal, M. (1996). *Double Exposures: The Subject of Cultural Analysis* (London and New York: Routledge).

Bal, M. (1996). "Reading Art?" In G. Pollock, ed., *Generations and Geographies in the Visual Arts: Feminist Readings* (London and New York: Routledge, 1996).

Bal, M. (1999). *Quoting Caravaggio: Contemporary Art, Preposterous History* (Chicago: University of Chicago Press).

Barthes, R. (1982). *Camera Lucida*, trans. R. Howard (London: Fontana).

Bauman, Z. (1989). *Modernity and the Holocaust* (Cambridge: Polity).

Bauman, Z. (2000). *Liquid Modernity* (Cambridge: Polity).

Benjamin, W. (1936). "The Work of Art in the Age of Mechanical Reproduction." In *Illuminations*, ed. H. Arendt, trans. H. Zohn (London: Collins Fontana, 1973), pp. 219–54.

Bennett, T. (1988). "The Exhibitionary Complex," *New Formations* 4: 73–102.

Bennett, T. (1995). *The Birth of the Museum: History, Theory, Politics* (London and New York: Routledge).

Berger, J. (1971). *Ways of Seeing* (London: Penguin Books).

Berger, M. (2004). *Museums of Tomorrow: An Internet Discussion* (New York: Issues in Cultural Theory 8).

Boone, S. A. (1986). *Radiance From the Waters: Ideals of Feminine Beauty in Mende Art* (New Haven and London: Yale University Press).

Breton, A. (1977). "Manifesto of Surrealism." In *Manifestoes of Surrealism*, trans. R. Seaver and H. R. Lane (Ann Arbor: University of Michigan Press).

Broude, N., and Garrard, M. D. (eds.) (1994). *The Power of Feminist Art: The American Movement of the 1970s, History and Impact* (New York: Harry N. Abrams).

Bruyn, J., Haak, B., and Levie S. (1982–9). *The Stichting Rembrandt Research Project* (3 vols.) (The Hague, Boston, London: Martinus Nijhoff Publishers).

Bryson, N. (1992). "Art in Context." In *Studies in Historical Change* (Charlottesville: University Press of Virginia).

Butler, S. R. (1999). *Contested Representations: into the Heart of Africa* (London and New York: Routledge).

Casely-Hayford, A. (2002). "A Way of Being: Some Reflections on the Sainsbury African Galleries," *Journal of Museum Ethnography* 14: 113–28.

Catanis, M. (1970). "Behind Every Artist There's a Penis," *The Village Voice* (March 19, 1970).

Chave, A. (1990). "Minimalism and the Rhetoric of Power," *Arts Magazine* (January 1990)

Clarke, C. (1997). "Africa: Art of a Continent" (exhibition review), *Art Journal* 56/1: 82–7.

Clifford, J. (1988). "Histories of the Tribal and the Modern." In *The Predicament of Culture: Twentieth-Century Ethnography, Literature and Art* (Cambridge, MA: Harvard University Press).

Clifford, J. (1997). *Routes: Travel and Translation in the Late Twentieth Century* (Cambridge, MA: Harvard University Press).

Coombes, A. (1988). "Museums and the Formation of National and Cultural Identities," *Oxford Art Journal* 11/2: 57–68.

Coombes, A. (1994). *Reinventing Africa: Museums, Material Culture, and Popular Imagination* (New Haven and London: Yale University Press).

Corrin, L. G. (1994). *Mining the Museum: An Installation by Fred Wilson* (New York: The New Press).

Cotter, H. (2002). "From the Ferment of Liberation Comes a Revolution in African Art," *New York Times* (Sunday, February 17), Section 2, 1, pp. 40–2.

Cottingham, L. (1997). Interview with Laura Cottingham. In *Environ 27 ans. Les Cahiers de la classe des Beaux-Arts* 113 (February).

Court, E. (1999). "Africa on Display: Exhibiting Art by Africans." In E. Barker, ed., *Contemporary Cultures of Display* (New Haven and London: Yale University Press), pp. 147–3.

Crimp, D. (1980). "On the Museum's Ruins," *October* 13.

Crimp, D. (1993). *On the Museum's Ruins* (Cambridge, MA and London: The MIT Press).

Culler, J. (1988). *Framing the Sign: Criticism and its Institutions* (Oxford: Blackwell Books).

de Beauvoir, S. (1960). *The Second Sex*, trans. H. M. Parshey (London: Jonathan Cape; orig. pub. 1949).

de Salvo, D. (1993). *Past Imperfect: A Museum Looks at Itself* (Southampton, NY: The Parrish Art Museum).

Debord, G. (1994). *The Society of the Spectacle*, trans. D. Nicholson-Smith (New York: Zone).

Derrida, J. (1996). *Archive Fever: A Freudian Impression*, trans. E. Prenowitz (Chicago: Chicago University Press).

Dominguez, V. (1992). "Invoking Culture: The Messy Side of 'Cultural Politics'," *South Atlantic Quarterly* 91/1: 19–42.

Duffek, K. (1989). *Lyle Wilson: When Worlds Collide*. Museum Note 28 (Vancouver: UBC Museum of Anthropology).

Duncan, C., and Wallach A. (1978). "MoMA: Ordeal and Triumph on 53rd Street," *Studio International* 1.

Duncan, C., and Wallach A. (1978). "The Museum of Modern Art as Late Capitalist Ritual: An Iconographic Analysis," *Marxist Perspectives* 4.

Eliade, M. (1964). *Shamanism: Archaic Techniques of Ecstasy* (Princeton: Princeton University Press).

Errington, S. (1998). *The Death of Authentic Primitive Art and Other Tales of Progress* (Berkeley: University of California Press).

Fabian, J. (1983). *Time and the Other* (New York: Columbia University Press).

Firestone, S. (1970). *The Dialectic of Sex: The Case for Feminist Revolution* (New York: Morrow).

Fisher, J. (ed.) (1994). *Global Visions: Towards A New Internationalism in the Visual Arts* (London: Kala Press).

Foster, C. (2000). "A Ship and its Cargo." In J. Mastai, ed., *Making Meaning* (Toronto: Art Gallery of Ontario).

Foster, H. (1985). *Recodings: Art, Spectacle, Cultural Politics* (Seattle, WA: Bay Press).

Foster, H. (1995). *The Return of the Real* (Cambridge, MA and London: MIT Press).

Foucault, M. (1972). *The Archeology of Knowledge*, trans. A. M. Sheridan Smith (London: Tavistock Publications).

Foucault, M. (1972). "The Eye of Power." In *Power/Knowledge: Selected Interviews 1972–1977*, ed. C. Gordon (New York: Pantheon Books), pp. 146–65.

Fraser, A. (1991). "Museum Highlights: A Gallery Talk," *October* 57 (Summer 1991).

Freud, S. (1910). "Leonardo da Vinci and a Memory of his Childhood." In *The Standard Edition of the Complete Psychological Works*, vol. 11 (London: Hogarth Press, 1953).

Garoian, C. (1999). "Performing the Museum." In C. Garoian, ed., *Performing Pedagogy: Toward an Art of Politics* (Albany: The State University of New York Press).

Gilman, S. L. (1985). *Difference and Pathology* (Ithaca and London: Cornell University Press).

Goldfarb Marquis, A. (1989). *Alfred H. Barr, Jr.* (Chicago: Contemporary Books).

Goldstein, R. (2002). "Managing the Unmanageable," *The Village Voice*, March 6–12, 2002.

Greenberg, C. "Avant-garde and Kitsch." In C. Greenberg, *The Collected Essays and Criticism*, vol. 1, ed. J. O'Brian (Chicago: University of Chicago Press).

Greenberg, R., Ferguson, B. W., and Nairne, S. (eds.) (1996). *Thinking About Exhibitions* (London and New York: Routledge).

Greenblatt, S. (1991). "Resonance and Wonder." In I. Karp and S. D. Lavine, eds., *Exhibiting Cultures: The Poetics and Politics of Museum Display* (Washington, DC: Smithsonian Institution Press).

Habermas, J. (1989). *The Structural Transformation of the Public Sphere* (Cambridge, MA and London: The MIT Press).

Habermas, J. (1990). *The Philosophical Discourse of Modernity: Twelve Lectures*, trans. F. G. Lawrence (Cambridge, MA and London: The MIT Press).

Harding, A. (1997). *Curating: The Contemporary Art Museum and Beyond* (London: Wiley Academy).

Hebard, A. (1997). "Disruptive Histories: Toward a Radical Politics of Remembrance in Alain Resnais's *Night and Fog*," *New German Critique: An Interdisciplinary Journal of German Studies* 71: 87–113.

Henderson, J. (1998). *Museum Architecture* (London: Mitchell Beazley).

Heresies Collective (1985). Editorial Statement. *Heresies* 18, 5/2.

Hiller, S. (1991). *The Myth of Primitivism: Perspectives on Art* (London and New York: Routledge).

Hooper-Greenhill, E. (1992). *Museums and the Shaping of Knowledge* (London and New York: Routledge).

Horrigan, B. (1996). "Dweller on the Threshold." In M. Renov and E. Suderburg, eds., *Resolutions: Contemporary Video Practices* (Minneapolis and London: University of Minnesota Press), pp. 165–72.

Johnson, G. A. (1993). "Structures and Painting: 'Indirect Language and Voices of Silence'." In G. A. Johnson, ed., *The Merleau-Ponty Aesthetics Reader: Philosophy and Painting*, trans. M. B. Smith (Evanston: Northwestern University Press).

Jones, A. (1996). *Sexual Politics: Judy Chicago's Dinner Party in Feminist Art History* (Los Angeles: University of California Press).

Kanfer, S. (2002). "How to Trivialise the Holocaust," *City Journal* (April 3).

Kasfir, S. L. (1995). "Field Notes: Reimagining Africa," *Museum Anthropology* 12/1: 45–53

Kelly Trabulsi, M. (1968). *Painted Reliefs*. Exhibition Invitation, Jafet Memorial Library, American University of Beirut, June 21 – July 5.

Kelly, M. (1981). "Reviewing Modernist Criticism," *Screen* 22/3: 41–62. Repr. in Kelly, *Imaging Desire* (Cambridge, MA and London: MIT Press, 1996).

Kelly, M. (1983). *Post-Partum Document* (London and New York: Routledge).

Kelly, M. (1989). "Mary Kelly in conversation with Griselda Pollock at the Vancouver Art Gallery," June 1989. In *VAG Document 1*, introduction by Margaret Iverson (Vancouver: Vancouver Art Gallery).

Kelly, M. (1995). "A Conversation on Recent Feminist Art Practices," *October* 71.

Kelly, M. (1996). *Imaging Desire* (Cambridge, MA and London: MIT Press).

Kelly, M. (2001). *La Balada de Kastriot Rexhepi, Musica Original de Michael Nyman*. Exhibition catalogue including an interview by Trisha Ziff and essay by Jorge Reynoso (Mexico: Museo Universitario de Ciencias y Arte, Ciudad Universitaria).

Kelly, M. (2001). *The Ballad of Kastriot Rexhepi with an Original Score by Michael Nyman*. Exhibition catalogue including a conversation with Elsa Longhauser and essay by Maurice Berger (Santa Monica, CA: Santa Monica Museum of Art).

Kirshenblatt-Gimblett, B. (1998). *Destination Culture: Tourism, Museums and Heritage* (Berkeley: University of California Press).

Kirschenblatt-Gimblett, B. (2000). "The Museum As Catalyst." In *Museum 2000. Confirmation or Challenge* (Riksutställningar: Svenska ICOM och Svenska Museiföreningen).

Kleeblatt, N. L. (ed.) (2001). *Mirroring Evil: Nazi Imagery/Recent Art* (New Brunswick, NJ and London: Rutgers University Press).

Krane, S., and Benglis, L. (1990). *Dual Natures* (Atlanta: High Museum of Art).

Krauss, R. (1973). "Sense and Sensibility," *Artforum* (November).

Krauss, R. (1996). "Postmodernism's Museum Without Walls." In R. Greenberg, B. W. Ferguson, and S. Nairne, eds., *Thinking About Exhibitions* (London and New York: Routledge), pp. 340–8.

Kristeva, J. (1973). "The System and the Speaking Subject." *Times Literary Supplement* (October 12), pp. 1249–52.

Kumsa, M. (2000). "The Space In-Between." In J. Mastai, ed., *Making Meaning* (Toronto: Art Gallery of Ontario).

Kwon, M. (1997). "In Appreciation of Invisible Work," *Documents* 10 (Fall).

Lippard, L. (1983). "Classified: Big Pages from the *Heresies* Collective. In *Events: En Foco, Heresies Collective*, June 11 – July 20 (New York: The New Museum of Contemporary Art).

Lippard, L. (1995). *The Pink Glass Swan* (New York: The New Press).

Lipton, E. (1978). "The Violence of Ideological Distortion: The Imagery of Laundresses in Nineteenth-Century French Culture," *Heresies* 6.

Lukács, G. (1971). *History and Class Consciousness: Studies in Marxist Dialectics*, trans. R. Livingstone (Cambridge, MA and London: The MIT Press).

Lukács, G. (1977). *Aesthetics and Politics* (New York: Verso).

Lynes, R. (1973). *Good Old Modern: An Intimate Portrait of the Museum of Modern Art* (New York: Atheneum).

MacCormack, C. P. (1980). "Nature, Culture and Gender: a Critique." In C. P. MacCormack and M. Strathern, eds., *Nature, Culture and Gender* (Cambridge: Cambridge University Press).

Maleuvre, D. (1999). *Museum Memories: History, Technology, Art* (Stanford: Stanford University Press).

Malraux, A. (1965). *Le Musée Imaginaire* (Paris: Gallimard).

Malraux, A. (1978). *The Voices of Silence*, trans. S. Gilbert (Princeton: Princeton University Press).

Marx, K. (1843). "On the Jewish Question." Cited from *Early Writings* (London: Penguin Books, 1975).

Mastai, J. (1995). *Women and Paint* (Saskatoon: Mendel Art Gallery).

Mastai, J. (1997). *Social Process/Collaborative Action: Mary Kelly 1970–1975.* (Vancouver: Charles H. Scott Gallery, Emily Carr School of Art and Design).

McEvilley, T. (1992). *Art and Otherness: Crisis in Cultural Identity* (Kingston, NY: Documentext).

Merleau-Ponty, M. (1993). "Eye and Mind." In G. A. Johnson, ed., *The Merleau-Ponty Aesthetics Reader: Philosophy and Painting*, trans. M. B. Smith (Evanston: Northwestern University Press).

Millet, K. (1970). *Sexual Politics* (New York: Doubleday).

Mirzoeff, N. (ed.) (2000). *Diaspora and Visual Culture: Representing Africans and Jews* (London and New York: Routledge).

Mitchell, J. (1966). "Women: The Longest Revolution," *New Left Review* 40.

Mitchell, J. (1975). *Psychoanalysis and Feminism* (New York: Vintage).

Mitchell, J., and Rose, J. (eds.) (1982). *Feminine Sexuality: Jacques Lacan and the École Freudienne*, trans. J. Rose (New York: Norton and Company).

Molesworth, H. (1997). "Work Stoppages," *Documents* 10 (Fall).

Molesworth, H. (1999). "Cleaning up in the 1970s: The Work of Judy Chicago, Mary Kelly, and Mierle Laderman Ukeles." In M. Newman and J. Bird, eds., *Re-writing Conceptual Art.* (London: Reaktion Books).

Morrell, C. (1974). "Interview with Juliet Mitchell," *Spare Rib* 22.

Mulvey, L. (1975). "Visual Pleasure and Narrative Cinema," *Screen* 16/3 (Autumn).

Oberhardt, S. (2001). *Frames Within Frames: The Art Museum as Cultural Artifact* (New York and Washington: Peter Lang).

Olofsson, U. K. (1970/1). "Beautiful Moments: An Art Exhibition with a Shock Effect," *Museum* 1 (UNESCO).

Owens, C. (1980). "The Allegorical Impulse: Towards a Theory of Postmodernism," *October* 12 and 13.

Phillips, R. B. (1995). *Representing Woman: Sande Masquerades of the Mende of Sierra Leone* (Los Angeles: Fowler Museum of Cultural History).

Phillips, R. B. (2002). "Where is 'Africa'? Reviewing Art and Artifact in the Age of Globalization." Review essay in *American Anthropologist* 104/3: 11–19.

Pollock, G. (1988). *Vision and Difference: Feminism, Femininity and Histories of Art* (London: Routledge; new edn. Routledge Classics, 2003).

Pollock, G. (1990). "What's Wrong With 'Images of Women'?" Originally pub-
lished in *Screen Education* (1977) and revised as "Missing Women: Rethinking
Early Thoughts on 'Images of Women',￼" in C. Squiers, ed., *The Critical Image*
(Seattle: Bay Press, 1990), pp. 202–20.

Pollock, G. (1992). *Avant-Garde Gambits: Gender and the Colour of Art History*
(London: Thames and Hudson).

Pollock, G. (2002). "A History of Absence Belatedly Addressed: Impressionism
with and without Mary Cassatt." In C. W. Haxthausen, ed., *The Two Art
Histories: The Museum and the University* (New Haven and London: Yale
University Press), pp. 123–42.

Pollock, G. (2004). "Mary Kelly's *Ballad of Kastriot Rexhepi*: Virtual Trauma and
Indexical Witness in the Age of Mediatic Spectacle," *parallax* 10/1: 100–12

Pollock, G., and Rowley, A. (2006). *Now and Then: Feminism/Art/History:
A Reading of documenta 11*. CATH Documents, no. 3; also on <www.leeds.ac
.uk/cath/documenta11/aah.html>.

Price, S. (1989). *Primitive Art in Civilized Places* (Chicago and London: University
of Chicago Press).

Pryor, N. (2002). *Museums and Modernity: Art Galleries and the Making of Modern
Culture* (Oxford and New York: Berg).

Putnam, J. (2001). *Art and Artefact: The Museum as Medium* (London: Thames
and Hudson).

Rancière, J. (1998). "The Cause of the Other," trans. D. Macey, *parallax* 7.

Randolph, J. (1991). *Psychoanalysis and Synchronized Swimming* (Toronto: YYZ Books).

Randolph, J. (1992). "Technology and the Preconscious." In J. Randolph, ed., *The
City Within* (Banff: The Banff Centre), pp. 35–46.

Redford, R. (1959). "Art and Icon." In *Aspects of Primitive Art* (New York:
Museum of Primitive Art).

Robins, C. (1977–8). "The AIR Gallery: 1972–1978." *Womanart* (Winter).

Rogoff, I. (2002). "Looking Away: Participations in Visual Culture." Unpublished
paper presented at *Museums After Modernism* (Toronto: Centre CATH, Leeds
University).

Rosenblum, R. (2002). "Mirroring Evil? No, Mirroring Art Theory." *New York
Observer*, April 16.

Rubin, W. (1984). "Modernist Primitivism: An Introduction." In W. Rubin, ed.,
"Primitivism" in 20th-Century Art: Affinity of the Tribal and the Modern, 2 vols.
(New York: Museum of Modern Art), vol. 1, pp. 1–84.

Schama, S. (1999). *Rembrandt's Eyes* (London: Allen Lane).

Schor, M. (2000). "The F-Word: Contemporary Feminisms and the Legacy of the
Los Angeles Feminist Art Movement." *Documents* 17 (Winter/Spring).

Schwartz, G. (1993). "Rembrandt Research After the Age of Connoisseurship,"
Annals of Scholarship, 10 (3/4): 313–35.

Serota, N. (2000). *Experience or Interpretation: The Dilemma of Museums of Modern Art.* The Walter Neurath Memorial Lecture (London: Thames and Hudson).

Shelton, A. (2000). "Curating African Worlds," *Journal of Museum Ethnography* 12.

Shelton, A. (ed.) (2001). *Collectors: Expressions of Self and Other* (London: The Horniman Museum and Gardens).

Shelton, A. (ed.) (2001). *Collectors: Individuals and Institutions* (London: The Horniman Museum and Gardens).

Silverman, K. (1983). *The Subject of Semiotics* (Oxford: Oxford University Press).

Silverman, K. (1996). *The Threshold of the Visible World* (London and New York: Routledge).

Simon, R. I., Rosenberg, S., and Eppert, C. (eds.) (2001). *Between Hope and Despair: Pedagogy and the Remembrance of Historical Trauma.* Culture and Education Series (Lanham: Rowman and Littlefield).

Solomon, M. (ed.) (1973). *Marxism and Art: Essays Classic and Contemporary* (New York: Knopf).

Spring, C., Barley, N., and Hudson, J. (2001). "The Sainsbury African Galleries at the British Museum," *African Arts* 34/3: 18–37.

Stein, S. (1985). "The Graphic Ordering of Desire: Modernization of a Middle-Class Women's Magazine, 1914–1939," *Heresies* 18: 7–8.

Stocking, G. W., Jr. (ed.) (1985). *Objects and Others: Essays on Museums and Material Culture* (Madison: University of Wisconsin Press).

Tucker, M. (1977). *Memory.* May 10–21 (New York: The New Museum of Contemporary Art).

Tucker, M. (1977). *New Work/New York.* June 25 – July 13 (New York: The New Museum of Contemporary Art).

Tucker, M. (1978). *Bad Painting.* January 14 – February 28 (New York: The New Museum of Contemporary Art).

Venturi, R., Scott Brown, D., and Izenour, S. (1977). *Learning from Las Vegas.* (Cambridge, MA: MIT Press).

Vergo, P. (ed.) (1989). *The New Museology* (London: Reaktion Books).

Vogel, S. et al. (1988). *Art/Artifact: African Art in Anthropology Museums* (New York: The Centre for African Art).

Wallis, B. (ed.) (1984). *Art After Modernism: Rethinking Representation* (New York: The New Museum of Contemporary Art).

Wilding, F. (1977). *By Our Own Hands: The Women's Artists' Movement, Southern California, 1970–1976* (Santa Monica: Double X).

Williams, J. L. (ed.) (2001). *Rembrandt's Women* (Edinburgh: The National Gallery of Scotland; New York: Prestel).

Williams, R. (1975). *Television: Technology and Cultural Form* (New York: Schocken).

Wollen, P. (1993). *Raiding the Icebox: Reflections on Twentieth-Century Culture* (Indianapolis: Indiana University Press).

Women's Workshop/Artists' Union (1974). *Spare Rib* 29.

Yee, L. (ed.) (1995). *Division of Labor: "Women's Work" in Contemporary Art* (Bronx: The Bronx Museum of the Arts).

Zucker, B. (1979). "Making AIR," *Heresies* 7, 2/3 (Spring).

Index